INHUMANE SOCIETY

INHUMANE
SOCIETY

The American Way of
Exploiting Animals

Dr. Michael W. Fox

Introduction by

Cleveland Amory

St. Martin's Press/New York

Design by Amelia R. Mayone

Library of Congress Cataloging-in-Publication Data

Fox, Michael W.
  Inhumane society : the American way of exploiting animals / Michael W. Fox : introduced by Cleveland Amory.
      p.   cm.
   ISBN 0-312-04274-4
   1. Animal welfare—United States.   I. Title.
HV4764.F695   1990
179'.3'0973—dc20   89-70299
                                                                      CIP

First Edition
10 9 8 7 6 5 4 3 2 1

For Deanna and all our relations

Contents

Acknowledgments

I am grateful for the assistance and support of many colleagues in the animal protection movement, who are too many to list. Especial thanks to my executive assistant Ellen Truong, to Joy Hague, to my associates Gail Black and Dr. Melanie Adcock at The Humane Society of the United States, and to the Society's president, John A. Hoyt. Without the wisdom, understanding, and encouragement of my wife, Deanna, this book would have been incomplete, if ever actually completed. Thanks also to my hard-working copy editor Debra Manette, and to my editor at St. Martin's Press, Bob Weil, whose interest and sensitivity have proven invaluable in completing this work, which is the culmination of fifteen years of research and investigation in the field of animal protection and reflects almost thirty years of experience as a veterinarian and animal behaviorist.

Introduction

My friend Michael Fox has in this book taken on a veritable host of animal enemies. And these, as I know from personal experience, will not hesitate to fight back. But let them make no mistake—Michael comes well armed for the fray. He is not just a doctor but a double doctor—a doctor of Science of Animal Behavior and Ethology as well as a veterinary doctor with a Ph.D. in Medicine.

In his very first chapter double doctor Fox defines his field of battle as "the institutionalized, industrial-scale exploitation of animals." He believes, and states firmly, that human well-being and animal welfare are "intimately related," and he persuasively argues that "the degree and extent of animal exploitation, suffering, and environmental desecration today are symptomatic of a dysfunctional society." And, if this isn't enough for you, steel yourself for his master bite. "Our industrial society has," he says, "from its inception been built on a scientific-technological–economic paradigm that is ultimately counter-productive, *un*egalitarian, abusive to animals, destructive to the environment, and hazardous to human health."

Warming to his work, Dr. Fox presents the fields in which, as he puts it, "An informed society must make the decision to determine where and when justice and mercy must prevail in our relationships with animals and nature"—just as it does, or at least should, "in our relationships and transactions with each other." He begins with the incredibly cruelty-filled field of farm animals and makes clear why, to so many of us, vegetarianism has become "the ethical imperative." From this he moves to what for so long has been the almost equally abusive field of laboratory animals. Here he quotes, for example, from the

American Psychology Society's "Code of Principles"—that "Research procedures subjecting animals to discomfort shall be conducted only when such discomfort is required, and is justified, by the objectives of the research." *Discomfort*, mind you! Yet Dr. Fox remains scholarly: "This sounds so clear and simple," he says, "yet on second reading it is a credo of sheer utility and instrumental rationalism where animals can be simply a means to any end that the human imagination chooses to justify."

As for Dr. Fox's own belief in this perhaps most controversial of all animal fields, he states simply, "I would question psychological and all other experiments on animals that do not totally benefit them."

The author's next main field embraces our whole ecological crisis, from rain forests and factory-scale fishing to habitat destruction, hunting, and even zoos. Of the latter he asks that they at least justify their existence by sufficiently informing and even shocking the public into compassionate concern and political action. "I know of no zoo," he states sharply, "that exhibits crippled but otherwise healthy animals that have been maimed by trappers and hunters."

In the field of companion animals, Dr. Fox's range is equally wide. His book takes on not only inbreeding and overbreeding but even purebreeding. As a student of the "pariah dog" in India, he believes, as do I, that the best dog or cat is none other than the mutt. You will also find in this chapter some fascinating statistics—as, for example, that in the majority of U.S. households, caged birds, tropical fish, or the huge numbers of hamsters, guinea pigs, or gerbils never see the light of any veterinary care.

Finally, speaking of veterinarians, I found the most memorable part of this book Dr. Fox's analysis of his own profession. "I decided," he writes, "to become a veterinarian at an early age to help alleviate and prevent animal suffering." His profession has not lived up to his hopes. "I feel," he writes on, "that I and the profession have failed to alleviate, to any significant degree, the suffering of animals under humanity's dominion."

He feels that a good place for the veterinarian to start is to look at the oath taken on being admitted to the profession of veterinary medicine. This oath now starts, "I solemnly swear to use my scientific knowledge and skills for the benefit of society through the protection of animal health, the relief of animal suffering," and so on. Dr. Fox's suggestion is that the oath should read "Being admitted to the veterinary profession, I solemnly swear to use my scientific knowledge and skills for the benefit of *animals through relief of suffering* . . ." and so on.

My own suggestion is that these veterinarians, after they have their new oath, should read this book.

—CLEVELAND AMORY
President, The Fund for Animals
February 1990

Preface

This book has grown from the heart of my concern as a veterinarian to help relieve much animal suffering. In veterinary school I was not taught about the causes and cures of this suffering, or even introduced to it as a professional concern.

This suffering arises from how animals are perceived and treated for various purposes; exploited if you wish, as they themselves rarely benefit from the consequences of human dominion, except perhaps those delicate mutant creatures we use for research purposes and as pets, or entrust to others to raise for us to eat.

These highly domesticated and genetically, hormonally, and environmentally manipulated creatures—from mutant mice and miniaturized dogs to high-yield dairy cows and bulimic broiler chickens—could never exist in the wild independent of human "assistance." Yet ironically while they seem to benefit from veterinary and other treatments, they actually suffer from a host of health problems that arise as a consequence of how they are treated; and all to what end, as we make them ever more dependent on us.

This book is not an indictment of veterinarians or of farmers, vivisectors, pet owners, hunters, and others whose lives entail some relationship with other animals, either directly, as with the fur trapper, or indirectly, as with the woman or man who wears a fur coat. Rather it explores and reveals the *animal side* of these various relationships. In speaking for the animals I may seem presumptuous, but as a veterinarian and animal behaviorist, I am not unfamiliar with their condition and problems.

According to veterinarian Calvin Schwabe, as he so eloquently reasons in his book *Cattle, Priests & Progress in Medicine*, the first scientific step in human medicine was made by the priests of ancient Egypt. Besides ministering to the physical and spiritual ills of the populace, they were also responsible for the health and well-being of the sacred animals of the temple gardens, especially cattle, and the people came to revere these deities as the cow goddess Hathor and the bull-god Apis. As Professor Schwabe observes, these priests were the first veterinarians, and it was this priestly caste that helped found a truly comparative medicine. By learning how to treat animals for various maladies and from animal autopsies, they gained an understanding of how to treat people more effectively.

During the Middle Ages in Europe, progress in medicine ceased. Animals during these dark ages were seen as inferior to humans and so unrelated that knowledge about their diseases had no relevance to healing the afflictions of a spiritually superior humanity.

Time has largely changed this attitude. Animals are now used as models of human disease, and some progress in comparative medicine has been made for the benefit of both animalkind and humankind. But the belief in human or spiritual superiority (which was *not* espoused by the early Egyptian veterinary-priesthood; otherwise animals would not have been deified and revered) continues today. A more compassionate and democratic relationship is needed with the animal kingdom. Its holocaust mirrors the consequences of the human community's lack of compassion and democratic spirit.

In this book I have attempted to set forth a new paradigm, a new way of relating to and treating our fellow animals and indeed the living Earth itself. This new way, the way of respect, compassion, and understanding, is the covenant restored in a biblical sense. In a medical and veterinary sense, it is holistic, preventive, and environmental medicine.

This process entails healing our relationship with creatures and creation emotionally, theologically, politically, and economically. We will then begin to heal ourselves and the rest of the animal kingdom in the process.

Many eminent and dedicated thinkers and doers are beginning to address these problems: artists, philosophers, poets, and more recently ecologists, economists, and agriculturalists to name but a few groups. The veterinary profession, like other professions and occupations that depend on society's exploitation of animals, has been relatively silent in responding to the holocaust of the animal kingdom caused by our collectively harmful dominion.

Until we address this issue, we will not heal the Earth. Until we include the animal kingdom in the human agenda of our daily lives and local and global influences, the Earth will not be restored. This is because animals are part of the same earth community as we, so that when we harm them, we inevitably harm ourselves. The fate of the animals and of humankind are thus interconnected. The natural world will become transformed into a toxic bioindustrial wasteland, run by a global technocracy caught in the down-spiral of human need and greed and the rising costs of adapting to an increasingly uninhabitable planet.

This is my dark vision. I have closely followed recent developments in genetic engineering biotechnology as applied to plants and animals, and the utopian vision of the future wonder-world of many biotech companies is quite clear: The natural world will become a bioindustrial "theme park."

The first genetically engineered animals patented were "Oncomice"—cancer-prone mice developed by Harvard University for duPont Chemical Company, a major manufacturer of pesticides and other chemicals.

The American government ruled against putting animal genes into people but has endorsed and financed putting human genes into mice (to make them into medical models for human diseases) and into pigs to make them grow faster and bigger (but it made them sickly with weakened immune systems and crippled bodies). Genetic engineers have now developed techniques to make severely overworked cows produce 20 to 40 percent more milk—in a time of global milk surpluses!; sheep that will not abort their lambs even if they are in too poor physical condition to raise one; lambs whose growth regulation has been disrupted so they become freakish giants; and pigs whose appetites have been so altered that they never want to stop eating. Farm animals are also being engineered to produce human drugs in their serum and milk, heralding a new era of pharmaceutical farming.

As the screw turns, so future generations seem bent on exploiting animals and the rest of creation on the same grounds of necessity, economy, and divine right that are so widely voiced today.

I do not speak for the veterinary profession, because they have not reached a consensus. Rather I speak for the animals. I hope that this book will help them by moving us all away from an _inhumane society_ in the direction of a sane and humane planetary stewardship.

—Dr. Michael W. Fox
The Humane Society of the United States
Washington, D.C.
March 1990

*One does not meet oneself until one catches
the reflection from an eye other than
human.*
—Loren Eiseley, *The Night Country*

*Every form of life is unique,
Warranting respect regardless of its
worth to man, and to accord other organisms
such recognition, man must be guided by a
moral code of action . . .*
—World Charter for Nature
adopted by the General Assembly
of the United Nations,
October 28, 1982

Foreword

An illustration of a dog afflicted with rabies, in an old book that I came across as a child, moved me very deeply. There was something about the abject terror of this frenzied and dying soul that touched mine so deeply that I resolved to become an animal doctor at the young age of eight years. It was no coincidence that dogs were my loyal, trusting, and always accepting playmates. I took in wartime strays and spent my pocket money on food for them and various medications to cure them of nature's afflictions, such as worms and mange. I was aware of how various diseases made them and other creatures suffer, and it became my heart's desire to learn how to alleviate that suffering by going to a university to study veterinary medicine and surgery.

Before coming to the United States, I studied at the Royal Veterinary College, London, England, from where I graduated, and undertook further studies to earn a Ph.D. in medicine and a D.Sc. in animal behavior, but this is another story. Suffice it to say that I realized my childhood ambition only to discover that much of the suffering of animals was not caused by nature but by *people*. And the preventives were not to be found in wonder drugs and vaccines but in the heart of compassion's wisdom and empathy. My battle was not so much against disease as it was against human ignorance and indifference toward the animal kingdom—a disease in itself.

It took me several years of "disindoctrination" to realize that humanity had broken its part of the covenant to "dress and to keep" the natural world in all its beauty and diversity; and

3

that much of the suffering of animals (not to mention human beings) arose as a consequence thereof, because humanity abused its power of dominion over the rest of creation.

From this perspective, I realized that the veterinary profession was in part responsible for the broken covenant: It profited from animal exploitation and thus helped maintain the status quo, did not challenge such cruel practices as factory farming and the doping of lame racehorses, or take a strong stance against the propagation of genetically defective "pets," the trapping of wild animals for their fur, and the vivisection of animals in laboratories for such trivial purposes as scientific curiosity and cosmetics testing.

Indeed the magnitude of animal suffering caused by humankind is far greater and more insidious and pervasive than that caused by "nature"—the elements, parasites, predators, and infectious microorganisms against which most animals have evolved some immunity and other natural defenses. They have no protection against traps, poison baits, harpoons; no way to cope with confinement stress on factory farms, and no escape from the cages of zoos and laboratories.

While most veterinarians still wage war against disease, a radical shift in perception is taking place. There's nothing wrong, evil, or "fallen" about nature. *It is human nature that is the problem*, and the suffering of the animal kingdom and the destruction of the natural world under our inhumane dominion are symptomatic consequences. Collectively, humanity is not in its right mind and heart in relation to the rest of God's creation. The covenant, particularly in the United States but elsewhere as well, has been broken.

Sometime in our lives we are all confronted with the suffering and death of animals as a consequence of human actions. No matter how insulated we are from the reality of what some now call the holocaust of the animal kingdom, we cannot ignore it. One new member of The Humane Society of the United States who attended our 1987 conference in Phoenix confided that she was ignorant of what was going on until she saw on television stolen videotapes taken of lightly sedated baboons at the University of Pennsylvania having their skulls crushed in the name of medical progress. This kind of thing simply should not be happening. Yet it is.

My own rude awakening—or at least my first, because there have been many—occurred when I was about five years old. I was playing around one of the ponds in my neighborhood, a favorite place full of the surprises of aquatic life, when I saw a sack floating in the water.

Treasure, I thought as I pulled it to the bank with a long stick. But when I opened it, I found a litter of dead kittens. So soaked and bloated were they that I did not quite realize what they were at first. Then I realized that someone had deliberately, one by one, put them into the sack and had then thrown them into the pond to die. I learned that other people—grownups—must have a different attitude toward animals from mine, for I could never have drowned a litter of kittens in an old sack.

Around this same pond the following springtime, I had another rude awakening. I discovered the burst remains of several frogs, easily caught in their vulnerable breeding season, strewn along the muddy bank. I knew no wild creature could cause such wholesale destruction. Then I saw the hollow, broken straws of thick grass stems that had been thrust into the frogs' mouths. Boys—my peers and sometimes playmates—had blown up the frogs; blown them up into four-legged, eye-bulging, yellow-green balloons until they burst apart. I realized then that it was not just adults but also children like myself who could be cruel in their indifference toward animal life and animal suffering.

Rude awakenings can come at any time in one's life. The first awakening can leave an indelible scar or an open wound that never heals. More often the scar seems to fade, not with the waning memory of the first awakening but with the acceptance of the social norm of human cruelty toward animals, if not indifference toward their suffering.

When the status quo is legal yet seems at odds with one's

own feelings and ethical sensibility, a deep rage at the injustices of the world arises. It seems as if there are two worlds: in one those who care for frogs and kittens can never belong, and in the other there is respect for all life and an ethical consistency in our relationships with the other living beings that are an integral part of the community of moral concern. In the latter, animals are protected by laws of the land—which rarely need to be enforced—because human actions are governed by ethical sensibility and guided by empathetic sensitivity.

This world of peace, justice, and respect for the integrity and future of creation seems to be disappearing before our very eyes. Even my wonder-filled playground ponds are now all gone, filled and paved over beneath a labyrinth of suburban housing developments.

The rude awakening can also evoke feelings of alienation and despair. These emotions, along with anger, are neither unnatural nor unhealthy. They and the overwhelming sadness over the tragedy of reality have to be worked through. The reality created by people's perception of animals and all natural creations as mere "things," devoid of inherent worth and thus unworthy of moral consideration, is a cause of deep concern.

How ironic it is that those who do hold the well-being of creatures and the beauty and mystery of creation close to their hearts should suffer as a consequence! Yet in their rude awakening lies hope beyond the burdening emotions of sadness, anger, alienation, and despair.

Humanitarians can all take heart from the fact that there are many instances of people making significant, even radical, changes in their lives following a "rude awakening." Public sensitization and education, based on factual media coverage of animal welfare and environmental issues, *can* make a difference. Public apathy and indifference are less of a problem, I believe, than lack of knowledge about such issues and what one can do to help.

It is a fact that many people who are confronted with animal cruelty and suffering simply tune out. For some, reality may be too painful. Others may erect a kind of protective indifference to the holocaust of the animal kingdom. All humane educators need to consider this alienation. They should not be afraid of alienating an already alienated public. Rather they should draw them into the circle of concern for creatures and creation, because, in the final analysis, altruistic concern is enlightened self-interest—the way to a better society and a world where peace, justice, and the integrity of creation may be better ensured for future generations to enjoy.

Sometimes I wonder if some people feel too much. They seem overly sensitive to others' suffering: to the distress of helpless creatures, such as the sight of a grasshopper drowning in a swimming pool; a photograph of a coyote struggling to free itself from a trap; or a cat writhing in its death throes after being hit by the car ahead.

And I know of people who suffer when they see a forest desecrated by loggers, a once-prairie plain turned into rectangular monocultures of wheat and corn, a river poisoned into an open sewer by industrial waste.

Those people who feel nothing should surely not be misjudged as being morally wrong or evil. Their lack of feeling is a kind of emotional-perceptual impairment that warrants sympathetic help because it can lead to ethical blindness.

Being overly sensitive—"too emotional"—is a very relative thing. What is at issue is how well we deal with the many feelings that are evoked by the distress and suffering of our own kind and of fellow creatures. It is not simply a question of how fully we identify with them.

Feelings of outrage, horror, apprehension, helplessness, frustration, and even guilt need to be acknowledged as part of the experiential process of complete empathetic identification. We must do so because these emotions can have a profound influence on one's motivation and effectiveness. Understanding why we feel the way we do about some issue or concern can help improve our effectiveness and motivation—it can even radically change the direction we take in our lives. Our feelings do profoundly influence our perception and the kind of truth we live by and for. And that truth can gain in strength of conviction when we share our feelings and concerns with others in an open and nonjudgmental way. Then, and only then, will those who, for example, currently have little concern for the plight of animals and the desecration of the natural world undergo a radical change in perception and begin to feel, to empathize. And when this process of empathetic identification begins, people's will is awakened. Without the will to change, there can be no motivation to make this world a better place for all creatures great and small.

I have written *Inhumane Society* to illustrate how humanitarians' concern for the welfare of homeless cats and dogs and for those countless numbers of animals that are cruelly treated by humanity is not a sentimentally misguided and thus irrational obsession. To be concerned for the welfare of animals in the United States and elsewhere, and for the global environment in which we live, are the eleventh and twelfth commandments of the animal rights and "deep ecology" movements.

These movements have grown out of the emotional yet rationally enlightened moralistic perspectives of the humane (animal welfare) and conservation movements. They represent the forefront of a more global, political, and spiritual network of movements and organizations, ranging from consumer and holistic health and solar and organic farming ideologies, to human rights, bioregional economic communities, and the peace movement. All share the ideology that we should treat others, including all living things, as we would have them and God treat us—with understanding, respect, and love. As will be shown, it is enlightened self-interest and a survival imperative to follow this Golden Rule.

This book does not deal with deliberate cruelty toward animals by individuals, which is, as recent studies have shown, a psychiatric problem that often occurs alongside child abuse and violent criminal behavior. The institutionalized, industrial-scale exploitation of animals and nature is a far more pervasive problem and, as will be shown, has far-reaching consequences on society, human health, and the environment.

It is within the framework of these broad political and ethical dimensions of animal exploitation that the issues of animal welfare, habitat conservation, and rights are best considered. The humane movement may then be more effective and also gain greater support and recognition for its contribution to the enlightenment and transformation of society. Human well-being and animal welfare are intimately related, because, as *Inhumane Society* shows, the degree and extent of animal exploitation, suffering, and environmental desecration today are symptomatic of a dysfunctional American society. By the millennium's end, global nemesis, rather than the birth of a golden age, seems inevitable. As Albert Einstein once observed, "We shall require a substantially new manner of thinking if mankind is to survive." This new manner of thinking must necessarily include ecological conscience and respect for the rights of all living things.

I have subtitled this book *The American Way of Exploiting Animals* to expose the complicity, indifference, and passivity, particularly in America but also elsewhere, of many people and professions contributing to the holocaust of the animal kingdom. And my own veterinary profession is no exception: Like people in general, and especially professionals involved in animal exploitation, they have become immunized against the atrocities that are occurring daily.

As students, veterinarians can become desensitized to animals' suffering and rights by having to perform surgical and other invasive procedures on perfectly healthy animals—often on people's lost or abandoned pets taken from animal shelters. It demeans students' own humanity to make healthy animals sick and operate on them as part of their education.

Little wonder then that many graduate veterinarians come to regard and treat animals as mere commodities and use their skills primarily to benefit the animals' owners and society first, often in violation of animals' rights. An extreme example is doping racehorses that are lame—and should be rested—so that they feel no pain and can be raced. Fortunately, the number of veterinarians in this country who do put animals first is increasing, as witness the recent formation of the American Association of Veterinarians for Animal Rights. I consider it my duty as a veterinarian to speak out against the animal holocaust, even though many of my colleagues have called me the "pariah" of the veterinary profession.

The humane movement, which was once dedicated solely to the elimination of pain, fear, and suffering in those animals that were under our dominion, has expanded its scope of concern significantly over the past decade. The intent of *Inhumane Society* is to show the scope of this movement today, particularly in the United States, and more importantly to demonstrate its social and political relevance to human health and well-being and to planetary survival.

First, the new animal rights philosophy has broadened the movement conceptually: Beyond the humane concerns over animal pain, fear, and suffering lie issues related to more basic rights, such as the right to life for endangered species. Another example of the principles derived from the new ethic of animal rights relates to the whaling industry: An explosive harpoon, for example, could conceivably cause death without pain, fear, or suffering, but would such technology make the killing of whales ethically acceptable? The animal rights argument that the value of a whale's life to itself has more intrinsic worth than have the various products derived from the whale's body to humans provides a strong basis for accepting that even the humane killing of whales is ethically unacceptable.

Second, the industrialized forms of propagation and exploitation of animals by agribusiness and biomedical research, have forced the movement into a political arena of confrontation and legislative battles on the local, state, and even national levels. Evidence has been accumulating that the situation is the exact opposite of the claims of agribusiness and the biomedical research establishment. Namely, that they do *not* contribute significantly to the greater good of either humanity or the environment. There are many examples. For instance, due to factory farming consumers now face health hazards introduced through the drugs given to control disease and to boost productivity in confined, often overcrowded, and stressed farm animals. And because most biomedical research is virtually useless in preventing the many chronic degenerative diseases that are related to poor diet and environmental pollution, much animal research is unnecessary and irrelevant. The appropriate corrective actions must instead be primarily social and political.

If we are to justify the exploitation of farm and laboratory animals, then we must be able to say that it contributes significantly to the greater good of society. But today the main beneficiaries of such exploitation are the industries themselves.

Humanitarians are in general agreement that we and the Earth will be well only when we can all begin to live in harmony and with reverence of all life. Human, animal, and environmental well-being are as inseparable ethically as they are interrelated ecologically and spiritually. The self-centered worldview of humanity in general, and of the major industries that exploit animals in particular, clearly violates these principles. I agree with American biologist and historian Carolyn Merchant who feels that, in the long run, the Earth will be restored to health only if mainstream values are reversed and economic priorities are drastically changed.

Regardless of the claims of science and technology that we are evolving toward some millennial age of plenty, without a revolution in values and attitudes, the quality of human life and all life on Earth will continue to decline, and could possibly end in our extinction. It is to be hoped that what will become extinct by the end of this millennium will be those attitudes and values that deny others—including animals and plants—equal and fair consideration and the mechanistic worldview of rational egotism that believes that animals are unfeeling machines. To treat living things and organic systems as if they are mere machines, even though such an approach "works," gives a false sense of power and security. This so-called Cartesian paradigm is a type of insanity, according to philosopher Morris Berman, because a mechanistic paradigm can only be applied destructively to living things and organic systems.

In the first chapter of *Inhumane Society*, the status of animals in our society is reviewed, followed by in-depth chapters describing how laboratory and farm animals are treated and wildlife managed, purportedly for the benefit of society. Basic reforms in animal care and in the kinds of exploitation that result in unnecessary suffering and destruction of species and of their habitats are detailed. Subsequent chapters examine how the plight of animals and the fate of the Earth are determined by the kind of society that we have built, showing very clearly that the fate of the animal kingdom is inseparable from our own. The holocaust of the animals today will be ours tomorrow. But this is not inevitable provided we, collectively as a species and individually as planetary citizens, awaken to the plight of animals and of the environment, and act with responsible compassion. This enlightened self-interest is the supreme challenge to humanity at this time. If we begin to assume the responsibilities of self-dominion and humane planetary stewardship, there is room for optimism.

CHAPTER 1

The Status of Animals in the

United States

In our society, people's status is defined either as their condition in the eyes of the law or their rank in relation to others. I believe the legal and social status of animals in human society is not based on any objective, scientific criteria or ethical rationale, but rather on their individual value to that society. This value has its roots in tradition (how a species has historically been viewed or treated); utility (how vital or profitable is its role in our lives); and emotion (how rare, appealing or beautiful it is). The use of these arbitrary criteria has caused tremendous and illogical variations in how different species are treated.

Consider, for example, the disparities between the way we view coyotes and their cousins, the domestic dog. Despite their close biological relationship, the two species could not be treated more differently. Traditionally coyotes have been condemned as "varmints" or pests. We have hunted them for their pelts or for recreation, and our emotional reaction to them has rarely included compassion. As a result, anyone who systematically traps, starves, burns, gases, shoots, or poisons coyotes is condoned (on the false and unethical premise of economic necessity), but anyone who treats a stray dog the same way would violate state and federal anticruelty laws and incur society's disapproval.

Because they are producers of food and products and are therefore not "real" animals (in the sense pets are "real"), farm animals can be kept five to a cage two feet square, tied up constantly by a two-foot-long tether, castrated without anesthesia, or branded with a hot iron. A pet owner would be no less than *prosecuted* for treating a companion animal in such a manner; an American president was, in fact, morally censured merely for pulling the ears of his two beagles. But such patent cruelties are common and routine practices in farm-animal husbandry, despite those animals' great biological and psychological similarity to species kept as pets.

Is it logical and scientifically valid for society and the law to accept that wildlife and farm animals are treated with fewer restraints than laboratory animals? Is it ethically tenable to prosecute a pet owner for doing to a companion animal—a term I prefer to "pet"—what a state predator-control officer does to coyotes or a farmer to a sow? Such social and legal inconsistencies do not stand up philosophically, in terms of logic and reason; nor do they stand scientific scrutiny, because the physiological and psychological *similarities* are greater among rats, cats, and pigs than the differences. Thus there is no scientific basis for such discriminatory treatment. Scientific evidence supports the philosophical argument that such animals are sentient, have needs, interests, and intrinsic worth.

An even more unreasonable example is how laboratory animals can be experimented on by untrained students and supposedly qualified researchers while companion animal owners may not inflict such treatment on their cat or dog. Students or researchers are spared from prosecution because their activities are presumed—rightly or wrongly—to be of ultimate value to society. As a consequence, laboratory animals are accorded fewer rights than are companion animals, because of their presumed greater usefulness to man.

Our legislators should scrutinize closely these socially and legally accepted inconsistencies. Practices or customs that *benefit society* should stand philosophical and objective (scientific) scrutiny. Otherwise how are we to be sure that what is socially acceptable is ethically justifiable? The fact that farm, laboratory, and companion animals are kept for different purposes does not logically justify such inconsistencies. Why should an animal that is to be killed and eaten, or made to suffer and sacrificed for knowledge's sake, or harvested or exterminated (as are many wild species) have less protection than do companion animals? Obviously the difference lies in the greater emotional value that is placed on companion animals, a valuation that unconditional supporters of biomedical research, hunting, trapping, predator control, and factory farming criticize as anthropomorphic. For the sake of consistency, it might be argued that society should not prosecute someone for burning a cat with a branding iron, keeping a dog permanently held by a short tether, or destroying a litter of pups with a fire bomb. That would eliminate consistencies all right, but companion animal owners—because of their emotional attachment—and animal protectionists would undoubtedly disagree.

I believe farm animals should be treated with as much respect and care—if not more—than companion animals, because it is we who will ultimately kill and consume them. The same may be said for laboratory animals, whose suffering and death purportedly benefit society by providing knowledge to alleviate human sickness and suffering. And as it is we who intrude on wildlife's world and create "pest" and "predator" problems, we should rectify those problems only by the most humane and ecologically sound means. It is neither rational nor ethical to allow companion animals to enjoy greater social status and legal protection than others simply because they satisfy our sentimental, emotional, and traditional needs.

At long last, the well-being of farm animals is being brought to the attention of the public. In fact, according to American agribusiness publications, the issue of farm animal welfare was "the issue of the eighties; and it's not going to go away." They also recognize that it is an "emotional issue." While public concern over the farm-animal welfare may be highly emotional and to some extent anthropomorphic, if democracy and justice prevail, the general public is where the final decision will be made.

A new law passed in Sweden in 1988 prohibits cruel "factory" livestock and poultry practices, outlawing veal crates, battery cages for laying hens, and tethering of pregnant sows. However, most countries are opposed to such humane reforms, arguing that costs to consumers would be increased. This kind of thinking, where economic interests take precedence over ethical concerns, is illustrative of how the industrial-scale exploitation of animals has become a socially accepted norm in so-called civilized society.

The ultimate choice of which predator control and farm husbandry practices and other treatments are acceptable cannot be based on sentimentalism on the one hand and economic justifications on the other, but rather on scientific study, ethics, and commonsense morality.

As a final illustration, consider the rabbit. A rabbit can be perceived, and therefore treated, in a variety of ways, which influence its social and legal standing. It could be a cuddly pet, a subject for high-school dissection or research, a menu item, or the source of a pair of fur mittens. It could be a farmer's pest, a sportsman's "worthy adversary," or a greyhound trainer's lure. But nowhere is the rabbit valued intrinsically, in and for itself. Our own perceptions and underlying needs, values, and projections create a spectrum of attitudes that determines a rabbit's ultimate social and legal standing. But does the rabbit not suffer equally whether it is a pet, a laboratory animal, or a "pest?" Isn't it just as cruel, given the rabbit's ability to experience pain, to torture it in a laboratory or in an open field as it is in a home? Not according to the law!

Most exploiters of animals believe the concept of giving rabbits fair and equal consideration (under the rubric of animal rights philosophy) is utterly preposterous. Yet no less preposterous is the fact that society's attitudes toward animals show no consistent morality or legality.

Surely, as long as our society continues to accept the fact

that animals may be exploited and are a means to human ends, an ethical contract must be made to balance our need to exploit with a moral obligation regarding the animal's intrinsic nature and worth. Such a contract has its foundations in all the world's major religious traditions (which are too often ignored) of justice and mercy; in compassion, understanding, respect, benevolence, and love; and also in the emerging philosophy of animal rights. These humane tenets provide the necessary balance to the inherent limitations of employing the scientific method per se to determine animal welfare, suffering, emotional states, and so on. When such balances are made, the conditional exploitation of animals may prove to be socially, legally, and ethically justifiable, rather than based on unfeeling and unthinking utility, self-centered emotional and perceptual inconsistencies, and intellectual rationalizations.

It is neither ethical nor unethical for a wolf to kill a deer: On the contrary, such predation is an expression of natural and ecologically harmonious behavior. It is based on the bioeconomics of necessity and superiority of power and intelligence of one species over another. There is virtually no overriding element of choice; chance and opportunity dictate the outcome. Similarly for people, our superiority of power and intelligence over other animals allows us to exploit them for reasons of economy and to satisfy diverse social needs. But while a wolf may have no choice, and no ethical constraints, *people have the additional power of choice or discrimination.* This power has the potential to free us from the biological constraints and dictates of sheer necessity and utility. It must be modulated by ethics and enlightened self-interest that employs the least harmful means to secure the "greatest" good for all.

People may make the ethical choice of being vegetarians and not hunting or wearing the furs of trapped and ranch-raised animals. But there should be no choice about whether or not animals should be treated humanely (and even killed humanely). This is an ethical imperative, a moral injunction. There *are* certain ecological and humane arguments in favor of killing animals under certain circumstances (to control populations of wild animals and to euthanize sick or crippled ones). But killing them for purely self-serving reasons, or making them suffer needlessly, as in biomedical research, is not rooted in any ethical principles but rather in presumed divine right and superiority, and choice based on custom, expedience, alleged economic necessity, and social progress.

Consequently there is no simple resolution to the rightness or wrongness of humans exploiting animals. It is a question of choice; whether or not we wish to assert dominion over them for self-serving ends. Because we have the power and freedom of choice, we can liberate ourselves from the ultimately self-limiting, if not degrading, necessity of exploiting animals to satisfy exclusively human ends. We can be benevolent and compassionate toward other creatures, irrespective of ethics and morality. To accept this freedom of choice and to seek *alternatives*, by reducing the numbers of animals that are killed, exploited, and made to suffer is a first step toward our becoming more fully human. The power of choice is far greater than the power of domination because it leads ultimately to freedom and liberation, rather than the self-limiting dictates of socioeconomic necessity.

Reasons of convenience, expedience, esthetics, ethics, economics, and ecology may constrain us to exploit or not to exploit animals. The choice is ours to make. Arguing that it is custom or tradition, and therefore morally and socially acceptable, to continue to exploit animals unconditionally is ethically untenable. Conformity to consensus values—the Eichmann syndrome—has no ethical boundaries and is one of the most pervasive causes of man's tyranny over others. Boundaries can be established, but it requires radical courage and the insight of the iconoclast to do so—qualities few societies have ever tolerated. We should adhere to the ethic of respecting the right of all animals to equal and fair treatment.

Many people involved in animal exploitation, as other Americans in the past who were engaged in slavery, see any change as a threat to the economic status quo. But injustice and inhumanity must be confronted and opposed. I believe that we should employ all ethically reasonable means, *including nonviolent civil disobedience*, to reduce the extent of animal exploitation and to improve the treatment of those animals that continue to be exploited. As we begin the 1990s, the American way of animal exploitation is finally being challenged across the United States and also in Europe. And the unholy alliance of multinational agribusiness, petrochemical and medical–pharmaceutical industries is being exposed. (This alliance is exemplified by the profits from pesticides that ultimately poison the food chain, and the profitability of treating people afflicted with diseases linked with such environmental contamination.) Concern for animal protection and rights equals and strengthens concern for nature, for environmental degradation and pollution, for the deformations and diseases of our children and the sickness of consumers and those in hazardous workplaces, such as slaughterhouses, chemical factories, and nuclear power plants.

As nature has been enslaved, so atomic energies have been harnessed and the genes of life identified, cloned, and rearranged to meet human voracity—voracity that now threatens the integrity and future of creation. The animal protection and rights movement is a natural outgrowth of an enlightened and compassionate human response to the realization that we must change those industrial processes and consumer dependencies that have enslaved the world and now threaten the planet with extinction.

The history of this movement can be traced to biblical times. The Old Testament tells the farmer to care for his stock before satisfying his own needs and to rest the soil and help it regenerate, feeding wildlife in the process. Yet civilization after civilization destroyed the good earth and left deserts behind. Then came the Industrial Revolution. The Age of Reason rode on the traditions of patriarchy and a transcendant monotheism that placed a male god over men and women, animals and nature under those men. The descendants of this male mentality that endorsed human slavery, the subordination of women, of nature, and of fellow animals (who they claim have been created for man's use) now empower the same industrial process that is their nemesis. It is a nemesis brought about by an arrogant disregard for the rights, interests, and inherent value of others, whether races, plant and animal species, or the Earth itself.

Perhaps the rest of the universe is observing, in silent witness, the demise of the human species, or awaiting its transformation into a truly humane and *sapient* species. The widening of the circle of compassion to liberate fellow humans from slavery, to emancipate women, and now to free animals from the tyranny of human chauvinism is a positive sign of such a transformation in progression today.

THE LANGUAGE OF ANIMAL EXPLOITATION

A detailed, cross-cultural linguistic analysis of terminology related to various forms of animal exploitation might give considerable insight into how professional and vested interest groups perceive and value animals and how sensitive they are about what they do. Dairy cattle, breeding sows, and laying hens have been called production units and biomachines. Language may be "laundered" to assuage guilt, gain public respectability, or avoid public ridicule. Many species that become too numerous are called pests that must be "exterminated," yet humans have caused that very overabundance, as of blackbirds and pigeons. Seals, deer, and other wildlife are "harvested," as if they were apples, rather than slaughtered. Recently farm groups were distressed when, in its school curriculum guide, the National Association for the Advancement of Humane Education asked school children what animals they had eaten that day. The aim of the exercise was to help children become aware of the extent to which animals contribute to our lives. Livestock and poultry industry representatives would have preferred the children being asked what kind of meat or other animal produce they had eaten. Thus language can be used to distance us from reality and responsibility.

Scientists often use the term sacrifice regarding the killing of laboratory animals. It is a significant choice of terms, implying the animals die for human benefit or for knowledge's sake. I find other terms demeaning as well: "pets" for such companion animals as cats and dogs; "specimens" for zoologists. Most noncompanion animals, even though they, like we, do have gender, are rarely referred to as "she" or "he" but in an epicene way as an "it." They are deanimalized further by such terms as "that" rather than "who" or "whom." English teachers, writers, journalists, and others might also help clean up our vocabulary where demeaning inferences are made about fellow creatures in describing essentially human traits and short-comings: swine, sloth, bitch, brute, and beastly. Rapists are often called "animals," policemen "pigs," and so on.

Our use of language does not serve only to distance us from animals but also tends to reduce them to the level of insensitive objects. It gives an aura of respectability to ethically questionable forms of animal treatment—even sanctioning the "sacrifice" of animals in laboratories and poisoning of "pests."

In ironic contrast, owners of "pets" often anthropomorphize their animals by giving them human names, such as "Bob" or "Suzie," as distinct from purely descriptive names like "Fluffy," "Ginger," "Spot," or "Scamp." Giving human names may or may not reflect the status of the animal as an integral member of the family. It may also be due to perceiving the animal as having certain human attributes, which may or may not be scientifically valid.

Perceiving and appreciating the animal in its own right is more difficult, however, when we lack an understanding of its intrinsic nature and when there are negative associations (such as wolves being vicious killers). Furthermore, when animals are perceived as mere commodities—for food, for fur, for scientific study or other use—the language used by those who exploit them often discounts the nature and existence of the animals themselves. For example, some farm-animal production scientists (who perceive pigs primarily as productive biomachines) find it laughable to consider the "pigness" of pigs, because it is productivity and profits that must remain paramount. Pigs are mere production units, items of commerce. Yet thanks to the "pigness" of pigs, we have profits, pork, ham, and bacon.

While the pig may be sacrificed for food and profit, should its right to develop and to express and experience its "pigness"—its essential nature—be denied before it is killed?

In sum, the question is not whether or not it is right or wrong to exploit animals and nature. Rather we must conscientiously identify those areas of exploitation where ethical transgressions may be evident. As an informed society, we must determine where and when justice and mercy must prevail in our relationships with animals and nature.

CHAPTER 2

The Jungle Revisited

Upton Sinclair's exposé *The Jungle*, a book about the horror to man and beast alike in the slaughterhouse, shook the nation in 1905.[1] But aside from minor improvements in worker safety and the abolition of killing animals with a sledgehammer, nothing has really changed since the book was first published. *The Jungle* has spread and Sinclair's documented revelations pall before the industry's "business as usual" status quo. From slaughterhouse and poultry packing plant union-busting, repetitive-motion injuries to minimum-wage workers (and zero-compensation), to the "line hypnosis" of U.S. Department of Agriculture meat inspectors who have only seconds to check every dead animal for disease and fecal contamination, we glimpse the tip of an iceberg. This is an iceberg that is more deeply immersed in corruption than ever before. We continue to see sales of contaminated and condemned meat to schools and other institutions; the firing of slaughterhouse and government whistle-blowers; epidemics of food poisoning from meat and poultry products contaminated with *Salmonella*, *E. coli*, *Listeria*, *Campylobacter*, and other fecal bacteria; diseased, dead, dying, and debilitated animals (called "4-D meat") along with condemned parts of other animals rendered down into tallow for soap and into meat meal that goes into most pet foods or is recycled and fed back to farm animals; larger and fewer slaughterhouses handling thousands of animals a day that are often transported under great stress for hundreds of miles because the killing business has become so overcentralized.

This jungle of atrocities—fueled by greed, indifference, and competitive pressures of the market economy—has spread from the slaughterhouse to family farm. Indeed, the family farmer, the good steward of the land, has become an endangered species, forced to "get big or get out." Those who have mortgaged their lives to stay in business have adopted cruel factory-scale methods of livestock and poultry production that would make Upton Sinclair turn in his grave.

The mass production, slaughter, and consumption of billions of animals result in a psychic numbing of our empathetic sensitivity. Farm animals are treated as mere commodities. This insensitivity spreads from indifference toward the rights and interests of those who work in the steaming bowels of the slaughterhouse to a total disregard for the fate of the family farm and the rights and interests of the consumer in having healthful and wholesome food. But those who suffer most prior to slaughter are the farm animals themselves, the enslaved victims and protein factories of a meat-based agriculture that is neither sustainable nor in the best interests of the nation's health and future prosperity.

DOWN ON THE FACTORY FARM

The agricultural technologist's dream of vast, fully automated "farmerless farms" is quickly becoming a reality—on a scale that simply could not be fathomed by Upton Sinclair in 1905. Farmers, in the traditional, cultural sense of the word, who husband the land and stock are now an endangered species, replaced by agribusiness corporate managers and specialists in chemical farming, genetics, nutrition, and other disciplines— "specialists" far more trained in the way of animal exploitation and inured to its consequences than was thought possible eighty-five years ago. One assistant manager of a large West Coast egg factory took me around the plant. As we talked beside one of the several sheds containing over 70,000 laying hens, he told me, "We don't regard the hen as a bird. It's a production unit, a black box. All we do is monitor input and output." He was a college graduate with a degree in computer science and his boss had a master's in business administration. Later, in his wood-paneled office, the manager admitted to me that while his egg factory, like most factory-farmed animal operations, was less efficient than a well-run small- or medium-size family farm and that his animals were less productive on an individual basis, bigness pays because of the economy of scale. Such capital-intensive systems are displacing the family farm. While they give short-term profits to few, the long-term consequences, as will be shown, are ominous.

The image of space-age livestock farming is widely promoted as hygienic, efficient, and in the best interests of the animals and consumers alike. What do we actually see? Rows of sows, cows, veal calves, or hens kept in small pens with labor-saving automatic manure removal and ventilation systems. Computers formulate diets and some are being designed to collate data from biotelemeter transmitters on or inside the animals that signal when the animal is ready to breed, requires veterinary attention, to regulate its access to food, and other behavior patterns. Electrodes have been implanted into animals' skulls by scientists seeking to stimulate the hunger centers in the brain. Appetite stimulants, especially arsenic (a potent human carcinogen), are widely used today, together with anabolic steroids, hormones, and other drugs to accelerate growth.

Special hybrid strains and genetically selected lines of animals are being produced to increase productivity and efficiency. And now with genetic engineering, animals *twice* normal size may be soon created; scientists have already done this with mice using the implanted growth hormone gene of a human. Why keep three cows when one super-cow can produce as much milk as three (by extrapolation, can you imagine genetically creating a human three times our normal size)? But there are limits to which these disease- and stress-susceptible hybrids can be pushed. Fast growing broiler chickens keel over and die, their hearts unable to keep up the oxygen demand of rapidly growing muscle "flesh." High-yielding dairy cows suffer from a variety of production diseases; fast-growing pigs become overheated when disturbed and drop dead—the so-called porcine stress syndrome. Such technology creates complex "domestogenic" diseases because many animals do not have the capacity to adapt. This necessitates more research and costly controls; symptoms alone are treated rather than the underlying causes.

While genetic, hormonal, and other manipulations make these space-age farm animals put on weight faster or produce more eggs or milk, they require assistance in adapting to the stressful, crowded factory conditions. Piglets have their tails amputated to prevent tail biting and cannibalism; poultry are debeaked and often declawed, and it has been proposed they even be fitted with rose-tinted contact lenses to reduce crowding stress. Keeping stock in semidarkness is another way of combating overcrowding. Light-dark cycles are manipulated to regulate feeding and hormones are used to synchronize breeding and even delivery of young. Artificial insemination is old hat, and sperm banks, test-tube babies and embryo transfer were developed on the space-age farm long before such biotechniques were available to people. High-yielding cows and sows are super-ovulated with hormones, operated upon, and their eggs are then fertilized and placed in regular recipient animals. This way super-utility lines can be spawned rapidly.

Even natural birth is considered counterproductive because of the attendant risks of disease contamination. Consequently, pregnant sows just ready to deliver are opened up and their offspring delivered by caesarian section under squeaky-clean conditions. These animals become the foundation stock of almost disease-free herds. Naturally they must be kept indoors all their lives, and both workers and visitors must enter an airlock, strip, shower, and wear sterile clothing whenever they enter the unit. Some space-age hog experts also believe that the natural mother is too inefficient, so piglets have been taken away soon after birth and raised on a robot "Autosow." This means that the mother sow can be artificially inseminated and produce another litter sooner.

The "Pig Mama" and "Autosow" are automated rearing systems for piglets taken from their mothers at one day of age. Initially these systems were developed to help save sickly "runt" piglets, but some animal technologists, dedicated to eradicating all of nature's inefficiencies, would have the natural sow mother replaced entirely. The mother's system is allowed no time to adjust; she becomes a reproduction machine.

Developers of these artificial sows claim that they can create a better system than nature has, for a sow may accidentally crush or cannibalize her piglets, a common problem in poorly designed farrowing crates. As the egg incubator replaced the broody hen, so the robot sow could come to replace the natural mother. These inventions are part of the industrialization of animal farming, which agricultural journalist Steve Turner[2] regards "as machines that effectuate corporate control of animal husbandry." They are the necessary adjuncts of the spread of this lobe of big-time agribusiness. And as the board room takes over ownership of livestock, the concept of food animals as creatures worthy of consideration, just for themselves, is peeled away as meat from the bone. Land grant universities, founded to improve the lot of family farms, Turner states, have instead helped put them out of business by helping develop capital-intensive systems that are cost effective only on large industrial-scale farms.

According to Turner, these innovations have created a central moral issue: "In precarious times for humans, simple laws of survival may make life understandably bad for domestic creatures. But when the reason for devising repugnant animal nurture systems is simply the desire for a higher return on investment, the social implications are ominous, bespeaking an imbalance between the dynamics of the economic system and the experience of life itself."

In essence, as farms become fewer and larger, respect for animals as individuals and as species gradually erodes. But, as Turner writes, "not until today's generation did that flagging respect disappear into contempt, the consignment of intelligent life to physical torture, genetic freakhood, and machine nurture, and only because its sole purpose is to produce protein and cholesterol and its by-products for human consumption." Turner is surely correct in concluding that "at some level, the debasement of other species to suit our dominant modes of money-making is an allegory—percolating up through the biological strata—for what we are doing to ourselves. Or at least, making ready to do."

Space-age farming biotechnology also includes the new "efficiency" system of feeding feces and slurry back to the animals. I was once shown an experiment by an animal scientist who wanted to conserve water for the pig industry so he was giving the pigs filtered slurry water (including animals' urine) to drink. But he found, to his frustration, the pigs got more parasitic worms! Sows have been fed some of the excrement of fattening pigs; cattle have been given their own feces mixed raw in their feed or in silage and have their rations enriched with poultry manure. Drugs from animals' medicated feed, which are excreted along with partially digested food, are hazardous contaminants of such fecal material. This drug-residue buildup is a health hazard to consumers, further aggravated by the rendering of dead and diseased animals, often heavily treated with drugs, into meat meal, which is also fed back to farm animals. In the old days, manure was recycled naturally back to the land to improve soil quality. Now there's so much because there are so many animals concentrated on factory farms that animal wastes are a major source of ground water pollution and also air pollution, contributing to acid rain and global warming (from methane).

Within all of this high technology, the animals are essentially production units; input (feed, costs, and so on) and output (performance) are manipulated and monitored with the ideal goal of minimizing input (as with lowest-cost feed formulation) and maximizing output. In the process, the animals are no longer perceived as living creatures. They are the biomachines of the factory farm that process and convert various materials into animal protein for human profit and gastronomic enjoyment.

Farm animals are raised under very similar factory conditions in Europe and North America. I have described them in detail in a textbook entitled *Farm Animals*. To mention just a few examples, milk-fed veal calves are kept in social isolation for sixteen weeks in individual wooden crates so narrow that they cannot even turn around, make normal postural adjustments, or even groom themselves satisfactorily. The calves are kept relatively immobile so that their meat will be tender, like newborn "baby veal." It must also be white, or it will not fetch a high price. In order to make the meat pale, the calves are deprived of iron, so that they are borderline anemic. They are also deprived of roughage (hay), because its iron content could darken the meat—yet the calves crave roughage as they mature. No straw bedding is provided, as they would eat it. Many calves are literally cripples and have great difficulty walking when they are uncrated and driven into trucks to go to the slaughterhouse.

Their mothers—dairy cows—generally have an easier life, but there is a trend to keep very large herds in feedlot-style corrals or in sheds on concrete slats. If they are kept indoors on these slats, their feet crack and become infected. In the open dirt-lot corrals, they are rarely provided with adequate shade or shelter, and the muck they wallow in causes serious udder and foot infections. The green pastures that they once grazed in so placidly have been lost to real estate development or have been plowed up to produce cash crops or feed for livestock.

Beef cattle in the United States and other countries are "finished" (fattened) for 100 to 120 days in open dirt lots, which are often overcrowded. The cattle are fed a "hot" diet high in concentrates and grains, which is stressful because cattle are basically consumers of roughage. This diet can lead to bloat, foot inflammation (laminitis), acid indigestion, ulceration of the digestive system, and subsequent infection of the liver. In order to reduce injuries in these overcrowded feedlots, the cattle are dehorned—have their horns cut off—without an anesthetic. They are also castrated without anesthetic and branded more than once with a red-hot iron. These brutal treatments adversely affect productivity but because of mass production—the economies of scale—there is little economic incentive to adopt humane alternatives.

Of all the practices down on the factory farm, the care of breeding sows that produce piglets that are fattened into pork, ham, and bacon, engenders the most concern. Rows of sows are housed indoors, often in semidarkness, on concrete slats without bedding. For several years they are either chained to the ground with a collar around their necks or shoulders, or are kept in narrow stalls in which they cannot even turn around. Living over their own waste is another health hazard and is a recognized occupational health hazard for people working in swine confinement buildings. When they are ready to give birth, they are put into metal farrowing crates that similarly restrict almost all activities: They can only stand up, lie down with difficulty, eat, drink, and evacuate. Such conditions would shock muckrakers like Upton Sinclair far more than anything they actually envisioned at the Chicago abattoirs in the early 1900s.

Such immobility and confinement results in many problems, including lameness, arthritis, obesity, infertility, and birth difficulties. Sows normally make a nest before they give birth. Frustration or privation of this and other basic instincts can cause stress and abnormal "neurotic" behavior patterns: excessive chewing or chomping on the bars of the crate or pen, for example.

Laying hens suffer considerably in modern egg factories. Four and sometimes five birds are confined in a wire cage twelve by sixteen or eighteen inches in size, stacked in long lines, usually in tiers of four or more. This is called the battery-cage system. Lights are dim and, as mentioned, the birds are debeaked to reduce cannibalism. This process must be repeated, often resulting in extensive damage to the birds' sensitive mouth parts, during their one- to three-year incarceration. In some egg factories, the birds are starved for up to ten days. This shock treatment, which kills many birds, is done to force them to moult and stop laying eggs. After a rest period, they are built up again and a second egg-laying cycle begins. Not all farms follow this practice. Instead, the birds are killed after their first laying cycle and are made into soups and pet food.

In contrast to the severe privation of laying hens, broiler chickens—those destined to be cooked and consumed—have considerably more freedom and have a mercifully shorter life of six to eight weeks. Broiler factories are low buildings up to 350 feet long, each containing 20,000 to 40,000 birds or more on a "deep litter" floor of wood shavings or other absorbent material. By the time the birds are ready for slaughter, they have little more than half a square foot of floor space each. Hysteria (mass panic), cannibalism, and heart attacks, possibly from overstimulation, are common problems. No perch space is provided for broilers. The litter, soaked with their droppings, creates an irritating, ammonia-rich environment, especially in humid weather, leading to eye disease, respiratory problems, and contact burns on the birds' skin called breast blisters. Catching these birds for transport to slaughter is no easy task and results in a high percentage of injuries, especially broken wings and legs. Because of these problems, research has been done on raising the birds in cages, but they develop abnormally with deformed limbs and fragile bones that break easily when they are handled.

ADAPTATION, WELFARE, AND PRODUCTIVITY

While artifical breeding methods have been widely adopted, the basic nature of farm animals has not been changed. Contrast a wolf, dingo, Chihuahua, and Great Dane—they differ widely in structure, but their basic behavioral repertoires and instinctual needs and emotions are virtually identical. Domestication has not changed their essential intrinsic nature (or *telos*). The argument that battery-caged hens, turkeys, pigs, and other farm animals are dumb, insensitive, degenerate forms ideally adapted to the conditions of total confinement factory farming is untrue. Some believe that turkeys are so degenerate that they have lost the instinct to to breed, hence they must be artificially insem-inated. The truth is that they have relatively normal sex drives but are physically incapable of breeding because of the huge breast muscles that have been selectively bred into them. These are structural changes, not alterations of the intrinsic nature of the farm animal—its basic needs, emotional reactions, and in-stinctual patterns. In nature, the animal's *telos* fits like a glove with its environment. This is called adaptation. But in total confinement on the factory farm, the animal is less fit and may have neither the freedom nor the environmental conditions con-ducive to satisfying its basic needs. The greater the privation, the greater is the challenge upon the animal to adapt. After a certain point, the animal is under chronic stress. Various treatments—debeaking, medication of feed with antibiotics, and reduced illumination—may reduce stress, but the very na-ture of intensive factory farming and the economic imperatives of mass production—where the measure of efficiency is how much meat or eggs can be produced per square foot of building space and amount of food consumed—subjects the animals to stress. Susceptible individuals and hybrid strains are likely to suffer more than others.

Many animal scientists erroneously speak of the animal's productivity (rate of growth, or milk or egg yield) as being the cardinal indicator of well-being and argue that if the animals were under stress, they would not be productive and so farmers wouldn't make any profits. In reality, many of the treatments reduce the physical expression of stress (as disease and injuries from fighting) while leaving the psychological distress. Further-more, studies have shown that animals given more living space and individual human attention are more productive than factory-farmed animals. But then, drug companies wouldn't profit.

Automation promised to free farmers from routine chores so that they could spend more time with the animals. Instead, farmers have acquired more and more animals, and human at-tention, a vital part of animal husbandry, has been all but elim-inated. This is especially true on large factory farms, where one person oversees thousands of animals. Disease incidence and mortality increases with increasing herd or flock size, but because of overstocking, running costs are offset and profits justify such overall inhumane and inefficient production. This economy of scale may be profitable and efficient in terms of direct costs and benefits to the producer, but there are indirect hidden costs to the consumer, the environment, and the animals themselves in terms of their overall welfare.

Productivity on the factory farm is not simply the biological index of the individual animal's feed conversion efficiency in relation to its rate of growth or egg or milk yield per day per unit of food consumed. Rather the overall production per pen or cage of animals is computed against the cost of labor, equipment, and feed. In sum, "productivity" is a misused term. In spite of agribusiness's claim to the contrary, it cannot be regarded as a valid indicator of animal health and well-being.

ENVIRONMENTAL AND SOCIAL ISSUES

Concern for the welfare of those billions of animals on factory farms goes much deeper than the surface phenomena of gross confinement, suffering, and unnecessary privation. It goes right to the heart of agribusiness whose values must be humanized. The indifferent treatment of farm animals is symptomatic of a lack of ethical awareness. As Wendell Berry shows in his book *The Unsettling of America, Agriculture and Culture*, the land is treated with the same impersonal indifference, and as a consequence we are destroying our life-support systems.[4] We must restore these essential humane, ethical, and ecological connections in our consciousness and actions, because our own good and future are bound inseparably with the quality of the earth and of our relationships with all life. It is called stewardship, the essence of husbandry.

Berry describes factory farming as follows:

> The damages of our present agriculture all come from the determination to use the life of the soil as if it were an extractable resource like coal, to use living

things as if they were machines, to impose scientific (that is, laboratory) exactitude upon living complexities that are ultimately mysterious.

If animals are regarded as machines, they are confined in pens remote from the source of their food, where their excrement becomes, instead of a fertilizer, first a "waste" and then a pollutant. Furthermore, because confinement feeding depends so largely on grains, grass is removed from the rotation of crops and more land is exposed to erosion.

If plants are regarded as machines, we wind up with huge monocultures, productive of elaborate ecological mischiefs, which are in turn productive of agricultural mischief: monocultures are much more susceptible to pests and diseases than mixed cultures and are therefore more dependent on chemicals.

If the soil is regarded as a machine, then its life, its involvement in living systems and cycles, must perforce be ignored. It must be treated as a dead, inert chemical mass. If its life is ignored, then so must be the natural sources of its fertility—and not only ignored, but scorned. (P. 90)

One may well wonder how agribusiness can make any profits from keeping animals under such conditions. Mark Kramer, in *Three Farms: Making Milk, Meat, and Money from the American Soil*, presents clear evidence that small farmers produce better food more cheaply than their big-time "factory style" counterparts do.[5]

Corporate farming, which Kramer sees as essentially a manufacturing process, is replacing independent family farming, a vital part of our culture. Those who live and work on the land and tend their crops and livestock personally have a greater sense of empathy and responsibility toward them than corporate employees, who are interchangeable, replacing skill with system and accepting corporate goals in place rather than personal ones.

Yet small farms have been caught up in the treadmill of industrial expansion. As Kramer outlines the problem, land owners, food processors, and banks operate in concert for the benefits of large farm operations. Banks are more willing to give loans to large corporations than to small farmers, and the present tax structure favors the corporate and large-scale factory farmer. Also centralized processing companies, which constitute an oligopoly over American food markets, prefer to buy from large corporate factory farms that can guarantee minimum supplies, which a small or medium size family farm operation cannot.

Agribusiness has a host of proponents to sell the notion of factory-style space-age farming to the public and to garner public funds for further research and development: technocrats, multinational corporations, investors, scientists, university research departments, public relations firms, and lobbyists. Various government agencies support the goals and aims of intensive livestock production, believing it to be progressive and in the best interests of the nation. However, these "best interests" are limited primarily to agribusiness corporations—feed, drug, and equipment manufacturers and suppliers, many of which are gaining control of the entire livestock industry and are either incorporating independent farmers into contract peonage or forcing them out of business. Costs to producers, consumers, and the environment are escalating. Without powerful coalitions of farmers, concerned consumers, environmentalist, conservation, and animal welfare groups, the trend will continue until the entire livestock industry is controlled exclusively by a few powerful oligopolies.

Agriculture also presents growing economic and political concerns that affect human welfare. Well-known social critic Ivan Illich, in *Medical Nemesis*,[6] writes:

> Beyond a certain level of capital investment in the growing and processing of food, malnutrition will become pervasive. . . . No biological engineering can prevent undernourishment and food poisoning beyond

this point. . . . This is but the application of a general law: when more than a certain proportion of value is produced by the industrial mode, subsistence activities are paralysed, equity declines, and total satisfaction diminishes. [The encroaching world famine] will not be the sporadic famine that formerly came with drought and war, or the occasional food shortage that could be remedied by good will and emergency shipments. The coming hunger is a by-product of the inevitable concentration of industrialized agriculture in rich countries and in the fertile regions of poor countries.★ Paradoxically, the attempt to counter famine by further increases in industrially efficient agriculture only widens the scope of the catastrophe by depressing the use of marginal lands. Famine will increase until the trend towards capital-intensive food production by the poor for the rich has been replaced by a new kind of labour-intensive, regional, rural autonomy. Beyond a certain level of industrial hubris, nemesis *must* set in, because progress, like the broom of the sorcerer's apprentice, can no longer be turned off. (P. 131)

HUMANE REFORMS

Humane reforms are clearly needed. Systems need to be designed that are more conducive to the farm animals' welfare and to the satisfaction of their basic needs. Even the five most basic "freedoms" of animals—to easily and comfortably stand up, lie down, stretch, turn around, and groom or preen—are too often denied to factory farm animals.

Public awareness is an essential ingredient of transforming factory farming from the dehumanizing and "deanimalized" status quo that agribusiness condones and defends. Right now

---

★This concentration in turn creates urban poverty as disenfranchised and unemployed rural populations migrate to urban industrial centers to subsist on welfare. Author.

some believe the effective step is to become a vegetarian or a "conscientious omnivore"—know "whom" you eat, how it was raised, transported and slaughtered. We should all endeavor to eat low on the food chain (i.e. eat less food of animal origin and more food of plant origin) to reduce the inefficiencies, waste, unethical animal exploitation, and environmental costs that excessive meat consumption requires. As citizen–consumers, we should push to protect the interests and livelihood of those independent farmers who care well for their land and stock. Codes of practice need to be established to elevate the standards of livestock production with a return to good husbandry or empathetic stewardship. While advances in agritechnology and space–age farm management need not be abandoned, they must be humanized and integrated with sound ecological principles of regenerative agriculture. The farm animals must be respected and treated as animals with rights and interests, not biomachines. It is also in our best interests to farm the land and raise livestock without further depleting wildlife and natural resources and without jeopardizing human health with chemicals.

As with any industry, reforms in factory animal farming will be difficult to instigate. Opponents will rationalize that factory farming is an efficient way to produce cheap animal protein and that humane reforms will cause inflationary pressures on the economy.

Yet it is easy to see why factory farming is not cost efficient. It has been built on the soft foundation of cheap and plentiful fossil fuels—needed to provide energy to grow crops, transport feed and livestock, and make petroleum-based pesticides, herbicides, and fertilizers for the crops used to feed the animals. These fuels are no longer cheap. In terms of energy expenditure, factory farming of livestock is grossly inefficient; seven times more fossil fuel is required to produce one kilogram of meat than to produce one kilogram of grain protein, and sixteen times more labor.

And while humane reforms may be costly initially, when changes have been made, long-term profits rather than losses may be predicted. Professor David Sainsbury of Cambridge University in England has demonstrated that laying hens kept free in half-open barns are healthier, more productive, and more profitable than hens kept in cages. Dr. Bob Fritschen with the U.S. Department of Agriculture in Nebraska has shown that total confinement of hogs is less efficient than keeping fattening hogs in half-open climatic houses and that hogs in total confinement actually develop "building fatigue," which is reflected in reduced growth rates. Numerous other research reports document how factory farming methods diminish production in other species as well. Why haven't such findings been incorporated on the factory farm? Partly because of the gap in communications between the laboratory and the farmer and among research institutions in different countries, but principally because these improvements in animal welfare do not offer a sufficient profit margin to make them seem worth adopting.

Furthermore, the question of farm animal welfare as presented in livestock journals has been clouded by a smokescreen of paranoid delusions that the growing and politically influential animal protection movement is bent upon putting livestock producers out of business, making all Americans into vegetarians, and establishing strict laws to dictate how one can raise livestock. What *is* putting farmers out of business is agribusiness.

There are various ways around such obstacles at both national and international levels. The United States and Canada could follow the precedent set by the United Kingdom and establish a Farm Animal Welfare Advisory Council, consisting of industry representatives and those from animal science, veterinary medicine, and animal welfare. Codes of practice—at first minimal, subsequently optimal—could be formulated and enforced regarding how farm animals should be husbanded. Farmers could be better advised on building design and animal welfare as in Sweden, where a central veterinary authority provides free counsel. In West Germany (where the battery-cage system for laying hens has been recently judged inhumane), farm animals are included in the Animal Protection Act of 1972, which states that:

Any person who is keeping an animal or who is looking after it:

(1) shall give the animal adequate food and care suitable for its species; and he shall provide accommodation which takes account of its natural behavior;

(2) shall not permanently so restrict the needs of an animal of that species for movement and exercise that the animal is exposed to avoidable pain, suffering or injury.

We must strike a golden mean, economics notwithstanding, between meeting farm animals' needs and not subjecting them to such social and environmental-experiential privations and restrictions that cause suffering or reduce their abilities to cope with stress. In essence, their welfare is dependent on the degree to which they are able to adapt without suffering to the environments that we provide for them. The following basic guidelines have been suggested by the British Carpenter Committee[7] to govern the management of animals under human stewardship. No husbandry system should deny the environmental requirements of the animal's basic behavioral needs. These needs should include the following minimal environmental requirements:

- freedom to perform natural physical movement

- association with other animals, where appropriate of their own kind

- facilities for comfort-activities, e.g., rest, sleep and body care

- provision of food and water to maintain full health

- ability to perform daily routines of natural activities

- opportunity for the activities of exploration and play, especially for young animals

- satisfaction of minimal spatial and territorial requirements including a visual field and "personal" space

Deviations from these principles should be avoided as far as possible, but where such deviations are absolutely unavoidable, efforts should be made to compensate the animal environmentally.

The Animal Welfare Act in the United States and other countries should be amended to include provision for the welfare of farm animals along these lines. Producers might be adversely affected financially from the initial setup costs of these implementing reforms. Therefore, imports of animal produce from countries that employ cheaper, inhumane, or ecologically unsound methods of livestock production and maintenance should be restricted. International agreements and comparable humane codes of livestock husbandry are needed. The European Economic Community has already drawn up a series of articles defining the minimally acceptable codes of farm-animal husbandry for member nations.

If farm-animal produce is labeled—giving a grade of humaneness to designate how animals have been raised, for example—consumers could select products from humanely raised animals. Such a system operates in Holland, where producers of free-range eggs cannot keep up with the public demand for their "happy" eggs. An informed public can do much to improve the welfare of farm animals: They can demand government investigation, funding for applied research into developing optimal production systems, and regulations in the form of voluntary guidelines or codes or mandatory, legally enforced directives; they can also directly, through selective buying, support more humane and ecologically sound systems of animal and plant food production.

In many countries government agencies responsible for educating the public on matters of nutrition and health have been concerned primarily with promoting the interests of agribusiness. Such agencies must now establish programs, especially for schoolchildren and for low-income families, to educate people on how to prepare nutritious and balanced meals that are not based primarily on meat. Studies in the United States have shown that with the predicted increases in the cost of most meat and dairy products, poorer families will not be able to afford to buy such dietary staples. They need to be educated as to what less costly substitutes can be used in place of meat, and the market availability of high-protein alternatives such as beans, lentils, and soybean products should be improved. According to a number of studies, the nation's diet needs to be radically changed. Doing so will have positive repercussions economically and may help reduce the numbers of animals kept on factory farms. A growing consensus of expert opinion states we should consume less fat (in meat, eggs, and dairy products); less meat, salt, sugar, and refined flour; and more beans, grains, fresh fruits, and vegetables. (While fresh fish and other seafoods provide a good protein source, overfishing and ocean pollution make this an increasingly unreliable food source.)

NEW DIRECTIONS

Before he stepped down from office in 1981, Department of Agriculture Secretary Bob Bergland published an in-depth analysis of organic farming methods,[8] which clearly showed that they are cost effective. More recently the National Academy of Sciences published a detailed report entitled *Alternative Agriculture*, documenting the many shortcomings of modern agriculture, and demonstrating the economic viability of more humane, sustainable agricultural practices that have less reliance upon crop chemicals and veterinary drugs. Both reports clearly challenge current chemical-dependent agribusiness practices. Chemical farming is not self-sustaining because many varieties of high-yield crops are pesticide-dependent due to their genetic makeup and also because synthetic fertilizers and monoculture production impoverish the soil and make crops even more susceptible to diseases and pests. Similarly, intensively housed live-stock are more susceptible to diseases. Rather than adopting the sensible remedy of deintensifying production methods (by raising fewer animals with more space in a more healthful environment that provides for their basic behavioral needs), it is more expedient and profitable to treat the symptoms of poor animal husbandry and crop production respectively with drugs and pesticides that profit the monopolistic petrochemical and pharmaceutical companies.

The world population, which is expected to jump from 5 billion today to 8–10 billion within the next forty years, cannot support itself on natural resources alone. American agricultural technology will be of limited help. *We have already crossed that self-limiting threshold where the human population exceeds the carrying capacity of natural ecosystems.* Hence artificial ecosystems must be developed with appropriate science and technology.

But such development must not be at the expense of our efforts to conserve natural ecosystems and the integrity of the biosphere. Solar, wind, and biomass (plant alcohol) energy, integrated pest management, judicious application of biotechnology (genetic engineering), and labor-intensive mixed farming systems will be an integral part of future agriculture. The foundations established today by "organic" farmers are essentially labor intensive, technologically appropriate, sustainable systems that are resource–replenishing and recycling.[9] Organic farms are cyclical patterns of systems in co–creative harmony. Most present-day systems are linear, such as monocultures of corn or pig production with their incredible waste and pollution. As many past cultures and present-day organic farmers have shown, regenerative systems are more efficient and productive on a long term and sustainable basis. In fact, they are more appropriate to support the world's growing numbers of starving people than current factory-type agricultural practices. Yet the useful techniques and scientific advances generated by agribusiness should not be abandoned. Some of these advances may be applied in the development of large-scale regenerative farming systems. We must research and develop and phase out, as rapidly as possible, the ecocidal, linear, and entropic pattern of contemporary factory farming.

Factory farming is a highly controversial issue because it evokes many metaphors: the subjugation of life to the industrial system; the subordination of individual rights and autonomy to goals of efficiency and productivity; the maintenance and propagation of life under wholly unnatural conditions; and the dependence of life on drugs, vaccines, and technology.

Critics of factory farming may or may not be unconsciously bearing in mind the social relevance of these metaphors. Either way, the controversy over the rightness or wrongness of factory farming is highly political and socially relevant. Perhaps there is some wisdom, some atavistic survival instinct, in the abhorrence many have not only for the conditions under which farm animals are kept but for the human conditions also. Defenders of the animal industry are quick to judge all criticisms as anthropomorphic, utopian idealism. They dismiss any suggestions of alternative husbandry systems as a return to primitive, uneconomical methods, stating that consumers need and expect a cheap and plentiful supply of farm-animal produce. Surely neither the critics nor the supporters of factory farming are totally wrong in their perceptions. Animals living at high density, like us, need vaccines and drugs to control and treat disease. Science and technology can certainly help in helping animals—and us —adapt to our respective conditions.

But just as there are limits to the subordination of human rights for the good of society, so limits must be placed on the subjugation of animals in the service of society. An informed society must decide where the ethical limits should be set, economics and public benefits notwithstanding. The basis for our decisions must not be weighed by economic interests or science alone, but by ethics also, because our exploitation of animals incurs a moral obligation to maximize their well-being in return for their contribution to our own.

The inherent cruelties of intensive livestock and poultry

production have a ripple effect that harms consumers and others. These are summarized as follows.[10]

INHERENT CRUELTIES OF FACTORY FARMING

Cruelty: To the Animals

The stress, distress, and production-related diseases suffered by livestock and poultry raised in confinement are well documented.[10] Drugs are necessary to maintain the animals' health and productivity. A consumer health hazard due to residual drugs and antibiotics in the animals' meat, milk, and eggs results. Millions of animals are subjected to the documented cruelties associated with transportation to auctions and slaughterhouses. Cruelty is an unavoidable aspect of slaughter when large numbers of animals are processed. The processing of large numbers of animals also leads to inadequate inspection of the animal products, another consumer health hazard.

Cruelty: To the Consumer

Inadequately inspected meats contaminated with harmful bacteria, drug residues (including pesticides and other agrichemicals), and diseases pose serious threats to consumer health. It is well documented that a reduction in the consumption of meat products contributes significantly to a person's overall well-being. The following health problems have been linked to the consumption of animal products: food poisoning (*Salmonella* infections), allergies (to the antibiotics residual in meats), arteriosclerosis, breast and colon cancer, and osteoporosis.

Moreover, consumers should be very wary of

"Meat Week," which I have come to regard as Cruelty Week, for those who care for animals, for the good farmer, and for their own health. Meat Week is then a week to think twice about eating meat or any farm-animal product. Meat has come to occupy a central place in the American diet, but at best, given all the information I have provided, plus its overall cost, it is enlightened self-interest for this nation and all consumers to reduce the overall production and consumption of meat.

Cruelty: To Wildlife

Millions of acres are used to produce feed for livestock and poultry. This displaces wildlife, pushing many species toward extinction. This problem is aggravated by wholesale use of poisons to control "pests" and predators.

Cruelty: To Farmers Who Care

For economic reasons, farmers are forced to adopt cruel and unhealthful methods of livestock and poultry production. Thousands of family farmers have been forced out of business by large factory farms where cruelty is an integral part of animal management in order to maximize "efficiency."

Cruelty: To the Environment

The loss of nonrenewable resources such as topsoil through soil erosion, and the squandering of deepwater (aquifer) reserves for the raising of crops to feed livestock, and for export to affluent countries abroad as livestock feed is undermining American agriculture's ability to sustain itself. Wilderness areas in the United States, and tropical rain forests in Central and South America are destroyed primarily so the land can be used to raise cattle.

Cruelty: To "Third World" People

Native people and peasant farmers are encouraged to raise cash crops for export, some of which are used to feed poultry and livestock in the United States, while local peoples suffer from malnutrition.

Violation of Rights

The meat industry is just one segment of the American agribusiness food production system that violates others' rights in its monopolistic game of control and industrial-scale production efficiency. It violates the right of farm animals to humane treatment; the right of consumers to wholesome and healthful food*; the right of family farmers, rural communities here and abroad, and native peoples to self-determination; the basic rights of migrant farm workers, slaughterhouse workers, and producers under the peonage of production contracts have long been violated by agribusiness. The right of wildlife to a whole and healthy environment uncontaminated with poisonous agrichemicals and even the right of wilderness areas to water are also violated.[11]

Humans, animals, and the environment are not expendable resources, yet the technocracy of agribusiness treats them as such.

For many reasons, fish is not a viable dietary alternative to meat. No method of fishing is humane; many fish habitats (especially marine) are open sewers so fish flesh is contaminated. Also, commercially raised fish—trout, catfish, salmon, etc.—are treated with various drugs to treat and prevent stress-related diseases, which in turn contaminate both the fish and their aquatic environs.

_____

*Foodborne illnesses (from bacterial contamination of meat especially) cost the U.S. public $4.8 billion in 1987, according to USDA economist Tanya Roberts.

CHAPTER 3

"Agricide": Agriculture's Nemesis

Agriculture is cultivating the land with understanding and therefore respect: subduing the earth (which means bringing it under cultivation, according to *Webster's Dictionary*) and replenishing it (Genesis 1: 26–28). *Culture* is that which embodies and sustains those values that enable us to cultivate ourselves and nature alike, and even, as Plato and Aristotle believed, "to become like divinity as much as that is within our power." This takes the same degree of love and wisdom of one's own kind as it does of animals, plants, and this living planet, our ever-nurturing and (decreasingly) forgiving Mother Nature. As Taoist philosopher Lao Tzu said: "Love the Earth as yourself, then you can truly care for all things." Culture and agriculture are thus bound together by love and care—the essence of humane stewardship.

Wendell Berry[1] writes:

> An agriculture cannot survive long at the expense of the natural systems that support it and that provide it with models. A culture cannot survive long at the expense of either its agricultural or its natural sources. To live at the expense of the source of life is obviously suicidal. Though we have no choice but to live at the expense of other life, it is necessary to recognize the

limits and dangers involved: past a certain point in a
unified system, "other life" is our own.

The definitive relationships in the universe are
thus not competitive but interdependent. And from a
human point of view they are analogical. We can build
one system only within another. We can have agriculture only within nature, and culture only within
agriculture. At certain points these systems have to
conform with one another or destroy one another. (P.
47)

Currently agriculture, along with all the natural wisdom and
empathy that our farmer-ancestors and earlier hunter-gatherers
acquired (and, with such wisdom and empathy, were deeply
religious), is being lost—to high-tech agribusiness. From culture to technocracy: from sensibility to money, power, and
control. The evolution of factory farming is a natural consequence of our culture's materialistic and objectifying attitude
toward nature. Consequently, humanity no longer acts as part
of a unified field of being. By not acting so, we destroy this
unity, violating the ecological laws of nature and the ethical and
spiritual principles of our forebears. Factory farming is a second
Industrial Revolution.

FARM-ANIMAL WELFARE AND
"AGRICULTURAL NEMESIS"

Contrary to the claims of animal scientists and agribusiness
spokespersons, factory-scale animal production systems do not
feed the hungry world. In addition to poisoning our life-support
systems with pesticides and other agrichemicals, disrupting the
ecology, and depleting the soil of trace minerals, the United
States is now squandering nonrenewable agricultural resources
(soil, water, and overall environmental quality) in raising crops
to feed animals for domestic consumption and for export to
affluent countries, primarily as animal feed.

Factory farming, like biomedical research on laboratory

animals, is but another multinational industry that is insulated from public censure by its political, legal, and governmental protective structure. The public influence, self-serving policy decisions, and "ideological hypnosis" of this structure's scientists, economists, and other spokespeople all work to maintain the status quo of agribusiness, veterinary medicine, and other industries. All this occurs at the expense of taxpayers, the environment, and consumers' health.

As discussed in the last chapter, the physical and psychological well-being of factory-farmed animals are seldom considered on an individual basis; rather they are sacrificed in favor of overall productivity. And productivity and health are defined primarily in terms of the overall system's efficiency; the animals are merely conceptualized as the biomechanical components. Antibiotics, hormones, and other drugs are used to maintain health and productivity and to help animals cope with the stresses of intensive factory farming. To enhance efficiency, they are fed such waste products as cardboard, newspaper, and other industry by-products—and, as we discussed earlier, even their own excrement. Nothing is known regarding the consumer health consequences of this. Agribusiness and allied government agencies have rationalized and denied for too long the animal welfare and consumer health implications of drug-dependent farming. The nemesis of animal agriculture thus parallels the nemesis of chemically dependent crop farming.

THE AGRICIDE TREADMILL AND FARM-ANIMAL WELFARE

The factory farming of animals is, in essence, a product of the agricultural treadmill. As with the development and application of insecticides, the development of intensive confinement systems for raising livestock and poultry was not motivated by hunger or the threat of famine but by the treadmill effect of increasing capital-intensive rather than labor-intensive farming practices. After 1950, producers of fruit, cotton, and corn (for feeding livestock) became the largest users of insecticides. This chemical farming was required to protect capital-intensive farming and was the foundation for the involvement of the petrochemical industries in food production. As in the United States there have been food surpluses from overproduction year after year, it is ironic that chemical crop farming and factory farming of animals should have evolved. They have done so because of the treadmill effect of farmers competing to reduce production costs (and not, as agribusiness claims, to produce cheap and wholesome food for all) coupled with the lure of commodity price-support programs.

The consequences of this treadmill effect can be summed up in the one word: agricide. This is agriculture's nemesis. Meat has become simply a convenience food. Touted for its high, almost "complete" nutritional value (which no single vegetable product can provide by itself), meat has become a staple in American diets. Yet by combining vegetable products, a more nutritionally complete and healthful meal can be prepared without meat.

Some of the signs of agricide include: the bankruptcy of thousands of farmers; the virtual extinction of the midsize family farm and decline of rural communities; the loss of 5 to 6 billion tons of topsoil each year to erosion; the rapid depletion of deepwater aquifers used for crop irrigation; salination and depletion of soil nutrients; nationwide groundwater pollution from animal wastes and agrichemicals; ecologically unsound monocrop production and large concentrations of animals, which necessitate the excessive use of chemicals, harmful to humans, to control pests and disease.

Agriculture should operate on the principle that "We do not inherit the land; we borrow it from our children." Under agribusiness, our children will have little to inherit except a more polluted and exhausted environment. Yet the experts of our technocracy still believe that science can save us all: with stronger chemicals and genetic engineering to produce supercorn and giant pigs and cows. Science and government view reality only in terms of power—military, economic, technological, political, and medical. They seek power over life itself.

As we strive for absolute control over life, we lose the world, for as Lao Tzu[2] observed:

> *The Earth is sacred.*
> *You cannot improve it.*
> *If you try to change it, you will ruin it.*
> *If you try to hold it, you will lose it.*

AGRICULTURAL REFORMATION AND CULTURAL RESTORATION

Can agribusiness become cultured, governed by the highest ethical principles and by wisdom and empathy and not by the dictates of investors, short-term gains, market fluctuations, and other materialistic values and influences? The restoration of culture depends on this because our agricultural base is our life-support system, not simply the cornerstone of the industrial system.

One promise of our industrial future is genetic engineering, which agribusiness is already excited about. Many other potential industries may arise from this purported miracle of progress. But toward what end? What vision? Is it not one of absolute power and control over life—over the atom, the gene, over nature, animals, and even people who serve the industrial machine? Ever since humans acquired the power of fire, we have evolved from the fossil-fuel age of pyrotechnology to the age of nuclear power and biotechnology. While we may have greater material affluence, are we yet really civilized? Together, love and wisdom make us civilized. How prevalent are these attributes in agribusiness and allied industries?

Furthermore, the kind of diet agribusiness promotes—high in fat and animal protein, low in fresh vegetables, cereal grains, and legumes, and adulterated with preservatives and flavor-enhancing chemicals (which have become necessary because of overcentralized wholesale processing and distribution)—is not conducive to human health. Several expert analysts and study groups, such as the National Academy of Sciences, have linked such diseases as diabetes, high blood pressure, certain forms of cancer, arteriosclerosis,★ stroke, and arthritis to the agribusiness food industry. Yet it would be too simplistic and indeed unfair to blame agribusiness for these problems. Rather they are a consequence of a gradual revolution in agricultural practices over the past fifty years toward capital-intensive chemical farming and the production of vast grain surpluses, which then made it possible to raise more farm animals. We consumers now are in control of the counterrevolution; by changing our dietary habits toward vegetarianism we will help create market incentives for more healthful produce and in the process transform American agriculture to a more regenerative, ecologically sound system. And a more humane one, because farm animals will not need to be raised under such intensive conditions that cause stress and suffering.

A HUMANE REVOLUTION

Animal and human health and welfare are complexly interconnected. Human health will improve if we (1) start to revolutionize our agricultural practices through our government agencies (Environmental Protection Agency, U.S. Department of Agriculture, and so on); (2) begin to phase out the indiscriminate and wholesale use of pesticides, antibiotic feed additives, and other agricultural and farm-animal drugs; and (3) develop a healthful diet and a regenerative, humane and sustainable agriculture. Then far fewer animals will be needed in biomedical research. And with a reduction in the production and consumption of meat, eggs, and dairy products, less land will be used to feed these animals. Then there will be more grain for export to feed the hungry world. And as agriculture

★The processing of food can itself also cause health hazards. For example, the homogenization of milk releases an enzyme that enhances the development of arteriosclerosis. According to researchers, such milk is a greater health hazard than smoking cigarettes.

becomes able to get off the pesticide-herbicide-fungicide and synthetic fertilizer treadmill, vast quantities of oil, coal, and gas that were previously needed to manufacture pesticides, herbicides, and nitrogenous fertilizer will be made available for other uses. Also "marginal" lands could be returned to nature, for the benefit of wildlife. Worldwide aquatic and terrestrial ecosystems will also benefit from a reduction in farm animal wastes and in the use of harmful pesticides.

The food processing industry and the agricultural marketing system must also become decentralized, so that fewer chemicals are used to preserve perishable and "convenience" processed foods.

A humane and regenerative agriculture is one fundamental way that we can begin to replenish the Earth. It is also the only basis for a sound economy. Eating with conscience[3] is also an ethical imperative. It entails eating less meat and other farm animal produce, especially from animals treated inhumanely. If we eat less or no meat, the farm animal population will decline, which will help reduce animal suffering and, no less important, help reduce the amount of land, water, and other resources that are being exhausted in raising crops to feed the animals. By insisting that all animals be treated humanely, we help awaken the sensitivities of farmers and scientists that have been blunted by the economic pressures and values that drive agribusiness and the entire industrial machine.

Eating with conscience will also improve consumer health, help support the good family farmer, and encourage the restoration of agriculture and culture.

THE REAL COSTS

Agribusiness has stated that such reforms would increase the costs of food. This is a myth. The food we eat today is neither cheap nor wholesome. While market prices are low, the hidden and indirect costs of agribusiness are astronomical. Unemployment, depletion of the soil and deep-aquifer water reserves, human health-related costs, running government regulatory agencies, and doing research in medicine and agriculture cost billions of dollars each year.

Land reforms and equitable taxation are vitally needed, in order that everyone shares in the costs of social change entailed in achieving a more healthful environment and a more fulfilling life for all. More government funds are urgently needed, not simply to clean up toxic waste dumps but to educate and create jobs and cottage industries; to restore agriculture; to reorient biomedical research toward prevention; to augment this approach to human health through stringent controls on all industrial and agricultural chemicals, pollutants, and new developments; to restore the environment, the quality of our air, food, and water; to preserve natural resources and protect wilderness areas, unique habitats (terrestrial and aquatic), and viable colonies of indigenous wild animal and plant species.

Just as our life-styles and eating habits must change as agriculture changes, so must the quality of the tools, clothes, and other manufactured items improve. They should be made of natural materials, not synthetics that cannot be recycled. The synthesis and manufacture of synthetics further pollute our environment because they involve the use of massive quantities of diverse and dangerous man-made chemicals. And then we will not have to cause billions of laboratory animals interminable suffering in testing the safety of these chemical products.

We, the people, then, must restore the environment—revolutionize agriculture, industry, and medicine. As consumers and private citizens, we can do this: Indeed it is a survival imperative.

We can all do something to contribute to the peaceful and healing transformation of our species toward social and ecological harmony and world peace, provided we realize the virtue of personal as well as corporate and government responsibility.

This should not be construed as a wholesale indictment of science, technology, medicine, agribusiness, or industry, or of those individuals involved in these fields. Many of these people are dedicated to helping humanity in the creative process of our species' survival. We all fear death, suffering, and extinction, so much so that our collective anxiety has compelled us to completely objectify the world (through the quasi theology of science) and seek power and control over it. In the process we have almost lost the other kind of wisdom that our highly evolved sensory, emotional, and intellectual abilities have endowed us with. A greater recognition of the significance of the power of love (rather than the power of control over life) is needed. In *The Road Less Traveled*, psychiatrist M. Scott Peck defines love as "the will to extend one's self for the purpose of nurturing another's spiritual growth and one's own in the process."[4] It is a balancing of self-interest with respect for the rights and interests of others, including animals. This is the essence of transspecies democracy, the antithesis of biological fascism.

VEGETARIANISM—PERSONAL CHOICE OR ETHICAL IMPERATIVE?

I regard vegetarianism as more than a personal choice. I see it as an ethical imperative for several reasons. The human species is out of balance with the rest of creation not only by virtue of its numbers, but also as a consequence of destructive and ecologically unsound industries and consumer habits. While the problem of overpopulation is being slowly addressed, it cannot be corrected in isolation from these other concerns. Quite simply, we must recognize that it is ecological suicide for us to endeavor to maintain a meat-based agriculture and a primarily carnivorous diet.

We create irreparable damage to the ecology when we destroy natural habitats and displace and exterminate wildlife species to raise livestock and livestock feed. In nature there are always far fewer predator species, such as the wolf, than prey species. Now with a world population of 5 billion people, 1.2 billion cattle, 1.6 billion sheep and goats, and 800 million hogs, the loss of natural biodiversity of wildlife and wildlands is an inevitable consequence of such population imbalances, compounded by pollution, deforestation, and urbanization.

In sum, those who care for nature and for wildlife realize

that vegetarianism is an ethical imperative. Another reason for becoming a vegetarian is because of the cruel ways in which most livestock and poultry are raised, transported, and slaughtered. A simple beginning is to eat less meat and then only from humanely raised, certified organic (drug-free) animals.

When livestock are raised "intensively," they require more drug treatments (dips, worming, live vaccines, antibiotics, and other drugs) because they are more vulnerable to diseases than less-intensively raised animals. Hence organic farming, when it comes to livestock production, is by its nature more humane toward farm animals. This is because with less-intensive husbandry practices (neither overgrazing nor overcrowding) the animals suffer less stress and distress and need less drug treatments and preventive medications.

The public demand for meat will continue, but that demand will be conditional upon the healthfulness of such food. Those farmers who wish to continue livestock production into the twenty-first century are now beginning to see the connections between agriculture's contribution to human health problems and to the environmental crisis and are adopting organic, sustainable, and humane farming practices. (Organic farmers eschew pesticides, nitrate, and other chemical fertilizers and animal drugs alike.)

Aside from supporting organic farmers who practice humane sustainable agriculture, conscientious consumers can also eat lower on the food chain (by eating less food of animal origin and more vegetables, grains, nuts, fruits, and pulses) for reasons of economy and health. The higher up on the food chain one eats, the more contaminated is the food consumed because of bioaccumulation.

Several nutritional studies have shown the importance of reduced meat and animal fat (and butter) consumption. Pesticides, other agripoisons, and industrial pollutants, such as cadmium and lead, are concentrated in the tissues of farm animals, far more than in most nonorganically grown crops. Thus it is enlightened self-interest to shift toward a more vegetarian diet.

According to Masanobu Fuknoka, a Japanese farmer-philosopher and author of *The One Straw Revolution*,[5] "The ultimate goal of farming is not the growing of crops but the cultivation and perfection of human beings."

In one of my previous books *Agricide*,[6] I conclude that vegetarianism and organic, regenerative agriculture are significant steps toward the cultivation of human beings, if not of a Golden Age to come. In this Golden Age, high-tech innovations, even *appropriate* genetic engineering (using engineered microorganisms to manufacture many essential nutrients) will help humanity survive and prosper. But our survival will not be at nature's expense or in violation of the rights of all living things to a whole and healthy environment and to equal and fair consideration. Regardless of whether or not animals have a right not to be eaten, far too many are being produced and consumed today.

Vegetarianism is, therefore, an enlightened decision, if not a long-term survival imperative. Our national security, in part, depends on it. Producing and consuming less farm-animal produce, especially meat, are essential steps toward the overall restoration of our culture, agriculture, and environment. Vegetarianism (or at least eating less meat and only then from organically certified and humane farms), is probably one of the most significant contributions that a person can make to a greater good in these times.

CHAPTER 4

Science, Ethics, and the Use of

Laboratory Animals

An estimated 25 to 35 million animals are used in the United States each year for research, testing, and teaching purposes. Most of these are rodents, which are excluded from any protection under the federal Animal Welfare Act.★ Other animals, such as rabbits, cats, dogs, and monkeys, receive little protection under this act, because the U.S. Department of Agriculture does a wholly inadequate job of inspecting animal research facilities and an even worse job of enforcing the law when violations are found.

I speak from personal experience. The approved conditions under which laboratory animals are kept are generally deplorable. Cages are small. Large rhesus monkeys are kept for years alone in cages two feet by three feet. Deprived of social interaction and anything to manipulate, they develop abnormal "neurotic" behavior, such as stereotyped movements, self mutilation, repetitive masturbation, intense rage or fear, while some eat or drink excessively. Humans, of course, would act no differently under similar conditions. Cats and dogs are often kept

---

★The government's own animal research facilities at the National Institute of Health do *not* all meet the standards of this act, nor are they subject to U.S.D.A. inspection and compliance.

under similarly deprived conditions, with no exercise and infrequent human contact even though many were once house pets that reached laboratories through dealers and local animal shelters. Such extreme conditions affect the animals' behavior and physiology, thus making much research on them of questionable validity (except to other animals under comparable conditions).

In truth, today's standards for laboratory animal care are inadequate for two main reasons when considered in the new light of holistic medicine, which considers the totality of *body-mind-environment interconnectedness.* In terms of animal welfare, these standards give scant consideration to the animals' social, emotional, and environmental needs; they are unscientific and thus counter to progress in medicine because faulty results are obtained whenever the completeness of mind-body-environment is broken. Researchers have shown that segregation (as when an animal is isolated in a laboratory cage) introduces a variety of experimental variables that are *not* accounted for in the original design of the experiment. Thus the validity of research conclusions are dubious at best and probably of little relevance to the real-life conditions that actually cause health and disease. The lack of recognition of the holistic connections that collectively determine health and from which any meaningful parameters of normality must be derived reflects the narrow and scientifically unsound mindset of contemporary medicine, wherein therapeutic effectiveness, though profitable, all too often causes ten new problems in the course of solving the old one.

Scientists interpret abnormal behaviors of caged animals mechanistically, calling them "adaptive." They overlook the simple fact that these behaviors are indicators of biologically inappropriate environments. Besides placing in doubt the validity of their research, their empathetic ability, a vital part of diagnosis and healing, must be questioned. Researchers ignore the animals' psychological suffering and its significance. Perhaps empathy is no longer clearly understood or experienced (as it is now the vogue to interpret empathy as a reactionary type of sentimental anthropomorphism), and because the medical establishment's current worldview excludes the mental and environmental components of well-being. By focusing exclusively on the physical, the medical establishment considers laboratory (and farm) animals to be well as long as they show no gross physical abnormalities or organic pathologies under the current standards of care.

Recent advances in so called holistic or environmental, medicine, reveal the fallacy of this view. While the advances may not result in any immediate reduction in the number of animals being used in biomedical research, they do show that the costly over-reliance upon using animals to find cures for human diseases is imprudent, and that many illnesses are best prevented by adopting organic agriculture, sensible dietary habits and life-styles, and cleaning up a toxic environment. There cannot be physical well-being for man or beast alike, without mental well-being and a healthful environment that also satisfies behavioral and social needs. For the animal in the laboratory, as on the factory farm, these needs are not met, resulting in stress, distress and increased disease susceptibility.

The World Health Organization has defined health as "a state of mental, physical, and social well-being and not merely the absence of disease." These same criteria need to be recognized in the husbandry of laboratory animals. At best, their basic physical needs are satisfied.[1] Their mental states and social well-being are generally ignored; clean air, a cage, food, water, and the absence of disease are the narrow, mechanistic, and unscientific "necessities" currently recognized for both laboratory and farm animals.

Environmental health is another criterion of human health. Environmental medicine is a relatively new field developed to combat new and complex "technogenic" diseases associated with agricultural and other industrial chemicals that contaminate our air, food and water, impair our immune systems and increase our susceptibility to a host of diseases.

"SAFETY" TESTS

Laboratory animals are being used increasingly to test chemicals for their carcinogenic, teratogenic, and other pathological potentials. Such tests, like the "safety" tests for drugs, cosmetics, and other consumables, are so embedded in politics, corporate interests, and costly and ineffective bureaucratic regulations that chemicals known to cause cancer, birth defects, and other diseases are still being manufactured, widely used, and absorbed into our own bodies. Some that have been banned in this country are sold widely to Third World countries. And animal "safety" tests continue. In the process, the basic scientific fact of chemical synergy is overlooked ("synergy" means "combined action." In this context, the combination of two or more chemicals, even at "safe" levels, can have an additive effect, increasing their harmfulness to our bodies.) It is impossible for the 40,000 to 60,000 chemicals now in common use to be tested in combination to determine any reliable safety level. Animal safety tests amount to little more than a public relations campaign to dispel public concern and, at best, give a false sense of security. Clearly laboratory animals are being needlessly exploited in this field of research. They are made to suffer purely for reasons of profit.

RELEVANCE OF ANIMAL "MODELS"

It is ironic that the criteria used to define human health are almost as narrow as those employed to define laboratory animal health and welfare. As a consequence, the quality of biomedical research, the practice of medicine, and the quality of medical services available to the public are severely deficient on many counts. Psychiatric and social work services have low ratings with medical insurance companies. The biomedical industry has sold profitably to the public costly and iatrogenic drugs and diagnostic procedures (which only the more affluent and insured can afford) that address the symptoms of disease and not the causes. These causes are primarily mental, social, and environmental (especially improper as well as adulterated diets). Animal "models" mimicking human diseases in vivo are generally done in a vacuum, isolated in a sterile, impoverished environment. The animals are totally isolated from those social and environmental variables that are part of most disease syndromes, and are stressed emotionally as a consequence of social deprivation and environmental disruption. A tiny steel cage in a darkened, air-conditioned room is hardly a biologically appropriate environment for an owl monkey being used as a human model for malaria. Animal models are utilized primarily to find "cures" with drugs and vaccines and to study disease processes within the body. The former results give profits to manufacturers and do alleviate some human sickness; but without preventive health measures, especially clean air, water, food, and an adequate diet, sickness and suffering will continue and new diseases will appear. Studying disease processes in isolated animals results in seeing only part of the disease picture; knowledge of social and environmental influences are lacking.

Animal models therefore are of limited value. Some animal models cruelly and generally mimic human emotional disorders, such as prolonged social isolation, maternal deprivation, helplessness-depression, acute fear, and chronic anxiety. Some techniques used (and developed) on animals are, according to Amnesty International, also used on military prisoners and political dissidents. Psychologists perform some of the most inhumane animal studies. They refuse to admit that if their studies are relevant to human emotional disorders and distress, then it is likely that the animals they use may be subjected to great emotional suffering.

Even given better legislation and enforcement of laws to protect the welfare of laboratory animals, and better designed research studies that are more germane to improving human health, the question still remains: What animal research is valid and which studies that entail animal suffering are justified? In the final analysis, I believe the answer is clearly very few.

There are very few, if any, restraints on what a researcher may do to animals. While there is a peer review board for all federally funded research, a higher priority is given, especially for an established scientist, for "scientific knowledge" over animal welfare concerns. Alternative testing methods, such as microorganisms and tissue culture, receive little attention. And so we find psychologists and students with no formal training in veterinary surgery and postoperative care doing brain surgery on cats and monkeys; dogs and rats being given repeated inescapable shock ostensibly to find answers to help cure depression in humans; radiation, germ warfare, weapons testing, and burn studies in pigs, dogs, and monkeys—military research judged vital for national security; safety testing of new shampoos, cosmetics, and other nonessential consumables by placing various concentrations of test materials into the eyes of rabbits, causing severe pain and even blindness. Even when government tests on animals show some chemical to cause cancer, genetic damage, or birth defects, manufacturers often contest the findings. Results of tests in their own laboratories usually obtain quite different results, more consonant with the companies' interests. And so more animal tests are done before final judgment is passed.

Thousands of chemicals that are on the market have not yet been safety tested by the National Cancer Institute and other agencies. Others known to be harmful to human and animal health, are used widely, especially in agriculture and by chemical industries in the manufacture of paints, solvents, and other hazardous materials. And more animal tests are carried out on substances that are known to cause human health problems, such as alcohol, tobacco, and narcotics.

While some safety testing and basic and applied biomedical research on animals may be justified out of sheer necessity, "necessity" needs to be defined. It is an argument used to justify much frivolous animal research and testing.

JUSTIFYING ANIMAL USE IN RESEARCH

Scientists use one very powerful argument to defend and justify their right to use animals for research purposes. This is that the desire for acquiring knowledge—knowledge for knowledge's sake—is a cultural value. It is argued that all knowledge is of potential use to humanity and its pursuit should not be questioned and obstructed: Such obstruction would be against the best interests of society and also a violation of scientific freedom. This attitude has led to all knowledge of potential benefit to humanity being placed above such humane concerns as laboratory animal suffering. The means, no matter how much animal suffering is involved, justify the ends if there is benefit to society.

Yet all knowledge is not of equal value, and it is unscholarly to make such a generalization. Only certain essential knowledge, rather than trivial information, should be sought at the expense of animals' suffering. Perhaps scientists seek to defend and justify the pursuit of knowledge (scientific freedom), rather than the value of knowledge per se, because this pursuit may lead to knowledge that will benefit society. And it just as likely may not. Much research is repetitive and nonproductive. No research project can be guaranteed to give useful results.

Because scientific freedom and the promise of possible benefits to society are so rigorously defended, the means whereby such knowledge is obtained must be questioned. If there are alternatives to causing animal suffering, adopting such alternatives is a moral imperative and a scientist's responsibility. If no alternatives, such as tissue culture, are available, then the possible benefits of such knowledge to society must be weighed against the costs to animals in terms of physical and psychological suffering.

Human beings can and do suffer far more than animals in some ways, such as drug addiction, violence (notably rape and murder), depression, and schizophrenia. Thus some contend that it is acceptable to use animals in biomedical research because animals suffer less than humans. But this needs to be proven. And so I argue that the following ethical considerations should be adressed: namely, *if the pain and suffering to the animal would be greater than the amount of pain and suffering that a human might feel under the same experimental conditions, then the experiment should not be permitted.*

However, if we cannot ascertain how much the animal is in pain and suffering, then we should not experiment upon it. And scientifically, if we do not know these basic facts, then the value and relevance of the work aimed at ultimately alleviating pain and suffering in humans is most probably scientifically nvalid and of little relevance clinically. The variables of pain, suffering, fear, and deprivation must be controlled for, their intensity and effect on the animal must be known, otherwise the scientific validity and clinical relevance of data derived from animal experimentation will be minimal. Public censure of scientists who believe that any research is justifiable if the pain and suffering the animal undergoes will be greatly outweighed by the resulting alleviation of human pain will increase until they accept their responsibilities toward animals.

Researchers F. L. Marcuse and J. J. Pear[2] contend that the primary purpose and justification of scientists experimenting on animals is that the knowledge gained may be of *survival benefit.* How much this belief stems from unconscious anxiety and insecurity, which no amount of animal research is going to help, is worth consideration.

These scientists ask, "Should the good and well-being of humans be placed over that of animals?" The very question is based on the assumption that the good/well-being of animals and humans are mutually exclusive and that the two are somehow separate. It is this kind of "speciesist" thinking that underlies much human suffering as well as unnecessary animal exploitation and suffering. In a more empathetic and ecological, rather than anthropocentric, perspective, the good of humans and the good of other animals are mutually inclusive rather than exclusive. A thorough examination of the attitudes behind justifications for using sentient animals "for the benefit of humanity" might provide far more benefits than any that might derive from much animal experimentation.

Currently scientific and technological advances are conceived as the keys to our survival and prosperity. However, the Baconian dictum (advanced by the English philosopher Francis Bacon some 400 years ago) that knowledge (specifically science) is power (over nature) has led to an age of increasing anxiety and a greater need to control not simply nature but humanity itself. Abraham Maslow in *The Psychology of Science*[3] states that science "can be primarily a safety philosophy, a security system, a complicated way of avoiding anxiety and upsetting problems.

In the extreme instance it can be a way of avoiding life, a kind of self cloistering." It is considered heresy to question the values and perceptions of the scientific establishment, not because the validity of their data is beyond question but rather because of the widespread belief that science can solve all our problems. Such questioning, branded as "antiscience" and "antiprogress," exposes the anxiety of the times. The pain of this anxiety can be partially deadened by faith not in God but in the power of instrumental knowledge derived from science and applied technology.

Ironically, while many biomedical and agribusiness scientists believe in the theory of evolution, they label as anthropomorphic concerns about the suffering and emotional well-being of animals. Yet according to evolutionary theory, there probably is an evolutionary continuity of mental experience. Many of these scientists are neo-Cartesian creationists and fundamentalists dressed up in Darwinian clothes, giving mere lip service to evolutionary theory. If such were not the case, I believe there would be less indifference to and glib acceptance of the physical and emotional suffering and privation of animals in the modern world. Thus scientists condemn unnecessary animal suffering on the basis that it is "morally wrong" (because it is a sign of bad character) only when there is no overriding utilitarian justification. This is a weak argument. A stronger one, which they cannot accept, is that because of our physiological and emotional similarity to other species, humans should not treat them in ways that we would not treat our own kind. We should not cause pain or emotional distress, unless it is vital for their own well-being or for our own survival. Ethical limits need to be drawn, because ethically, the ends do *not* always justify the means.

The difference between a scientist and a nonscientist causing an animal to suffer is the difference between a societal judgment of necessary suffering (permitted under the law) and animal cruelty (punishable under the law). This difference is one of utility: of benefit to society and not of morality or ethics per se. And it is the public that gives the scientist such freedom (and responsibility) as well as financing most animal research.

But not all benefits to society are equal—some are indeed trivial if worthwhile at all. Thus all scientists who use animals in their research cannot make equal claims to scientific freedom without first being fully accountable in terms of the purpose and actual or potential value of animal sacrifice or suffering to society. Peer review of research proposals is highly questionable, as such peer groups do not necessarily represent prevailing societal values. For example, the American Psychological Association's code of principles (1971) states that "Research procedures subjecting animals to discomfort shall be conducted only when such discomfort is required, and is justified by the objectives of research." This sounds so clean and simple, yet on second reading is a credo of sheer utility and instrumental rationalism. Animals can be simply a means to any end that the human imagination chooses to justify. Based on such a creed, any peer-review system would be highly questionable.

Marcuse and Pear state that scientists should question the humaneness of their own and other's procedures with the same intensity that they question the scientific soundness of those procedures. But who is to encourage them to do so, and also to be more open with the general public and with animal welfarists? Marcuse and Pear believe that "the culture as a whole" has this responsibility. Certainly professional scientific groups seem incapable of doing so. This state of affairs will continue until scientific groups allow "the culture as a whole" to discuss and resolve ethical issues involving animal research. The doors have been closed for too long by such organizations as the National Society for Medical Research. And keeping the doors closed is to be out of step with the times. Now is the time for dialogue. Otherwise the biomedical and research community as a whole may suffer the consequences of a growing public disillusionment with science and medicine.

Many heralded the U.S. Animal Welfare Act of 1966 as a major step in the right direction to ensure the welfare of laboratory animals. Indeed, in contrast to other forms of institutionalized animal exploitation, laboratory animals undoubtedly have the best protection. But at best, this protection is minimal, and most of the animals used—rodents—are excluded from the act and therefore have no protection. Because of insufficient funding, the act is inadequately enforced. Many long needed amendments to the act should be implemented, such as: provision of exercise for caged dogs; improved housing for primates; improved postoperative care and use of analgesics; limits to be set to avoid unnecessary or unjustifiable animal suffering (especially in psychology studies) and needless repetition. The question of scientific accountability has yet to be answered. Many investigators hollowly assure the public that the act is adequate. The investigators themselves are protected by the professional consensus that tends to accept unconditional animal exploitation if the investigator is qualified (has an M.D. or Ph.D.), well known, and respected.

Control over the proliferation of laboratory animal tests and research studies is urgently needed. The concerns of keeping animals in small barren cages and the physical and psychological suffering that often result from invasive experimental procedures would be mitigated first by an overall reduction in the numbers of animals used. Significant reduction could be accomplished once the following recommendations made by the Carpenter committee, which I call a Bill of Rights for Animal Experimentation, are adopted:

i) A more intensified drive to find alternatives to the use of animals for research.

ii) More careful thought about experiments before undertaking those involving the use of animals, including consideration of whether the object of the experiment is likely to be achieved by the method used.

iii) Before embarking on a project entailing the use of animals, a research worker should satisfy himself that no alternative technique (e.g. cell culture) will meet the need of his investigation.

iv) Those engaged in experimentation on animals must ask themselves, in considering the ethical justification of a given project, whether the end to be realized is sufficiently significant to warrant such infliction of pain and stress as might be involved. This question, and it is a serious one, cannot be ignored, and a given presupposition for the answering of it must be that the animal should be treated as if it possesses rights.

v) Where the use of animals, after these safeguards have been taken, is regarded as necessary, careful thought should be given to deciding the number that will be required. Some species may be more appropriate than others in a given instance, either because the nearest approximation to man is a primary consideration, or because of a known specificity of response in a particular species or strain. At this stage economic considerations should not be paramount and scientifically appropriate species should be selected; the use of rare species should be avoided. In planning the number of investigations to be performed, care should be taken to limit the series to the minimum compatible with statistically valid results.

vii) Animals in research establishments should be under the permanent care of a veterinary surgeon and in particular those having undergone surgery should receive constant care and supervision.

viii) There should be discontinuation of experimentation for trivial purposes, e.g. for luxury goods such as adornment articles (there are already sufficient articles available to satisfy any actual need). Experiments designed to prove the obvious should be discontinued. There should also be discontinuation of animal research into products such as tobacco which man continues to take in full consciousness of the hazards of so doing.

As William Penn observed, "A good end cannot sanctify evil means; nor must we ever do evil that good may come of it . . . let us then try what love will do."

Several researchers are now breaking new ground in the area of disease resistance. Their findings, summarized by science writer Jean L. Marx,[5] lead to the conclusion that the pervasive anatomical and biochemical links between the immune and nervous systems help explain why mood (temperament and emotional stress) influences disease susceptibility. This is more than mere speculation and lends credence to the role of psychotherapy and "mind therapies," such as meditation and relaxation, in preventive medicine. That immune responses can be altered even by learning (classical conditioning) opens up new vistas that traditional (allopathic) medicine has too long ignored. The fact that a person's mental state clearly influences the immune system and disease resistance warrants a new look at our understanding and treatment of disease. We need also to take a hard look at the continued use of animals in biomedical research. I believe the overemphasis of animals as research subjects has retarded medical progress in many areas where laboratory animals either cannot be used (as in meditation) or are of limited use (as in clinical psychology as "models"). In sum, the more we assume responsibility for our own health and the health of the environment, the less vivisection can be justified.

I would question psychological and all other experiments on animals that do not intentionally benefit them. If the primary intention of the research is to benefit them, then we may learn much to benefit ourselves, as our bodily systems are very similar. But if the primary intention of animal vivisection is to find something of human benefit and any benefit to animals is purely coincidental, then it is surely not acceptable ethically; nor should it be scientifically. If the animal is to be a valid human model of human sickness or injury, then we should learn from already sick or injured ones. To artificially induce sickness as by injecting a virus (to make advances in medical treatment) or injury by breaking a leg (under anesthesia) to make surgical innovations is not scientifically sound because the models are too simplistic and not relevant to real-life conditions of infection and trauma in humans and animals.

And it is surely wrong to use animals that are only approximate human models, because the extrapolations may be very speculative. Such is the case when applying data from burned and scalded pigs to human burn victims. Our skin and ways of coping with pain and suffering are very different.

I have difficulty accepting the propagation of animals with genetic and developmental disorders that even closely model human genetic and developmental disorders. Such animals are usually highly inbred. But humans are generally not. Thus the etiology of these problems may be very different. Environmental factors probably play a far more significant role in humans, who, living longer than dogs, cats, and mice, are more likely to succumb to the effects of environmental teratogens and mutagens (such as chemicals and radiation) that damage the germ plasm or genetic integrity of sperm and ova. Such damage could cause germ-line-invaded (that is, heritable) and developmental disorders in humans comparable to analogous disorders in inbred dogs, cats, and mice. Researchers claim that from their research on purebred cats and dogs, they can advise the owners how to eliminate the problem from their breeding programs and thus the breeds benefit. However, *not* breeding purebred animals with extreme traits in the first place would be a better solution (see chapter 12).

Researchers also claim that they might, by studying these genetic diseases in companion animals (and by propagating them in research breeding colonies), come up with some remedial treatments—even corrective genetic engineering (which is already being applied to human patients) to help the animals.

Yet the ironic possibility remains that corrective genetic engineering will be used in humans instead of eliminating those environmental factors that were responsible or suspected of causing damage to sperm, ova, and developing embryos in the first place. And families will suffer the burden and stigma of genetic disease. The medical industry will continue to profit from, but not prevent, these problems, which are increasing dramatically in the human population (not from selective inbreeding but from other factors) and in purebred dogs and cats (from selective inbreeding) as they increase in popularity.

Thus it is difficult to justify research and expenditure on studying the heritability, diagnosis, and treatment of genetic diseases in inbred animals, because people are not inbred and the causality of their genetic disease problems is fundamentally different.

Certainly it seems wonderful that some genetic disorder in a human infant might be corrected thanks to extensive research on animal genetic "models." And some claim that this is progress—our way of adapting to an increasingly unlivable, poisoned environment. But it is not progress when we cause suffering and seek ways to alleviate it rather than to prevent it, as by cleaning up the environment so that fewer children are born with genetic damage and developmental disorders in metabolism, immunity, and even mental function.

This is not an impossible task. And government should recognize it as the primary task of the medical establishment and of biomedical research. Unfortunately, as in much agricultural research, biomedical research is aimed at benefiting industry by developing marketable "cures" and services rather than at benefiting society by developing nonmarket-oriented preventives that are aligned with appropriate and healthful industrial technologies and agricultural practices. This is because most research is funded by industry and supported ideologically by those who lack vision or conscience, or who are greedy for acclaim and profit.

While there are many areas of laboratory animal exploitation and suffering that need to be prohibited, such as military weapons testing and extensive burn studies, as long as the public consensus accepts the use of animals for essential biomedical purposes, we owe it to the animals in the name of both compassion and good science to ensure that they are treated humanely (analgesics and tranquilizers being used whenever necessary) and kept in conditions that guarantee their overall physical and psychological well being.

Not all would agree with Rudolph Bahro,[6] leading philosopher of the German Green Movement, who states, "We have not sufficiently understood the issue [of terracide—the destruction and pollution of the environment/planetary ecosystem] if we deal with the problems of animal experiments primarily in terms of sympathy and respect for life, much as these sentiments point in the right direction. We shall harm ourselves not only spiritually and morally, but physically as well, if we maltreat the animal and plant kingdom simply because we are afraid of disease and greedy for life." And, I would add, we also harm ourselves when we fail to see the connection between human sickness and our mistreatment of the environment and all who dwell therein.

But as Albert Schweitzer said, "Without a reverence for all life, we will never have world peace." Neither will we ever have world health.

I believe that it is ethically questionable and often bad science to routinely and deliberately make animals ill in the name of biomedical research and progress. It is bad science because artificially created animal models of human disease are generally inadequate and do not provide a complete picture, as most disease conditions have multiple factors and causes. And it is bad medicine when the primary focus is treatment-oriented and not preventive: The first medicine is prevention. The sacrificing of animals in the name of science and the greater good cannot continue unchallenged. Companion animals suffer many health problems, such as cancer, arthritis, autoimmune and immunosuppressed diseases, and also emotional disturbances. From these we could learn to better diagnose and treat such disorders in animals and analogous ones in human beings. This would entail a far greater cooperation between veterinary and medical schools and research institutions.

CHAPTER 5

The Nemesis of Science and Medicine

The use of laboratory animals to study the biological "mechanisms" of many of the major diseases that afflict humans forms the basis of profitable interventive, rather than *preventive*, medicine. Because the *primary* focus of such research and practice is not prevention, the primary beneficiary is not the public but the biomedical industry—at the expense of human health and animal suffering. Animal and human research studies have shown the connection between such diseases as cancer, arteriosclerosis, high blood pressure, heart attacks, diabetes, arthritis, birth defects, and stroke with such factors as improper diet, environmental pollution, and emotional stress. The solutions to these human health problems are not simple, cause-and-effect mechanistic ones that can be discovered in an animal research laboratory; they are primarily social, psychological, economic, and political.

Can society continue to justify the incarceration and suffering of laboratory primates, cats, and dogs, and other animals?

Contemporary standards of laboratory animal care are clearly inadequate and unscientific from the viewpoint of holistic medicine, which embraces the idea of *body-mind-environment* interconnectedness. Today's standards do not consider the animals' social, emotional, and environmental needs; they are also unscientific and thus counter to the progress of medicine because they disengage the normal nexus of mind-body-environment. This breakage (as when an animal is isolated in a laboratory cage) introduces a variety of new and uncontrolled experimental variables, which render the validity of research conclusions dubious at best and hardly relevant to real-life conditions of health and disease. It is from these physical, emotional, and environmental connections that meaningful parameters of normality must be derived. Contemporary medicine ignores these connections. Therapeutic regimen, though profitable, all too often causes more illness than it cures.

More and more scientists and physicians today are agreeing that much animal research is wrongly focused, leading to interventive, symptom-oriented medical treatments for human patients who would benefit more from preventive medical procedures. The best biomedical research "model" to demonstrate the need for a "paradigm shift" in laboratory animal research (and congressional funding) is drug addiction and alcohol poisoning studies in animals. These tests are supposedly done in order to develop pharmacological and psychological ways to treat such problems in people.

This paradigm will not shift until Congress is convinced that much unneeded and indeed worthless animal research is being done and that the suffering of these animals is morally unjustifiable. Ironically, the more animals suffer, the more we suffer indirectly. Interventive medical procedures, derived from often agonizing animal experiments, often have harmful (iatrogenic) side effects on human patients. And human suffering continues unabated—the social, environmental, political, and other factors that lead to physical and mental disease, drug addiction, and other critical problems are not addressed. This is because the current medical paradigm or mind-set is mechanistic and reductionistic rather than holistic. From a holistic perspective, drug addiction and alcohol poisoning studies in animals are neither scientifically valid nor medically relevant.

In sum, those who unconditionally support and condone all laboratory animal research—and especially drug addiction studies and psychological research "models," such as "learned helplessness" of human disorders—unwittingly contribute to *human* suffering. The research they endorse is not holistically oriented and thus cannot contribute to the *prevention* of human suffering and disease.

BIOMEDICAL RESEARCH REFORMS

The biomedical industry as a whole needs to be drastically reformed. Rather than capitalizing on human sickness and selling ever more costly "cures," planners and scientists should advocate disease prevention and health care maintenance programs. Unfortunately, today health is increasingly becoming only a by-product of the medical industry. This is clearly demonstrated by the self-serving way that research priorities are established and the narrow, mechanistic mind-set of the medical establishment, which is ultimately responsible for what has been termed the medical nemesis. And we, the people, are its unfortunate "beneficiaries."

The implanting of an artificial heart (developed first in animals) into a human patient made headline news as a medical "breakthrough." But regardless of its statistically insignificant contribution to public health and dubious cost effectiveness, such high-tech mechanistic medicine simply engenders yet another profitable new industry to manufacture replacement body parts. Another new frontier is fetal surgery. In contrast, holistic medicine eliminates the necessity of such heroic and costly interventive procedures.

In *The Social Transformation of American Medicine*, Paul Starr predicts that health care services and professional sovereignty will decline.[1] "Instead of public regulation," he believes, "there will be private regulation, and instead of public planning, there will be corporate planning." In sum, American medicine, like so many other expansionist, monopolistic industries, is becoming a corporate monopoly, which is the antithesis of democracy and free enterprise.

Americans now spend more than $350 billion per year—over 10 percent of the gross national product—on health care. And medical costs are rising at almost twice the rate of inflation. Physician Stanley Wohl has described the growth of high-profit multibillion-dollar hospital conglomerates and services that lead to an increase in medical insurance costs.[2] Large corporations expand their influence and monopoly by acquiring interests in hospitals and nursing homes. Nonprofit hospitals face dwindling state and federal support and take on an ever-increasing number of Medicaid, Medicare, and charity cases. While Wohl offers no real solutions, it is clear from his analysis that the less affluent and the uninsured have no guarantee of adequate medical services, while the more affluent and the insured are often subjected to unnecessary diagnostic and therapeutic procedures that profit the medical industrial complex and fuel the inflationary spiral.

The reformation needed in biomedical research, and especially research on nonhuman primates, cannot rely simply on stronger legislation and enforcement of current laboratory animal welfare regulations. Rather, a critical and objective appraisal of the relevance and morality of much research done on animals is needed. The several regional primate centers built and maintained at the public's expense should be looked into particularly.

It is imprudent idealism to oppose all animal research per se; advocating nonanimal alternatives and appropriate funding to develop such alternatives is far more realistic. However, everyone should question the necessity of all research on animals that does not aim at preventing the major diseases that afflict humanity.

Likewise antivivisectionists and others should oppose any kind of animal research that leads only to interventive, symptom-oriented medical applications in humans at the expense of research on disease prevention, especially behavioral and ecological medicine. The primary issue of animal pain, fear, and suffering, while crucial, must not be allowed to obscure the second fundamental problem: Our current policies permit the misallocation of research funds. As mentioned, research prioritization is basically flawed because, for political and economic reasons, the major causes of human disease—from industrial pollutants and agrichemicals, improper diet, contaminated food, air, and water, and emotional stress—are not being addressed. Sadly, preventive medicine, like the cleaning up of the environment, must be forced on industry, for it is not regarded as initially profitable.

An appraisal of biomedical research practices, goals, funding, and peer review is long overdue, considering that (1) cancer and other degenerative diseases are now reaching epidemic proportions,* in spite of the vast amounts Congress provides for laboratory animal research, and (2) the public must continue to pay more and more for medical treatment. When does society say enough?

In a memorandum (obtained from a "whistle blower") attached to his report on the animal rights movement for Harvard University, lobbyist David Loser urged that: "Every time there is a dramatic organ transplant or life saving open heart operation, the doctor doing the procedure should mention that it could not have been done without previous research on animals."

But my point is that *if the environment and our food, air, and water were cleaned up, along with our dietary habits, food-processing procedures, and agricultural practices, there would be little need for dramatic organ transplants or life-saving open heart operations.* Consequently, very few laboratory animals would have to suffer in various experiments, because the need for research to find cures for disease would decline. (With healthful dietary reforms, which include eating less meat, farm animals would not need to be raised as stressfully as they are today; because fewer would be consumed, they could be raised more humanely.)

---

*Each year an estimated 400,000 people are now diagnosed as having cancer, which is a symptom of *dis*ease and not a specific disease in itself.

PREVENTIVE MEDICINE AND THE POLITICS OF DISEASE

Great strides are purportedly being made today in biomedical research regarding cures for cancer, and many of these discoveries have come from research studies on animals and afflicted humans. These successes are widely publicized, as is the promise that *all* cancers will eventually be treatable. The millions of people who will be diagnosed as having cancer certainly have hope for some sort of cure.

Any questioning of the ethics of using laboratory animals in such seemingly vital research is perceived as being tantamount to ignoring human welfare and placing the needs of animals above those of people. To the public, these successes justify the continued and unrestricted exploitation of animals. The public has been conditioned to believe in biomedical science and technology as a kind of infallible truth and does not question the directions that such research and development have taken. And if and when people do become ill, they have the hope and promise of a cure, and relief and gratitude if they are cured.

According to physician Haydn Bush, more cancer cures occur in press releases than in actual patients. And cancer organizations receive more funds when more cures are reported.

While the federal government's National Cancer Institute claims that thousands more people are being saved from cancer than twenty years ago, other medical specialists, such as Dr. John Cairns, cancer analyst at the Harvard School of Public Health, and Dr. John C. Bailar, statistical consultant for the *New England Journal of Medicine*, have challenged these claims. Seemingly no progress has been made in cancer prevention. The success rates of many purported cures are dubious, partly because with advanced tumor detection techniques, some growths that are treated are not actually cancerous. Other cancerous growths could well have not killed the patients because of spontaneous remission, a far more common phenomenon—and mystery—than is generally acknowledged.

Dr. Alvin R. Feinstein and colleagues concluded that the

outcome of treatment for lung cancer between 1953 and 1977 among patients treated at two Connecticut hospitals was about the same, in spite of claims made by the National Cancer Institute and others that significant advances in treatment and survivability have been made.[3] Feinstein and coworkers stated that their results "are distressing because they suggest that the contemporary improvements of survival rates, at least among patients with lung cancer, is a statistical artifact." The difference in survival rates between the two periods they studied largely disappeared when statistical differences created by newer diagnostic procedures were eliminated.

Dr. John Cairns presents further evidence to cast doubt on the generalized claim that medical research is helping win the battle against cancer.[4] He cites studies from Norway that show that the life span of about a third of all cancer patients was not reduced as a result of the disease. He goes on to suggest that with earlier diagnosis, the purportedly improved survivability of patients being screened and treated for cancer may be exaggerated. This is because many forms of cancer could have remained dormant (that is, not metastasized or spread to other parts of the body) or even undergone remission. These cancers would not have been diagnosed twenty years ago. The inclusion of such nonfatal cancer cases in studies of cancer treatment and survivability clearly biases the results, giving the erroneous impression that real progress has been made because these cancer "victims" did not die. But as Cairns points out, there have been a few signal successes in treating certain more lethal forms of cancer, such as childhood leukemia with chemotherapy.

Other statistical artifacts can give misleading inferences as to the successes of cancer research and treatment. For instance, in the late 1940s the reported incidence of prostate cancer was 400 per million men per year; the figure rose to 700 in the late 1970s, while the death rate remained steady at 210 per million per year. The survival rate therefore increased, not because fewer men are dying but because more men are being classified as prostate cancer victims.

Chemotherapy—much of it based on animal research—is not proving effective in treating most forms of cancer, even though, according to Cairns, an estimated 200,000 patients are subjected to it and its harmful and sometimes fatal side effects. "All told," Cairns states, "adjuvant treatments now avert a few thousand (perhaps 2–3 percent) of the 400,000 deaths from cancer that occur each year in the U.S."

Cairns concludes that more emphasis needs to be given to cancer prevention, epidemiological research, diagnostic screening (especially for breast cancer), and antitobacco smoking campaigns. Significantly, nowhere in his article does he voice the need for more research on animals.

According to the March of Dimes, birth defects now afflict one out of every twelve infants born each year in the United States. Many experts now agree—and fear—that the epidemic increase in birth defects is caused by the chemical agents with which we have contaminated the environment. According to an editorial in *Mother Jones*, 56 percent of the children born near the notorious Love Canal toxic dump were mentally or physically disabled.[5] The editorial went on to state:

> . . . But official fear that too many new birth defects will turn out to have environmental origins—thereby forcing painful decisions about our society, industry, and lifestyle—fosters a pervasive lack of interest in systematically looking for those origins. . . .
> To others, the problem is scientific. For decades the conventional wisdom has been that human teratogens would be found by studying their effects on laboratory animals. Although billions of dollars have been spent worldwide on experiments that have sacrificed millions of mice, rats, and rabbits, in only two instances has a cause of birth defects in humans been found first in an animal; nor has this increasingly futile effort revealed anything about the basic biology of teratogenesis that can be now applied to preventing birth

FIGURE 5.1. Interrelationships Between Environmental Factors and Human Health

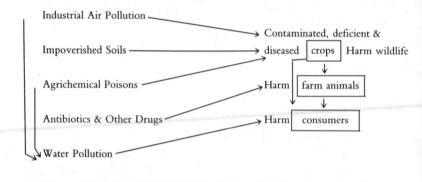

defects in humans. Causes of human birth defects have only been discovered through the examination of human populations.

Disease and suffering cannot be truly understood and combated if real knowledge about their precise causality is lacking, or if the causes are linked to economic and other material benefits. Is it not progress to be able to *prevent* cancer and other diseases rather than to possess only an armament of cures? Without preventive and health care maintenance programs, including environmental health and ecological medicine (see Figure 5.1), human suffering and sickness can only increase. This is because our environment, air, water, and food are becoming even more contaminated with agricultural and industrial chemicals and people are suffering the emotional stresses and privations of an increasingly dysfunctional society.

But what realistic options have we when the advances in preventive medicine have become ensnared in a politicized limbo? The U.S. Department of Agriculture, the Environmental Protection Agency, and other government departments are in a state of "bureaucratic gridlock" with the allied industries that are responsible for regulating, especially for food quality and environmental health—the two complementary pillars of health maintenance. Furthermore, research funded by the pharmaceutical and medical technology industries (for diagnosis as well as for treatment) is oriented primarily toward treating disease as it comes, rather than toward disease prevention, which is less profitable.

Disease prevention has been relegated to the federal government, while the war against human sickness remains the almost exclusive, legally protected monopoly of organized medicine and its associated biomedical research industry. But when establishment medicine and research focus primarily on interventive treatment-oriented cures and garners public funds to find these cures, we are faced with an aggressive attitude that envisions disease, and even life itself, as a perpetual battle. This attitude also extends into our dealings with other nations and with the forces of nature. Our adversary mentality is prepared to fight, or to self-righteously intervene or rescue, rather than to *prevent* the need for violent intervention through understanding and humility. Until a radical change in attitude occurs, physical and mental suffering and environmental problems will exacerbate, as will the demand for more research to develop better medical and technological "fixes."

While I am not denying that people who are sick should have the benefit of interventive and curative treatment, I do want to shatter the grand illusion that new cures (in the absence of concerted disease-preventive programs) always represent beneficial progress. Otherwise the quality of human life, and of all life on this planet, will continue to decline. We will become increasingly dependent on interventive remedies and ever more elaborate control systems, and on the exploitation of laboratory animals as "models" of our diseased states. Deteriorating health for all of us will become inevitable, if, for political, economic, and ideological reasons, society continues to ignore the importance of preventive medicine and the increasingly pathogenic state of the world in which we live.

Besides placing a greater emphasis on preventive medicine, we should question the current acceptance of orthodox (allopathic) medical methods. *Alternative forms of healing—homeopathic, chiropractic, acupuncture, psychotherapy-counseling, and so on—have been proven effective and practical for centuries.* Yet organized, monopolistic medicine has until recently opposed all nonallopathic therapies as "quackery," even making their practice illegal.

Too much emphasis has been placed on the side of domination and intervention. Interventive medicine has its place, not as a panacea but as a means of alleviating sickness and suffering whenever the immediate need arises. Preventive medicine, on the other hand, is the essence of *self*-dominion; it complements the humane stewardship through which we may indeed heal ourselves and in the process restore our planet for the benefit of all life to come.

What do doctors usually feel when they are called upon to help patients deal with cancer, sterility, or a deformed or brain-damaged child? Likely they are convinced that more research on animals will provide the key to new breakthrough cures—that we can all believe that science and technology will ultimately save us all. But what do these same doctors feel about the politicians and industrialists who, with their "expert" panels of scientists and armies of lawyers, permit such deadly poisons as lead, mercury, polychlorinated biphenyls (PCBs), and organophosphate pesticides to accumulate in our bodies and in the environment by establishing fictitious tolerance and acceptance levels for them in our air, food, and water?

According to a 1984 National Research Council's report, little or no information exists regarding the effects of almost 90 percent of all chemicals, including commonly used drugs, cosmetics, and industrial chemicals, on humans.[6] Adequate toxicity information was available for only 10 percent of the 3,350 pesticide ingredients now in common use; only 2 percent of 3,410 cosmetic ingredients; only 5 percent of some 8,627 food additives; 18 percent of some 1,815 pharmaceuticals; and 11 percent of an estimated 12,860 other commercial chemicals.

In sum, we have lost our right to control our own health and medical care; to determine the quality of food and agricultural practices; and to fully understand industrial activities and products and their impact on society and the environment.

INDUSTRIAL INTERESTS AND HUMAN HEALTH

Industry's public denial that agrichemicals and industrial pollutants pose serious risks to all is best illustrated in this statement from the ultra conservative *Parity Foundation* news magazine: "Is the notion of animal rights any more preposterous than the idea that DDT kills?" This denial is probably personal as well: The authors actually want to believe that agrichemicals are harmless, or at least that their benefits outweigh all costs and risks. This is an understandable defense mechanism, considering the variety and volume of profitable chemicals that now saturate the environment and contaminate the food chain. The Environmental Protection Agency has insufficient funds to monitor industrial pollutants and agrichemical use or enforce regulations, nor does it check whether states are adequately policing the use of registered and unregistered pesticides. Year after year the EPA rejects only a fraction of the hundreds of state-granted local declarations under an "emergency" clause permitting the use of hazardous unregistered pesticides; all the rest were permitted due to pressure from various senators, members of Congress, and state governors, ostensibly for the benefit of farmers but in reality to further the interests of the agrichemical industry (which budgeted $12 million in 1990 for lobbying efforts to prevent any steps to reduce pesticide use). Political and economic interests thus hold sway over scientific evidence, ethics, consumer interests, environmental health, and even the law.

In sum, the government jeopardizes the health of all by bending the law and discounting scientific evidence (from animal and human studies) to make it easy for farmers to use pesticides and other chemicals and by relaxing pollution standards and controls to reduce costs to industry. The health problems that arise, in addition to causing great human suffering, cost the public additional expenditures in tax-subsidized biomedical research, to find "cures" and in funding ineffectual government regulatory bureaucracies. The ultimate beneficiaries are agribusiness and other industries and the scientific-medical complex, which has new problems to solve and profitable cures to administer. This unholy alliance must be broken. But it is secure as long as the industries maintain their public image of being concerned with the public good, and as long as the populace continues to place its faith in science, medicine, and technological progress. Yet such faith is misplaced; the political influence of powerful banks and corporations, with the backing of allied professional organizations (as diverse as the American Medical Association and the American Farm Bureau Federation), ensure not the public good but the economic interests of a select few.

Politics and economics also influence what research may be done and who the beneficiaries will be. Much agricultural and farm-animal research conducted by land grant universities benefits large-scale corporate farming enterprises rather than operators of small and midsize farms, and in the process has contributed to the latter's extinction. Likewise, sophisticated advances in diagnostic and therapeutic biomedical technology (much of which entails extensive use of animals) are so costly to provide to the public that the primary beneficiaries are the rich and those who can still afford medical insurance. Furthermore, in less affluent areas, such advances are not available.

Political pressures on major granting agencies, such as the U.S. Department of Agriculture (USDA) and National Institutes of Health, play a major role in determining which research is to be funded and by whom it should be done. This pressure helps ensure whom the ultimate beneficiaries of public funds and resources spent on research will be. The USDA under Ronald Reagan even screened out scientists whose political and other ideologies did not conform with those of the administration and its industry supporters. Economics also determine research priorities in private industry; certain life-saving drugs and vaccines are not being developed, especially ones that might help third world countries, because sales would be unprofitable.

Laboratory animals should not continue to be subjected to unnecessary suffering, and the public should not be told that all such animal suffering is justifiable and essential if we are to enjoy good health for the rest of our days. When we begin to understand what health is, physically and psychologically, and assume full responsibility for our own health and for that of our planet (since the two are interconnected), then the wholesale exploitation of animals in laboratories will become unnecessary. Recent advances in human nutrition, preventive health care maintenance, physical fitness, and mental health are promising signs. They are undoubtedly more effective and realistic than wasting more animals and dollars finding cures for "techno-genic" and other diseases, such as cancer and heart attacks, complex diseases that are tied to ignorant and irresponsible disregard for environmental health, good sanitation, nutrition, and so on.

From all indices of well-being, modern medicine is not enhancing the quality of human life. The deep causes of sickness, greed, anguish, insecurity, and their consequences of violence, oppression, unethical dominion of animals and nature, violation of human and animal rights, and the destruction and pollution of the planet are the diseases of civilization, and are a challenge to all healers.

A person's (1) personality, attitudes, relationships, and general emotional state; (2) life-style (especially eating habits); (3) genetic background; and (4) the healthfulness of the environment (uncontaminated food, water, and air) all interact and determine how and which disease is expressed in the person's body. The medical industry is now beginning to tinker with genetics; it rejects the important contribution of psychiatry to people's general emotional state and barely touches life-style and the healthfulness of the environment. It ignores environmental issues because they conflict with the interests of other major industries that provide hospitals with a continuous supply of patients to be "cured" at great profit.

If there were a reduction in and a replacement of many medical treatments used to "cure" people after they have become ill, many fewer animals would be required in biomedical and psychological research. We need a medical industry that is less iatrogenic; less interventive (and thus less directly profitable to the medical industry), yet helps maintain a state of emotional and environmental health from which physical health naturally arises.

Dr. Robert Sharpe in his book *The Cruel Deception*[7] presents convincing evidence that the reduction in sickness and death from the major infectious diseases in the United Kingdom (mainly, tuberculosis, bronchitis, pneumonia, influenza, whooping cough, measles, scarlet fever, diphtheria, smallpox, and water- and food-borne diseases such as cholera, typhoid, diarrhea, and dysentery) was not accomplished through animal research. Since the middle of the last century, the dramatic increase in life expectancy can be attributed to improvements in nutrition, living and working conditions, hygiene, and sanitation. Chemotherapies, antibiotics, other drugs, and vaccines, all developed from animal research, really had no significant impact and were put into use when major infectious diseases were already disappearing from the population, thanks to advances in public health and preventive medicine instigated by humanitarians and social reformers of the nineteenth century.

The late physician and philosopher René Dubos[8] in the *Mirage of Health*, states, "by the time laboratory medicine came effectively into the picture the job had been carried far toward completion by the humanitarian and social reformers of the nineteenth century."

On the basis of that evidence, Dr. Robert Sharpe contends "*at most*, animal experiments had only a marginal effect on reducing the death rate, even on the unlikely assumption that animals were involved in developing all such medical measures."[9]

These communicable diseases are now something of the past and today's life-styles contribute to a new set of diseases that are difficult or impossible to cure but that are all largely preventable. These include cancer, stroke, obesity, heart disease, bronchitis, emphysema, alcoholism and drug addiction, diabetes, high blood pressure, sterility, birth defects, and genetic disorders.

We might ask, considering the wholesale use of animals in biomedical research over the past thirty years, if our overall health has improved as a consequence. Sharpe observes, "In 1951, a 45-year-old man could expect to live an extra 26.4 years whilst in 1981 he could a further 27.5 more years. Despite this small increase, evidence from America suggests that this is more than counterbalanced by more years of serious disablement. . . . There has been a progressive *increase* in the number of people reporting chronic sickness (defined as any long standing illness, disability or infirmity) between 1972 and 1982. This is supported by government figures which show an increase between 1967 and 1983 in the number of insured people incapacitated by sickness."

A study reported in the University of California, Berkeley, *Wellness Letter* of February 1986 supports these views[11]:

> A major five-year study at the Carter Center at Emory University in Atlanta recently identified the 14 primary causes of illness and premature death (deaths before the age of 65) for which preventive action can be taken. The causes included infectious diseases, infant mortality, drug abuse, cardiovascular disease, and cancer. Together the 14 problems are responsible for 85% of all personal health-care costs and 80% of deaths in America. They also account for 90% of the "potential years of life" lost in America (the term "potential years of life" is defined as the difference between age at death and age 65), which adds up to a staggering 8.5 million years of life lost annually. *Approximately two thirds of these deaths under age 65 are potentially preventable.* The clear conclusion was that we can turn ourselves into a healthier nation by making more effective use of the knowledge we already pos-

sess. We are not dependent on medical breakthroughs to achieve an enormous improvement in our nation's health.

Nor, I should add, are we dependent on the continuation of animal experimentation to improve our nation's health.

CHAPTER 6

Vivisection: Toward a Nonviolent Reconciliation

Many people today, including scientists and physicians, are questioning the suffering and killing of animals in the name of medical research. Congress receives more mail concerning the use of animals in laboratory experiments than on any other subject, according to Dr. Charles McCarthy, head of the Office for Protection from Research Risks at the National Institutes of Health. The mail runs 100 to 1 against the inhumane use of animals in research.

In 1984 I conducted a public attitude survey in my syndicated newspaper column *Animal Doctor* in the United States and via a news magazine in West Germany. Readers were asked if they agreed with Pope John II, who said in a public address that "it is certain that animals are intended for man's use." (I had written to him personally on this issue and in response simply received a copy of his speech—no scriptural or papal doctrine verification was offered.)

I received some 600 responses, and only four in the United States and three in West Germany agreed with the Pope.

Why is it, I wonder, that biomedical scientists have created a host of animal models of human disease, yet to my knowledge they have no animal models of human health? Is this a conceptual or cognitive limitation in the medical research paradigm? Or is it because the human condition is so dysfunctional and diseased that we are as limited in our ability to define health, naturalness, and normality as the vivisector is capable of fully empathizing with experimental animal subjects? If scientists felt empathy and a natural identification with animals, then deliberately inflicting suffering on fellow sentient beings would be unthinkable. Carl Jung, in his book *Memories, Dreams, Reflections*, recounts his reactions to animal experimentation. He found the study of psychology repellent because of vivisection, which was used merely for demonstration purposes.

> I could never free myself from the feeling that warm-blooded creatures were akin to us and not just cerebral automata. Consequently I cut demonstration classes whenever I could. I realized that one had to experiment on animals, but the demonstration of such experiments nevertheless seemed horrible, barbarous and above all unnecessary. I had imagination enough to picture the demonstrated procedures from a mere description of them. My compassion for animals did not derive from the Buddhist trimmings of Schopenhauer's philosophy, but rested on the deeper foundation of a primitive attitude of mind—on an unconscious identity with animals. At the time, of course, I was wholly ignorant of this important psychological fact.[1]

That we can accept vivisection is surely symptomatic of a dis-eased condition in terms of our relationship with other sentient beings and the Earth's creation. No amount of animal experimentation and suffering will ever cure this problem. Until society realizes that this dis-eased human condition accounts for us not living in harmony with the biotic community, we will never enjoy either health or world peace. To put an end to all forms of vivisection—to cease deliberately harming healthy animals and instead learn from and help those animals who are already sick or injured—is surely part of this healing process. It is not simply a question of animal versus human rights or of valuing a laboratory rat more than a sick child with some incurable disease. But defenders of vivisection generate public fear and support today by falsely claiming that there will be much human disease and suffering if animal research is stopped. Their strident claims echo those of agribusiness that contend worldwide famine if they were forced to adopt organic, humane sustainable agricultural practices.

VIVISECTION AND TERRORISM

There is a similarity between vivisection and terrorism that warrants some reflection. Both entail killing and suffering and a deliberate, indeed calculated, transgression of the Buddhist doctrine of *ahimsa* (nonviolence) and of the Golden Rule (of treating others, including animals, as we would have them treat us) in order to achieve some purportedly greater good. As a former animal researcher myself, I am no stranger to the altruistic rationalizations of the vivisector. One is that "the suffering of the few for the benefit of the many is justifiable." I now call this biological fascism.

The only animal model for human disease is man himself. Vivisection is a disease in itself that no amount of animal research and suffering and killing will ever cure. Metaphysically, this dis-eased condition is in part a reflection of the state of mind and social consensus that condones terrorism and war (the killing of human beings) on the one hand and vivisection (the infliction of suffering and killing of animals) on the other.

The antiterrorist and terrorist alike does violence in the name of peace, as the vivisector does violence in the name of medical progress. Such violence is accepted by society, if not as a necessary evil then as an altruistic act to further some greater good. Even though the deliberate infliction of harm is an evil in itself, in both instances, situational ethics that condone evil means for purportedly just ends override the absolute ethic of *ahimsa*.

Those who condone and engage in such acts of violence are not necessarily evil persons. Rather they are caught in a double bind that has its roots in a fundamentally unreconciled dilemma between how we value our own lives in relation to others and how we respond when we feel that our own lives and the lives of those for whom we care are threatened. In the diseased condition of paranoid terror, life threats become magnified to the point of distorting perception, feeling, and thought. Collectively, this pathology is manifested as a violent, sick and dysfunctional society. Terrorism (and its counterpoint, antiterrorism) is one symptom, and vivisection (with its counterpoint of war against disease) is another.

But there is a difference between anti-terrorism and vivisection. In vivisection, there are innocent victims: the animals that have been bred or captured and that are regarded as inferior, even as our own creations. In the secular, if not profane, world of medical science, they are not generally seen as manifestations of divine creation, as belonging to God and therefore "ours" only in sacred trust, to be treated with respect and love. And under the perceived threat of disease, suffering, death, and loss of our loved ones, we devalue the lives of animals, violating the sanctity of life by valuing our own lives over the lives of other sentient beings. The terrorist-assassin does the same.

A reverential attitude of heart and mind automatically precludes vivisection. One's own self is felt to be of equal sanctity and significance as the life of *any other* living being. This is the meaning of humility.

If such an attitude were to prevail, animal research would be restricted to the care and study of animals that are already sick and injured, for their benefit and for the possible future benefit of their kind. Coincidental but nonetheless significant benefits in the advancement of human health would arise naturally from the knowledge and skill gained from treating such animals.

A reverential attitude toward all life would preclude the use of normal, healthy animals in medicinal research; in stress, pain, and trauma studies; in toxicity and cosmetics testing; and in military weapon and biological warfare testing. Genetic engineering and selectively breeding sick and deformed mutant creatures would also be unthinkable.

But reproductive, nutritional, genetic, and other studies of endangered species to facilitate their viability and reintroduction into restored and protected natural habitats would be accepted, as the animals themselves would be the primary beneficiaries of such research.

Research on farm animals to enhance their productivity, efficiency, and adaptability to factory farm conditions would be something of the past, because the ethic of *ahimsa* mandates vegetarianism or at least a dramatic decrease in consumption of animal products by all industrialized nations. Concern for wildlife, both terrestrial and aquatic, necessitates such a shift toward vegetarianism in order to protect natural habitats and wild species displaced and exterminated by overfishing and by the conversion of land to provide feed for farm animals.

Veterinary research on the diseases of other exploited animal species, from "exotic" pets and purebred varieties of cats and dogs to racehorses and ranch-raised wildlife (including fish, alligators, turtles, deer, and fur-bearing mammals), would be terminated. An enlightened, compassionate society would not be involved in such forms of animal propagation and exploitation in the first place.

When people fear death and suffering and objectify certain other sentient fellow beings (human or nonhuman), they become empathetically disconnected from them, seeing them as less important, inferior, and expendable. This disconnectedness becomes generalized into sociopathic, zoopathic, and ecopathic behaviors, pathologies that collectively lead to "terracide," the destruction of the Earth. Institutionalized zoopathic behavior, as in vivisection, factory farming, and the wholesale harvesting of wildlife species, underlies the cultural and ethical disintegration of industrial society and its ultimate nemesis by way of materialism and secular humanism. Collective ecopathic behavior is exemplified by industry's destructiveness of the natural environment and by those values that place material gain over ecological sensibility, and which inevitably lead to economic instability and environmental disease. In sum, our ability to identify fully with the environment—with a lake, a forest, fellow creatures, and even our own kind—has become seriously impaired.

Vivisection, which is symptomatic of this cognitive and emotional impairment, contributes to the failure, *not* the ability, of medical science to *prevent* human suffering and disease. Prevention lies in part in medical science rectifying the cognitive and emotional impairment of a society that condones vivisection while poisoning the environment. The aphorisms "physician do no harm" and "physician heal thyself" have been preempted by the reductionistic and mechanistic approach of drug-dependent allopathic medicine. Such medicine has been promoted by the pharmaceutical-petrochemical multinationals and ideologically aligned medical establishment as the "first" medicine. With it has arisen the dependence on vivisection and the justification of laboratory animal experimentation for the purported good of society.

Recent developments in genetic engineering biotechnology, which entails considerable animal experimentation and suffering (see chapter 13), will only serve to hasten the demise of industrial society if they are not integrated with a more healthful, ecologically sound, and humane sustainable agriculture and with a more holistic, environmentally/ecologically oriented medical paradigm. The modern medical paradigm is inadequate because it barely addresses the environmental health problems associated with industrial pollution and agrichemical poisons. Applying new developments in medical science and genetic engineering biotechnology to help us adapt to an increasingly polluted, disease-enhancing environment is a massive denial and a waste of public resources and good minds. It merely sows seeds of false hope to an uninformed and indoctrinated public.

It is from this perspective that vivisection should be abolished. Although admittedly it has contributed to the advancement of medical knowledge, it now impedes further significant medical progress.

We cannot expect the terrorist to kill the terrorist within or to lay down the gun. Nor can we expect the dedicated vivisector to lay down the syringe, the scalpel, the electrode, or the laser. Without increasing public awareness, legislative pressure and consumer boycotts of all companies and industries whose products and services have entailed animal suffering, coupled with educational reforms that foster an empathetic and compassionate respect and a reverence for all life, the unjust and unnecessary suffering of animals in biomedical laboratories around the world will continue.

The Hippocratic Oath taken by every doctor becomes the "Hypocritic Oath" when the medical (and veterinary) profession remains silent on these issues. The abolition of vivisection should be seen as part of the healing process of a humanity that has become so empathetically disconnected that it is still at war with itself and nature, and condones costly military expansion and the killing of human beings in the name of security, peace, and justice, while the planet that we inhabit is dying. This is not an overstatement. To contend otherwise, or to believe that more animal research and new technological and legislative correctives will suffice, is a denial of reality. And to falsely claim that the antivivisectionist is sentimentally misguided and cares more for animals than for people is a gross injustice. As Albert Schweitzer observed, "Until he extends the circle of his compassion to all living things, man will not himself find peace." Indeed it would be a better world if the $2 billion that nations spend each day on military weapons was instead invested in public health, education, and environmental protection and restoration.

Denial and rationalization are two great obstacles to human progress, along with ignorance, arrogance, and greed. The end of vivisection could herald a new beginning where all policies and decision making at the personal, corporate, and political levels are based on the three principles of a humane, planetary society: namely, obedience to the Golden Rule; *ahimsa*, avoiding harm to all living things and to the natural environment; and reverence for all life. The integrity of creation and the future of humanity may then be beter assured. In the final analysis, animal liberation and human liberation are one and the same, because they are consonant and complementary with the ethics and morality of a truly civilized society.

ANIMAL EXPLOITATION: THE INEVITABLE CONCLUSION

The belief that all life is equal because all our planetary relations (both human and nonhuman) are sacred leads to the inevitable conclusion that it is unethical to value any one life over any other. Thus the life of the ant and the life of my child should be accorded equal respect. Likewise I extend the same respect and concern for my child to you and to yours as also to the ant; and also to our other relations, such as a rat, a river, a tree, and even the ground that we walk upon.

The sanctity of life is violated in that profane realm of secular human-centeredness where life is valued and respected primarily in terms of its utility. Animal lives especially are regarded as mere commodities and as means to satisfy purely human ends.

To give one's child and a rat equal respect as living beings with a life of their own is not to imply that one must or can love a rat as much as one's own child. But respect equally, yes. Certainly one may love a pet rat—or a wild one, for that matter—but the love for and the needs of one's own child are very different, if not more important. This is because we are naturally more connected and emotionally involved with our closest relations who need us more than rats and other creatures normally do.

Now more than ever the animal kingdom and nature as a whole are in dire need of not just our respect but also our nuturance and protection. When we let our concern and respect for these creatures be subordinate to our love for our children, then we justify vivisection for the benefit of our children and the destruction of nature for our own profit. We firmly believe that our children will suffer less from sickness from the knowledge gained through animal suffering and experimentation, and that they even learn something by dissecting fellow creatures without reverence or wonder.

This human-centered and utilitarian attitude toward animals arises from the profane dominion of a patriarchal and secular worldview. It is the sad and cruel reality of those who can still justify in the name of compassionate concern for their loved ones and humanity the suffering and death of animals in the research laboratory. They are sacrificed to the false gods of science, knowledge, and progress. This justification is more out of fear than love. Such sacrifice to gain control over life and mastery of the Earth's creation is done to assuage the fears and anguish of a life- and death-fearing society. Until we come to terms with the nature of suffering and the inevitability of death, the suffering of animals in vivisection laboratories will continue. Collectively we demean our own animality and spirituality (or divinity) when we accept and never question the deliberate torture and killing of our closest cosmic relatives, our animal kin.

THE HYPOCRISY OF ANIMAL "WELFARE"

Animal "welfarists" decry the deliberate killing of whales and seals, trapping, and trophy hunting as being "unnecessary" and not essential to the good of society. Such activities are therefore considered unethical and immoral. This rational conclusion is, however, human-centered and utilitarian because it implies that other forms of violence against animals may be necessary and therefore justifiable, if not unethical. Animal welfarists accept the mass slaughter of animals for human consumption and the suffering and killing of animals in the name of medical necessity with the patronizing proviso that the animals should be treated as humanely as possible.

The utilitarian justifications are not objective, because they are biased by subjective self-interest. This subjective consensus leads inevitably to the kind of moral relativism and situational ethics that justify violence and the suffering of others for the good of society. Yet objectivity is a prerequisite of good science and medicine and of sound agricultural and other social policies. To accept *any* form of violence against animals on the grounds of human necessity is, in the final analysis, chauvinistic and patronizing. To engage in violence against animals that are causing harm to us, as in coping with a locust plague or a rabid dog, is a very different matter from the industrial-scale, utilitarian exploitation of wild and domestic animals. How we choose to respond to such actual and potential danger of urban rats to our families and predators to our flocks and herds should be based on the ethical principles of respect for all life and *ahimsa*. Often less violent solutions to pest and predator control are not as harmful environmentally and to our own health and safety than the violent knee-jerk responses of poison baits and pesticide sprays. In the final analysis, to endeavor to act nonviolently and with respect for all life is enlightened self-interest.

Albert Schweitzer explained that "The utilitarian principle where animals are valued in terms of a resource of usefulness to man strengthens further man's separateness from other living things." Only when there is separation can we kill without reverence and compassion. And, ironically, the more we act in such destructive and violent ways, the more disconnected we become. This vicious cycle is not seen because, through a kind of protective psychic numbing, we become insensitive to the splitting of identification with our victim as a subjective, sentient, and significant other.

Over a billion animals are used worldwide in biomedical research each year. Many suffer as experimental models of cancer and genetic disorders (which are in part environmentally induced by pesticides in our food), and others are models of major diseases of civilization, such as alcoholism, drug addiction, malnutrition, and heart attack. A heart only for humanity, not for animals, makes such experiments possible if not ironically necessary. Perhaps within the irony lies the ultimate cure.

Preventing one will help prevent the other. But have we yet the courage to dare to try to give up vivisection?

The movement is reaching "critical mass," and public sentiment is shifting from self-concern to concern for what we are doing to fellow animals and to the environment. A laboratory beagle puppy is ceasing, very slowly, to be seen as a research "subject," an "object" of property and even as a separate and inferior species. More people are seeing the imprisoned and tortured animals in laboratories as our Earth relations, aspects of being or of the one life. As we are to a large measure defined if not determined by our relationships, the end of vivisection will mean that we have become a more compassionate species, more responsible and responsive to the needs of others, including the planet itself, and that we have become a less violent inhabitant in the process.

CHAPTER 7

The Economics of Conservation

A growing fear of the apocalyptic consequences of continued environmental destruction and pollution is stimulating the increasing concern for conservation and planetary survival. Deeper, more spiritual values are beginning to emerge in these troubled times. As René Dubos observes in *The Wooing of Earth*, we need the wilderness for our biological and psychological welfare, even though we do not live in it. By experiencing wildness in nature, we learn more about ourselves and our hidden potentialities. It "helps us become aware of the cosmos from which we emerged and to maintain some measure of harmonious relation to the rest of creation."

According to Dubos, the current ecological crisis is rooted in people's failure to anticipate the long-range consequences of their actions. And the consequences "have recently been aggravated by the power and misuses of modern technology." He contends that modern people pay no attention to environmental values because people are no longer linked to the Earth, as are animals and as were ancient peoples. The relationship between man and nature should be epitomized not by domination but by respect and love.

Dubos states later that:

> The demonic force . . . is not scientific technology itself, but our propensity to consider means as ends— an attitude symbolized by the fact that we measure success by the gross national product rather than by the quality of life and of the environment. . . . science and technology provide us with the *means* to create almost anything we want, but the development of means without worthwhile *goals* generates at best a dreary life and may at worst lead to tragedy.[1]

We can work, as landscape architects and ecological engineers, to protect and even enhance nature's potentials and diversity of plant and animal species, satisfying our own basic needs in the process. This is humane stewardship, the restoration, dressing, and keeping of the Garden of Eden: Paradesia. Clearly, the entire scientific, technological, industrial, and economic structure of the world's "developed" civilizations needs to be restructured. It must break free from the shortsighted conceptual linearities of converting nonrenewable resources into nonessential consumables regardless of the real environmental costs and long-term consequences. *Development must be consonant with conservation.* So many foreign aid programs operated by international agencies, such as the United Nations Development Program, Food and Agriculture Organization, and the World Bank, have done more to destroy the environment and to limit the future options of many underdeveloped countries than their original, traditional systems of agriculture and industry. Soil and water conservation, reforestation, and population control plus appropriate agricultural practices and cottage industries are far more essential in terms of economic independence, future options, and restoration of the land than encouraging or coercing third world countries to adopt large-scale industrialization, to grow cash crops for export, and to deplete their natural resources through inadequately regulated mining and logging.

The fruits of such programs is and has been poverty, famine, and accelerating environmental degradation.

An "ecocentric" view—an awareness of the global inter-connections among people, cultures, ecosystems, and the environment—and the impact of our values, actions, and life-styles—is now a survival imperative. Dr. Norman Myers, in *The Sinking Ark*, illustrates this point as follows[2]:

> It is simplistic to assert . . . that species are driven extinct through the ignorance or stupidity or wanton destructiveness of modern man. Species disappear be-cause of the way we prefer to live, all of us. For ex-ample, the expanding appetites of affluent nations for beef at "reasonable," i.e., noninflationary prices, en-courages the conversion of tropical moist forests into cattle ranches—and tropical moist forests harbor 40–50 percent of all species on earth, including plants that may offer drugs to combat a scourge of affluent na-tions, cancer. Hence an economic dimension that goes to the core of the problem straight off: which affluent-world conservationist does not enjoy the humble ham-burger with its humble price?

Environmentalist Robert Allen in *How to Save the World* clearly summarizes the urgency of the situation when he writes[3]:

> Time is running out. With every year that passes more essential resources are destroyed, while human de-mand for those resources increases. In the next 20 years the world population is expected to increase by almost half, from just over 4000 million to just under 6000 million. Yet at present rates of destruction these people will have to make do with a third less farmland and only half the present area of productive tropical forest. Because remedial action takes so much time, it must be very well focused, concentrating only on the highest priorities, and it must be taken at once. A world strat-

egy is needed to determine those priorities, indicate the main obstacles to achieving them, and propose ways of overcoming the obstacles. This is precisely what the world conservation strategy does.

The diverse and usually self-serving priorities of nation-states and multinational corporations must become secondary to the highest priority that affects us all, and that is the common cause of conservation and of protection of national resources and our life-support systems.

SAVE THE FORESTS

Tropical rain forests are now being destroyed at an estimated fifty acres per minute. These biomes are one of the Earth's richest genetic resources and are a vital "lung" for maintaining the atmosphere that we breathe. Local interests, such as extensive deforestation for logging and agricultural development, must be refocused much more broadly.

More and more people are beginning to realize how vital it is for us to conserve and properly manage these forests. According to Robert Allen in *How to Save the World:*

> Environmental disasters, such as floods, droughts and outbreaks of pests, are invariably blamed on nature or on the deity. They are called natural disasters or acts of God, as if there was nothing people could do about them and no way they could have had any hand in their making. Yet nature is generally the great preventer and mitigator of disasters, and an increasing number of floods, droughts and similar afflictions have either been caused or exacerbated by the violence people do to natural areas.
>
> Forests are the prime example of natural areas that contribute heavily to human welfare by acting as environmental buffers. Forests influence local and regional climates, generally by making them milder.

They help to provide a continuous flow of clean water; some forests, notably tropical cloud forests, even increase the availability of water by intercepting moisture from clouds. Watershed forests are particularly important because they protect soil cover on site and protect areas downstream from floods and other harmful fluctuations in streamflow. Removal or degradation of watershed forests and pastures can cause great human suffering. Without the sponge-like effect of their vegetation, which retains moisture and releases it slowly, the flow of water becomes erratic, leading to both floods and water shortages. The increased rate of water run-off causes additional damage by stripping the soil away, depriving agriculture of nutrients while clogging reservoirs, irrigation systems, canals and docks with silt, and smothering coral reefs.

Forests throughout the world are now being devastated by clearance for fuel, logging, agriculture, overgrazing, mining, and badly managed road building. Unless very effective conservation and reforestation programs are implemented immediately, effective restoration may be either impossible or too expensive.

SAVE THE OCEANS

The oceans are being destroyed by pollution, overfishing, and the elimination of coastal wetlands, which play a vital role in marine ecology. Robert Allen presents extensive documentation on the inefficiencies of modern factory-scale fishing practices. For every ton of shrimp caught, three tons of fish are thrown back into the ocean. Accidental killing of nontarget animals is an acute problem, leading to the depopulation of sea turtles, dolphins, seals, sea birds, and sea cows, and has prevented or slowed the recovery of several fish stocks. Allen believes that this incidental take of nontarget species equals pollution as a threat to living marine resources. Over a million sea birds are killed incidentally each year, and in salmon gill nets in the North

Atlantic and Pacific an estimated 20,000 porpoises are killed annually. Vast forty-mile long drift nets are now destroying even more ocean creatures especially in the Pacific ocean, pieces of which often break off to become floating graveyards for decades.

Coastal wetlands, including estuaries, swamps, salt marshes, and seagrass meadows, *must* be protected from pollution and land "reclamation" (for industrial and agricultural use) because they provide nutrients and habitat for many marine organisms, including the fry of cod, plaice, and herring. An estimated two-thirds of the world's fisheries are directly dependent on the coastal wetland biome. Coral reefs similarly are threatened by offshore drilling, oil spills, industrial pollution, dredging, and silting (from increasing soil erosion on land), yet they are vital to the marine ecology.

Many scientists and historians have shown that past civilizations have died out primarily not because of war (which often had a stimulating influence), but because of environmental degradation especially from the combined effects of deforestation and livestock overgrazing. And with this came droughts, floods, soil erosion, economic ruin, famine, and pestilence. Consider these lands that once supported noble and advanced cultures—ancient Egypt, Greece, and Rome; Persia with its garden Paradesias; the rich kingdoms of Nigeria and India; the Chinese dynasties.

Natural climatic changes are not solely to blame for these devastating consequences of imprudent human activities, as all these civilizations arose after the end of the last Ice Age. The Earth's hydrological cycle is disrupted when the rhythms of nature's "wheels" are drastically changed ostensibly by industrial progress, as by extensive deforestation, diversion of major waterways, and today's waste of water pumped from deep aquifers (much of what is sprayed over plants is lost in evaporation). The social, political, and economic consequences of these "ecocidal" activities were catastrophic to past civilizations. And these same symptoms are spreading to other more technologically "advanced" industrial-age civilizations, particularly in the

United States, which seem incapable of understanding and learning from history and from nature.

Taoism sprang from the ecological and other social crises of ancient China. Its modern analogue, the science of ecology, has emerged out of a growing awareness of the environment and of our destructive impact on it. Pessimists may see such philosophy and science as emerging too late to save their respective civilizations. In fact, what does survive is not the civilization (which is always changing anyway), but those individuals who are able to adapt to change and challenge and who do not succumb to conformity, helplessness, sickness, or insanity. Regardless of natural or manmade environmental changes that influence a country's socioeconomic structure, health, and wealth, they are able to continue to live responsible, meaningful, and relatively healthful lives. Modern survivalists pay less attention to their material security than they do to their own spiritual, mental, and physical health, and to an overall cognizance of what is going on in society. The denial of our ecological problems constitutes the collective insanity of the times.

To recover personal autonomy and responsibility, we must awaken ethically and take appropriate political action. The perception of a coming apocalypse gives us three choices: extinction, survival in a planned and engineered hell, or politically determined limits on industrial nemesis that is founded on an international agreement about procedural rules and basic values, consonant with the principles of environmental quality, economic sustainability, social justice and the integrity of earth's creation.

LIVING IN HARMONY

The biosphere is a living system that nurtures and sustains many interdependent life forms. These life forms have discrete niches within a "seamless web" of interconnecting ecosystems through which energy flows and consciousness evolves. Each life form and ecosystem is in a state of unstable equilibrium, and each is governed or regulated by an interplay of vectors and variables that we recognize as natural "laws." These laws are biophysical phenomena such as entropy and syntropy (destruction and regeneration), adaptation and subspeciation, sustainable self-regulation, co-evolution (evolving in mutual interdependence), energy transformation, and succession. Individual species also have recognized roles; some are regulators (carnivores, pathogens), others are energy transformers and synthesizers (plants, algae and herbivores), and still others are biodegraders (fungi, microorganisms, and carrion consumers of dead organic material). Their interrelationships may be one of parasitism, symbiosis, or commensalism (sharing the same resources). Then there are opportunist and pioneer species, which have the biological capacity to adapt to a wide variety of conditions. Man has the technological capacity to do so also. Once the door is opened by some natural vector, such as a beaver, pioneering opportunists can rapidly transform ecosystems, as in a natural succession of swampland into a willow and alder biome. Species such as the beaver (and man) may be regarded as *successional catalysts*, facilitating the cycles of natural succession and locally increasing biological and ecological diversity. René Dubos has eloquently shown how early agrarian man, in clearing the vast European forests with fire (a natural agent of succession) and ax, increased nature's diversity and released its potentials to create new biomes, open meadows, and so on.

The Maasai in East Africa had, until recently, a similar positive ecological effect with their cattle. Like the European farmers, they helped "freeze" their human-shaped biome, preventing retrogressive succession by destroying invading trees and shrubs. Fauna that depended on the latter had natural sanctuary in adjacent woodland and forest, while other wildlife and plants that preferred the open grassland meadow or savanna became commensals with humans and their domestic stock. Our earlier relationship with nature as a symbiotic hunter-gatherer thus changed to one of commensalism and natural cocreative stewardship. The low biomass and extractive power of our species and stock, our virtually nonexistent technology and the nomadic habits of some peoples helped reduce the rate of entropy until the advent of colonialism, urban industrialism and more recent Western technology and medicine. These resulted in population explosions, disease, larger herds of cattle, overgrazing, and other disruptive cultural and environmental problems. The Maasai culture is now on the verge of extinction. Some Maasai are now violating their religious taboo of not tilling the soil and have become sedentary agrarians like their Kikuyu and Bantu neighbors.

The Maasai are an invaluable cultural model of humans creating a commensal niche for their cattle and living primarily symbiotically with them (rather than as carnivores who kill). Their main sustenance is the fermented blood and milk that they collect daily from their stock. Only the warriors kill and eat the meat of wild and domestic animals. Some highly efficient and self-sustaining, primarily agrarian, cultures, such as the Asian and Andean irrigation and terrace farms and Hopi desert farming systems, are models of ecological stability and sustainable productivity. Also, "subsistence" coastal fishing cultures, and more recent relatively self-contained intensive farming systems of the Amish and British (Norfolk) crop-rotation systems have a minimal negative environmental impact. All these systems are characterized by minimal capital investment. The major energy inputs are in the form of human labor and animal draft power and manure.

In contrast, modern European and North American agricultural practices and economies are highly extractive and are not self-sustaining because they require vast amounts of energy input (artificial petrochemical fertilizers and so on) in order to be productive. Spectacular profits have resulted from the practice of raising the same crop year after year—monoculture—rather than crop rotation. In the process in arid regions deep-water aquifers have been depleted by artesian well crop irrigation and polluted by run-off from pesticides and fertilizers. But these short-term gains are now being offset by shortage of water, water pollution, soil erosion, exhaustion of soil nutrients, salinization, and desertification.

This artificially enhanced level of productivity is beyond the natural carrying capacity of the land, hence the need for energy inputs (especially fertilizers) derived from finite global resources. Most agriculturalists contend that this is essential for two reasons: to balance trade deficits in the world market economies and to exchange grains for other essential raw materials and resources (and for political power); and to provide food for a burgeoning and hungry world population whose biomass may well be beyond the biosphere's natural carrying capacity.

However, these ecologically unsound agricultural practices are parasitic rather than commensal or symbiotic, and the Earth cannot sustain this high rate of extraction. A new technological "fix," such as genetically engineering faster-growing corn or pigs or more efficient ways of deep-sea fishing, is not the right answer. Modern systems of agriculture and livestock production create many domestogenic diseases. Hence the need for pesticides, predaticides, parasiticides, herbicides, antibiotics, and antiviral vaccines. Farmers find themselves on an inescapable drug treadmill to keep at bay catastrophic pestilences. Through their chemical warfare against the forces of nature, they create further health and environmental problems, even "biological deserts." This is very different from destroying trees that invade the meadows and herding the flocks with domesticated dogs to keep away predators. Hybrid, fast-growing, and high-yield crops and livestock are even more susceptible to pests and diseases and the fertilizers and formulated feeds used may lower their resistance even more.

But once we begin to "think as nature acts," to paraphrase the late Gregory Bateson, pests and pathogens can become allies rather than adversaries. We need not always assume the offensive and react destructively, but we should rather endeavor to work cocreatively, harnessing nature's potentials. Crop rotation and integrated pest management, with areas of land preserved to harbor beneficial insects and birds, are enlightened alternatives of ecologically sound stewardship. Plankton and algae, grown in sunlight and fed on biological waste materials (including human excrement), could be the amino acid–rich food and fertilizer of the future whose potentials we might cautiously enhance through genetic engineering.

Regional population control through family planning, soil and water conservation, and the improved farm animal health and husbandry to make flocks and herds smaller but more productive, especially in third world countries, reforestation, and the recycling of plant, human, animal, and nontoxic industrial wastes and by-products are obvious partial steps toward a sustainable future. Changes in consumer habits (eating less meat) and in agricultural practices (such as crop rotation and tilling methods) and energy conservation are inevitable. We should not exhaust our land and resources to provide food and fiber to barter for political influence abroad, for "luxury" raw materials, foreign exchange, and consumer products (nonsubsistence materials), or for materials to build more and more lethal military weaponry.

Until there is a fundamental change in U.S. agricultural policy at home and abroad, these obvious solutions will be impossible to implement. The more we continue to deplete the Earth of its resources and turn once-rich fields and ranges into arid and exhausted wastelands, the more likely nations are going to compete and aggress rather than to cooperate and restore the biosphere.

If we do not think and act ecologically—"terrocentrically"—we, like the Maasai, will soon be extinct. When we think and act ecologically, and return to nature and learn from it, we may restore the Garden of Eden—a very different garden, supporting a vast human population that has developed appropriate technologies to sustain a cooperative world community and enrich the Earth at the same time without unnecessary destruction or gratuitous exploitation of any living creature.

As the late Indira Gandhi observed, "Everything is interdependent. Man, Animal, and Environment, whatever the economical or political context. Everything is related. Whatever happens now to animals will eventually happen to man. The conservation of our inheritance deserves the same natural care as our economical development."

CHAPTER 8

Wildlife: An Endangered

"Resource"

Several aspects of wildlife exploitation and conservation warrant scrutiny from a humane, ethical viewpoint as well as from ecological and utilitarian perspectives. The care and welfare of wild animals in captivity needs considerable improvement, especially with the regard to the relatively sterile cages that many primates and carnivores are kept in. Also, in terms of conservation, zoos need to take very great care to avoid the problem of inbreeding, which, as research at the National Zoo in Washington has shown, can very quickly lead to increasing health problems, birth difficulties, and infertility notably in captive ungulates (hoofed animals such as antelope).

The collecting of wildlife for educational and research purposes (taxonomy and so on) also needs more careful scrutiny, because collectors in certain biomes can have a significant impact on indigenous species. Better standards are also needed for the care and maintenance of captive fur-bearing mammals.

The fur ranching industry also should be questioned in terms of the ethics of raising animals and destroying them for purposes not essential to the greater good. Various species of wildlife are also kept as pets. Very strict regulations controlling the propagation of these animals for sale as pets would be advantageous not only to prospective owners but also to the species. Also, the capture of native wild species and the importation of exotic species into this country by the pet industry should be prohibited. As much as 80 percent of a shipment of birds, for example, can die between being caught and eventually finding a way into someone's home. To protect the poultry industry from Newcastle disease, the USDA often must destroy large numbers of imported birds infected or exposed to this disease.

Releasing rehabilitated and orphaned animals back into the wild is another problem area. Animals that are imprinted onto people or carnivores that do not know how to hunt may not adapt when released. State authorities who insist on taking away orphaned animals that people have raised should bear this in mind. Once an animal has been humanized, it may not be capable to care for itself in the wild. There is also a problem with releasing wild animals, such as raccoons, that have been humanely caught into wildlife refuges. It can facilitate the spread of disease, and territorial species may not be able to secure territory, which would prejudice their survival.

In contrast to fur ranching, some bioregions offer more positive advantages in ranch-raising wild ungulates. These herbivores, such as antelope, can thrive where nonindigenous livestock, such as cattle, sheep, and goats, will destroy the vegetation and trigger desertification. For example, in Kenya, Dr. David Hopcraft has shown that indigenous ungulates are highly productive, producing seven times more meat and three times more hides per acre compared to domestic cattle. Cattle require water and overgraze; the grasses that they trample and graze are not adapted to them. Furthermore, cattle need to be dipped to control insect-borne diseases every two weeks, while indigenous natural herbivores do not need such preventive medication. If people must eat meat, ecologically more sound alternatives to cattle in many bioregions should be sought.

However, the ranch-raising of exotic animals for trophy hunters, as is occurring in the state of Texas, is ethically questionable. Another very questionable practice is the introduction of alien and exotic species. The nutria, a South American aquatic rodent, can create havoc with natural waterways. This species was introduced for its value as a fur-bearer and encouraged by state wildlife departments ostensibly to help keep weeds down in lakes and waterways. All such interferences in the natural balance of ecosystems should be carefully scrutinized, because the end results are often disastrous. Similarly, the release of wild pets, such as the clawed toad and tropical fish, could have a serious, negative environmental impact, as has occurred in Florida.

Predator and pest control practices have come under considerable fire from conservationists and animal welfare groups. More biologically appropriate methods of predator and pest control need to be researched and implemented. Integrated pest management, for example, and better conservation of wilderness areas around cropland in order to provide natural predators for crop pests are more ecologically sensible alternatives to the continuous use of pesticides. Similarly, predators such as the coyote should not be controlled with non-selective devices—traps, cyanide guns, and poison baits. Indiscriminate predator control can have a significant impact on nontarget species, including eagles, bobcats, and other wildlife, not to mention companion animals that happen to be roaming free. A more biological approach to predator control would include introducing donkeys, or llamas, and guard dogs, which have all been effectively used to frighten coyotes away, as well as using improved methods of shepherding.

Hunting is part of the American way of life. Hunting groups are to be congratulated for protecting many wildlife areas from other human interests that would have damaged the ecosystems irreparably. Yet nonsubsistence hunting, hunting for pleasure, and trophy hunting (including the trophy hunting of marine fish, such as the marlin) are highly questionable activities. Subsistence hunting and maintaining a sustainable yield for human consumption of certain species may be ecologically sound. However, when natural "competitors" such as the wolf and mountain lion are eliminated by wildlife departments in order to reduce competition for the hunters, the system becomes ecologically unsound and ethically untenable. Hunters often argue that it is in the interests of animal welfare to shoot deer, for example, rather than to let them starve in winter. This is untenable. Deer, elk, and other ungulates are physiologically and behaviorally adapted to cope with seasonal starvation.

According to Humane Society records, the number of hunted animals killed every year in the U.S. (including ducks and geese) exceeds 200 million, a figure that does not include millions more that are injured and later die.

Hunters need to be educated in how to kill animals as humanely as possible. This would certainly rule out less accurate methods of hunting, such as bow hunting. Some bow hunters believe that using a curare-tipped dart to paralyze the prey might be acceptable. This alternative needs to be debated further.

Trapping is one aspect of wildlife exploitation that raises special ethical and welfare concerns. The steel leghold trap, which is responsible for the maiming and death of some 22 million animals each year in the United States, is an inhumane way of holding an animal prior to its being killed by the trapper. Trap lines are often not inspected for twenty-four or forty-eight hours. The padded offset trap might cause less injury than a regular steel-jaw trap but still causes terror. Even if humane methods are developed, the ethical issue of killing wildlife for their fur remains to be answered. While it is argued that hunting and trapping removes a population surplus of wildlife that might otherwise die in winter from starvation, wildlife management actually creates this surplus for human use. Hunting and trapping do not help preserve the balance of nature when there is no balance to begin with.

The artificially created overpopulation of "game" species (often at the expense of nongame species) necessitates, but does not justify, hunting and trapping to prevent serious ecological damage by excess deer or other game. Strictly speaking, in terms of bioenergetics, there is no "surplus" in nature: Nothing is wasted. The amount of suffering and pain trapped animals endure make commercial trapping unacceptable. And the right of wildlife to life versus our right to such luxury items as furs warrants critical scrutiny. Furthermore, certain fur-bearing mammals, such as the lynx and bobcat, are not adapted to human predation. Their reproductive rate does not increase in response to human predation, and unregulated trapping could lead to regional species extinction. The same may be true for the otter. When we combine the impact of trapping with the destruction of habitat due to irrigation, construction of dams, real estate development, deforestation, and agricultural prac-tices, it would appear that trapping is a form of wildlife ex-ploitation that, as it is not being adequately and humanely regulated, should be prohibited.

Similarly, the cruel "harvesting" of marine mammals for their fur (seals are simply clubbed to death) and whaling using explosive harpoons should be prohibited. Considering the mul-tifactorial influences of pollution, overfishing, destruction of marine estuaries, and oil spills on the marine environment, the present quota system for the taking of certain species of whale and seal is based on inadequate data. Moratoria should be es-tablished until it can be proven that sustainable yield quotas are based on sound, scientific evidence. However, even if sound evidence can be presented, the ethical question regarding these mammals' right to life remains.

Other aspects of wildlife conservation and exploitation that raise ethical issues include the selective destruction of feral spe-cies that are not indigenous to a given area but that have gone wild and adapted to a locale, such as the burros in the Grand Canyon. This particular question pits the humane ethic of re-verence for life and the right of wild animals to exist against the sensible, ecological imperative of maintaining the natural diversity and integrity of a given biome. As will be argued shortly, the latter ecological principle overrides the principle of individual rights. Thus feral species should be removed or de-stroyed.

A very serious problem is the control of wildlife diseases that are variously communicable to human beings and domestic livestock (such as rabies) and also those diseases, such as foot-and-mouth disease and distemper, that can affect wildlife. Careful wildlife management programs can greatly help in these areas, but more research is needed into the dynamics of such diseases, which may become more of a problem through human interference. The giving of live vaccines to wildlife may be ecologically unsound, but the only way to save some endangered species. Thousands of buffalo have been killed by government agents in the United States to protect the cattle industry because buffalo may harbor _Brucellosis_, a disease transmittible to cattle.

Wolf populations in North America have been decimated by distemper and parvovirus, transmitted by free-roaming domestic dogs.

It is ironic that species such as deer and bobcat have survived for millions of years yet now wildlife biologists insist that they must be "managed." No one managed bobcats and wolves during their 3 million years of existence. That wild animals need to be managed now (shot, trapped, and poisoned) is a fabrication to sanctify their exploitation scientifically or a necessity because we, and not they, have disrupted their once-healthy ecosystems; or both. The primary task of wildlife management programs should be to preserve viable, natural wildlife populations and the ecosystems on which they depend. Current wildlife management is scientifically unsound, either creating or perpetuating "ecopathology." According to Humane Society records, U.S. National Wildlife Refuges (of which there are some 400 encompassing some 90 million acres) are not refuges at all. On them over half a million animals are shot each year by hunters, 146,000 are trapped, trees are felled, recreation vehicles run amok, cattle are grazed, and pesticides are sprayed.

For conservationists and those concerned with wildlife park and wilderness area management, the "freezing" of ecosystems in order to protect endangered species is a dilemma of considerable magnitude. For example, in parts of Africa the elephant is destroying much of its habitat. This could lead to a population crash, a change in the vegetation, and then a gradual buildup again of the vegetation and elephant population. Should one cull the elephants to stop this natural succession, or is it really a natural succession? The problem could be a consequence of the elephants being confined to a very small area and unable to move out of the parks to other feeding areas. But against the relentless pressures of agricultural expansion, an increasing human population and poaching, the elephant, like the rhinoceros, in the absence of worldwide conservation support, may soon be extinct.

OTHER OVERLOOKED WILDLIFE CRUELTIES

We tend to overlook numerous instances of cruelty toward animals. This is partly because we care less about some animal species than others and partly because we do not even regard some creatures as animals.

Let us take fish for a start. Fish are animals, but perhaps because they are coldblooded or lack facial expression, most people do not question the humaneness of catching them on hooks, keeping them alive on a stringer, or letting them suffocate in the air after they have been caught in a net. However, research has shown that fish can suffer and that they have feelings. Fish have benzodiazepine receptors in their brains, just as we and other animals have. These receptors are blocked by such anxiety-relieving drugs as Valium, which means that fish, like us, have a biochemical system in the brain that can evoke feelings of anxiety. Fish attempt to escape when alarmed, and some, when frightened, actually change color. Ironically, one animal scientist reasoned with me in defense of his avid interest in fly fishing that fish surely don't feel pain, fear, or anxiety because when they are caught on a hook they swim away, pulling on the line. A human being would not pull away, he argued, but instead would stand still or move toward the rod so as to reduce the pain and tension on the fishing line. But if this man really knew fish, he would have realized that a terrified fish usually swims away and into deep water when alarmed or in pain.

The pain resulting from injury by the hook contributes less

to the fish's suffering than fear according to Dutch scientist John Verheijen and co-workers. They based their conclusion on observations of the behavior of carp after being caught on a hook and when the line was pulled taut. Fish hooked but not held on a taut line ate again soon after release; those subjected to line pressure avoided food for a considerable time afterward.

Some fisherpeople put worms on their hooks as bait without a second thought. Yet Swedish researchers have found that earthworms, like us and other animals, have a biochemical reaction to injury that helps dampen pain, so that they are not totally incapacitated. When injured, their nervous system secretes pain-killing opiates. That they, as we, have evolved such a way of coping with pain indicates that earthworms must surely feel pain and have feelings. Otherwise they would not possess this inborn opiate analgesic reaction and squirm wildly when first impaled on a hook!

All living things can be physically harmed, so it is natural that they should be averse to that which could harm them and evolve ways of avoiding injury and death. We recognize this as the survival instinct, or will to live. And while many life forms may not be objectively aware of that which could injure or kill them, or subjectively experience fear and anxiety, we should recognize their right not to be harmed or killed and their will to live.

Sometimes animals seem to act stupidly, as when a moth injures or kills itself by flying into a candle flame. In reality, the creature is reacting to a wholly unnatural stimulus that it has not evolved any way to avoid. Yet when moths are alarmed, they will attempt to escape, often flying in an erratic pattern so that they are difficult to catch, or else they fall to the ground and play dead, the camouflage markings on their wings making them almost invisible. They clearly have a will to survive.

It disturbs me that so many people use ultraviolet lights to attract insects that are then killed by an electrical current. These backyard and patio bug zappers should be abolished, because they also kill harmless insects, many of which are beneficial to the garden and are a food source for birds and other creatures. Only a minute percentage of the billions of bugs killed every year by these devices actually bite people. Mosquitoes, black flies, and other biting insects can be best avoided by using insect repellents, citronella candles, porch screens, and so on, and by people not going outdoors early in the evening when the insects are most active.

The wholesale and unregulated use of insecticides and herbicides also kill billions of innocent creatures including birds, earthworms, butterflies and other insects. I wish that more people would turn at least a part of their sanitized lawns into flower and "weed"-filled patches of meadow to attract insects, birds, and other wildlife. It has been estimated that more pesticides and herbicides are used in cities and suburbs than by the entire agribusiness industry. Many of these poisons are known to cause cancer, birth defects, and genetic damage. Perhaps this is nature's way of getting back at us for abusing our power of dominion and for being so insensitive to the rights and lives of other creatures who share with us the will to live.

Many pets have died following exposure to these poisons, some of which are even used in and around the home to control cockroaches, mice, rats, fleas, and the like. Pesticide-emitting flea collars, powders and sprays, and Vapona and other chemically impregnated fly-killing devices release poisons into the home that are hazardous to all who dwell therein. Humanitarians are appalled by the glue traps that are marketed to kill mice and various insects. They die slowly and terribly, unable to escape from an adhesive-covered bait board. We should extend our circle of compassion to embrace all creatures and begin to feel for the flies and other insects struggling to be free from sticky fly paper. There are humane alternatives. We can make our homes "pestproof" and not baited and poisonous traps for the creatures that might inadvertently enter therein. And we can think twice about going fishing, putting worms on hooks, and other unthinking acts of cruelty toward our fellow creatures.

PESTICIDE POISONING OF ANIMALS

Companion cats and dogs often suffer immediate poisoning when they come into contact with sprayed lawns, garden shrubbery, sidewalks, and roadside vegetation. Cats are especially at risk because they will ingest any pesticide residues picked up on their fur in the process of grooming themselves. Aerosol inhalation is another route of poisoning, especially when the pesticides are applied by spraying, particularly on windy days.

Backyard pets, from dogs to rabbits and ferrets in outdoor cages, are also at risk, as are goldfish and other fish kept in outdoor ponds. So are indoor pets, especially cage birds, if windows are accidentally left open and air conditioners not turned off when pesticides are being sprayed in the immediate vicinity.

These dangers are further compounded and animals are placed at even greater risk if they have been recently treated with pesticides (as to control fleas) by their owners. Again, because of their extreme sensitivity to pesticides, cats are especially at risk.

Symptoms of pesticide poisoning range from the acute to the chronic, and are often difficult to diagnose specifically because in many instances they mimic those of various infectious diseases. Hence the reporting of pesticide poisoning in companion animals is sporadic, and actual morbidity and mortality rates are difficult to determine.

In order to minimize risk, local authorities should set their own requirements for the proper and safe application of pesticides. The public and private sectors involved in pesticide application should be apprised of these requirements. Wildlife, especially birds, should also be considered because these animals are at risk especially when they are foraging most in order to feed their young.

The following are some of the symptoms in companion animals that have been linked with exposure to various pesticides (excluding rat bait poisons): weakness, depression, anorexia, vomiting, diarrhea, muscular tremors, disorientation, convulsions, coma, anaphylactic shock and death, dyspnea (difficulty in breathing), cardiac abnormalities, liver dysfunction, suppression of the immune system and increased susceptibility to infectious diseases, abortion, and birth defects in offspring.

Dogs and cats are also at risk when rat-bait poisons are improperly applied. Dogs are especially vulnerable when they have easy access to poison bait, which when ingested usually causes fatal internal bleeding. A person improperly applying pesticides to private property (lawns and orchards), public property (parks, highways), and other areas such as private or public golf courses and recreational areas and waterways (canals and streams) could put both wild and domesticated animals at risk.

In addition, we should all be concerned with the indiscriminate toxicity of most pesticides commonly used today (they are poisonous to nontarget species as well as those that they are intended to kill). Futhermore, the wholesale and indiscriminate use of pesticides will mean chronic, cumulative poisoning in wild and domestic animals and the buildup of resistance in short-lived, rapid-breeding target species. This results in the "pesticide treadmill": More and stronger pesticides are needed to control pests, while nontarget species, including the human population, are placed at greater and greater risk. Every community should address the adverse ecological impact of pesticide poisoning of beneficial nontarget species, notably insectivorous birds and plant-pollinating bees.

Much more public support of urban wildlife enhancement programs and land preservation and protection policies is needed. People in suburban and urban areas should be discouraged from feeding wildlife because of the possible population disruption and because, for example, attracting many birds to a bird feeder could accelerate the spread of certain diseases. Feeding may also disrupt the physiology of migratory species and thus jeopardize their survival. In rural areas and hunting preserves, the practice of supplemental feeding of game in the winter should be questioned.* It leads to an excessively high population, beyond the normal carrying capacity of the biome, especially with deer. Manipulating wildlife populations in order to provide a greater "surplus" for hunters and trappers is deplorable. It is more akin to farming wildlife than to sound ecological management.

The ultimate national question is whether natural resources, including wildlife habitat, can have multiple uses (for recreation, conservation, ranching, hunting, mining, etc.) Spokespeople under the Reagan administration equated environmentalism with being against the national interest. In fact, to be a conservationist was akin to being unpatriotic. However, economic imperatives notwithstanding, the nation's needs for certain raw materials, especially minerals and fuel and uranium, should not be jeopardized, but rather should be guided so that ecologically sound practices are followed and local communities of people, such as the Navajo and Hopi, are neither dislocated nor destroyed. No country can allow material and military interest to stand in the way of environmental quality or the interests of wildlife and minorities. A major flaw in the multiple-use concept of public lands in the United States is that different bureaucracies handle the different uses. Ultimately the land itself is not being properly managed because of lack of integration and coordination between different state and federal bureaucracies.

Throughout the world, there are unique biomes: the Serengeti plains, the Four Corners of the Colorado plateau, the Amazon and New Guinea rain forests, tundra, coral atolls, lakes, and ocean regions. A world park concept needs to be developed in order that all nations will collectively provide funds to stop the plunder, destruction, and pollution of these vital parts of the biospheric ecosystem and of the flora, fauna, and nonrenewable resources therein. These biomes, of priceless and unique biological content, are rapidly disappearing due to the inadequately regulated activities of undeveloped nations and

---

*Supplemental feeding is essential, however, if their winter rangeland has been overgrazed by ranchers' cattle and sheep.

multinational global enterprises alike. International biopolitics of conservation and protection will continue to fail unless the excessive demands and consumption patterns of developed nations are curtailed, acid rain and global warming reduced, and the vast expenditure of financial resources into armaments and nonessential consumables is redirected to protect our future.

Dr. John W. Grandy writes,[1]

> If we as a nation cannot preserve life for *its* own sake, then we ought to at least demand the preservation of endangered and threatened life forms for *our* own sake. . . . the preservation of life on earth is inextricably tied to biological diversity, that is, the diversity of life and genetic information that is contained in all of the species that inhabit this planet. This diversity of genetic information is continually renewed and revitalized through breeding and evolution. Extinction, which results in the permanent loss of genetic material and evolutionary potential, thus threatens the health of a wide diversity of eco-systems and the survival of all life.

The worldwide commercial exploitation of wildlife represents another destructive industrial-age activity that is clearly counterproductive and not in the best interests of our own species or of those we wantonly destroy.

Wildlife management programs should be designed to consider species' rights and the role of that species in the ecosystem. The moral injunction to maintain the natural diversity of a particular ecosystem (that is, the one absolute right of all life to a healthy biosphere) should also be considered, otherwise we are no longer talking about or practicing wildlife management or stewardship but instead practicing a form of agricultural management and seasonal harvesting.

Recently ecological and economic arguments have been presented to justify conserving wildlife species, particularly as genetic resources and for tourism. But in the final anaysis, the most convincing argument is a moral (or spiritual) one. The real challenge is to preserve both species and communities and to be able effectively to monitor, control, and predict the impact of direct and indirect human influences, ranging from trapping and hunting quotas to the effects of acid rain and other pollutants. Can this be done? Do we have the necessary scientific tools, the right attitudes, and local, national, and international cooperation? A nation of hungry people cannot give wildlife conservation a high priority. When the political and economic climate necessitates short-term gains and rules against long-term planning, management, and conservation, natural resources may be exhausted and indigenous species eliminated.

Humane alternatives and ecologically more harmonious pratices need to be researched and practiced. Hunter education can help make the slaughter of "game" species more accurate and therefore more humane. Improvements in trap technology and trapper education can make the restraint of fur-bearers more humane. However, the ethics of nonsubsistence hunting, trapping, and managing wildlife for human recreation and profit make such practices highly questionable. I believe the harvesting of wildlife is acceptable only if it is essential to restore and preserve the balance and integrity (that is, normality) of the biotic community, if no other alternatives (such as the reintroduction of predators) is feasible. And then it must be done humanely.

The challenge, and the very core of this ethical issue, is how to maximize human good without violating the basic rights of wildlife and the absolute right of the biosphere/biome in question. As humane alternatives are needed in the use of animals in biomedical research and in the husbandry and slaughter of farm animals, so we need to develop and implement ecological alternatives to restore and preserve the biosphere. Crop rotation and mixed grazing in agriculture is one example. Ranch-raising indigenous wild ungulates for human consumption is another, although conserving wildlife for tourism can provide far greater revenues especially for third world countries.

It is often said that hunting and trapping removes surplus

offspring that would otherwise die and be "wasted." Yet it is an ecological fact that nothing in nature is "wasted": A dead tree, bobcat, or deer is still part of the ecosystem, and its organic remains are an intrinsic part of the biodynamics and energetics of that system. Nothing can be removed without some price to something or someone. The ultimate challenge is for us to minimize the impact and to model and monitor long-term consequences (which are nonlinear and multifactorial) rather than to base policies on inadequate data, shortsighted goals, and humanocentric and potentially ecocidal cost-benefit analyses.

As some critics have observed, wildlife management has become wildlife *mis*management, more akin to ranching and promoting "feature" species for human consumption. The time has surely come to stop confounding wildlife conservation with management (that is, wildlife ranching) for exclusively human use. Those who wish might then get back to the business of restoring and monitoring ecosystems, which is no easy task. It would surely be simplified and enhanced if those wild species that hunters like and the fur trade require were propagated under controlled conditions on game and fur ranches. This is important, I believe, because by the time the United States and other nations reach a consensus over the rights of animals and of the right of all life to a whole and healthy biosphere, there may well be little left.

According to Professor Stephen Kellert's study of American attitudes toward wildlife, the majority of people surveyed favored protecting wildlife even at the expense of jobs, housing, and development projects. For example, 76 percent thought cutting trees for lumber and paper should be done in ways that help wildlife even if it resulted in higher lumber prices. When asked about possible sources of funding for wildlife management programs, the public indicated stronger support for taxes on "consumptive" activities, such as buying fur, than on "nonconsumptive" uses, such as birdwatching. Eighty-two percent favored a sales tax on fur clothing from wild animals; 75 percent favored entrance fees to wildlife refuges and other public wildlife areas; and 71 percent favored increasing the amount of general tax revenues of wildlife management. The same number favored sales taxes on backpacking and camping equipment; and 54 percent favored taxes on birdwatching supplies and equipment.[2]

Kellert's findings reflect the growing public concern for intrinsic worth of wildlife. But when national sentiment is in direct opposition to local or state attitudes, what is the democratic solution? Should wildlife "belong" to or morally and legally fall under the jurisdiction of state or federal authorities, or do all Americans have an equal share because wildlife is part of our national heritage? By analogy, the snow leopard or some other endangered species may not be valued in and for itself by the government of the country in which it exists, yet is not the snow leopard (or the sperm whale in "neutral territory" in midocean) part of our world heritage?

Animal rights and the absolute right of all life to a whole and healthy environment take us beyond personal, state, and national vested interests, which may result in unethical exploitation of wildlife species, unjustifiable suffering, and unsound and potentially ecocidal environmental impacts. Humanity is at a transitional point. Humanocentric values, perceptions, and priorities must be cast in a broader ethical framework of responsible stewardship. Wildlife and habitat are part of the same global community as mankind. Consequently we must develop a very different worldview that embraces those moral codes and ethical constraints that will protect the interests of all life on Earth, not simply the interests and rights of human beings.

A major factor contributing to the extinction of wildlife and destruction of their habitats has been the so-called development programs for third-world countries. Many of the export-oriented industrialization programs have been funded by the World Bank and International Monetary Fund and range from dam construction to cotton plantations, cattle ranches, and large-scale commercial forestry and fishing. It is now well documented that these programs have increased local poverty, disenfranchisement, displacement, and malnutrition and have ignored ecological constraints. The net result has been for the poor to feed the rich and at great cost of nonrenewable resources (becoming ever more dependent on food imports in the process), which makes poverty and famine their children's inheritance and social, economic and ecological bankruptcy inevitable.

His Holiness the Dalai Lama has stated[3] that:

> Peace and survival of life on earth as we know it are threatened by human activities which lack a commitment to humanitarian values.
>
> Destruction of nature and natural resources results from ignorance, greed and lack of respect for the earth's living things.
>
> This lack of respect extends even to earth's human descendants, the future generations who will inherit a vastly degraded planet if world peace does not become a reality, and destruction of the natural environment continues at the present rate.
>
> Our ancestors viewed the earth as rich and bountiful, which it is. Many people in the past also saw nature as inexhaustibly sustainable, which we now know is the case only if we care for it.
>
> It is not difficult to forgive destruction in the past which resulted from ignorance. Today however, we have access to more information, and it is essential that we re-examine ethically what we have inherited, what we are responsible for, and what we will pass on to coming generations.
>
> Clearly this is a pivotal generation. Global communication is possible, yet confrontations more often than meaningful dialogues for peace take place.
>
> Our marvels of science and technology are matched if not outweighed by many current tragedies, including human starvation in some parts of the world, and extinction of other life forms.
>
> Exploration of outer space takes place at the same

time as the earth's own oceans, seas, and fresh water areas grow increasingly polluted, and their life forms are still largely unknown or misunderstood.

Many of the earth's habitats, animals, plants, insects, and even microorganisms that we know as rare may not be known at all by future generations. We have the capability, and the responsibility. We must act before it is too late.

Pope John Paul II's encyclical *On Social Concerns* (Sollicitudo Re: Socialis, December 30, 1987) is the first papal encyclical to address concern for the environment. In paragraph 34 he states that:

Nor can the moral character of development exclude respect for the beings which constitute the natural world, which the ancient Greeks—alluding precisely to the order which distinguishes it—called the "cosmos." Such realities also demand respect, by virtue of a threefold consideration which it is useful to reflect upon carefully.

The first consideration is the appropriateness of acquiring a growing awareness of the fact that one cannot use with impunity the different categories of beings, whether living or inanimate—animals, plants, the natural elements—simply as one wishes, according to one's own economic needs. On the contrary, one must take into account the nature of each being and of its mutual connection in an ordered system which is precisely the "cosmos."

CHAPTER 9

Wildlife and Nature Liberation

WILDLIFE MANAGEMENT AND ANIMAL RIGHTS: RECONCILING IDEOLOGICAL DIFFERENCES

For many years, there has been an ideological difference between wildlife conservationists and animal protectionists over concern for animals as populations versus concern for individuals. Conservionsts generally see caring for and attempting to rehabilitate orphaned and injured wildlife as a waste of time and resources, especially for common species.

This difference persists today between environmental ecologists and animal rightists. For instance, the latter would contest the slaughter of feral species, such as the wild horses of Australia and the southwestern states of America, while the former would rationalize such action as a good conservation program. Animal rightists oppose in principle the ranch raising of wild animals, while many environmental ecologists contend that this practice serves both human interests and the interests of conservation. Likewise, conservationists would condone the "harvesting" of various wildlife species by Amazonian Indian and Arctic Eskimo communities, provided it is done on a "sustainable" basis. The animal rights position stands in direct opposition to native peoples' rights and traditions. However, native peoples' claims can be challenged when their hunting, trapping, sealing, and whal-

131

ing activities are no longer at a purely subsistence level. These rights are not inviolable when any of the animal products obtained are sold, traded, or otherwise distributed outside of their communities in exchange for nontraditional and nonsubsistence material goods, such as televisions, snowmobiles, and so on. In other words, native peoples who are culturally contaminated by the consumer values of "civilized" society and who are encouraged to contribute to various industries—as by trapping animals for the fur trade and killing walruses to make ivory carvings for the tourist trade—can have no special claims to continue killing wildlife on the grounds of custom and native rights.

Pollution, overfishing, mining, logging, agricultural expansion, and so on, are endangering both native peoples and wildlife alike.

RAISING WILDLIFE IN CAPTIVITY

To ecologist-conservationists, encouraging the propagation of wild species of economic value in the wild and in captivity may appear sound and sensible. But to animal rightists, no matter how ecologically sound such practices may be, it is fundamentally wrong to exploit animals, even if this means there will be less depredation on existing wild populations. And, in general, encouraging the abundance of select species in the wild, such as deer, and introducing nonnative species, such as nutria, for "recreational" and other commercial purposes means displacing other species.

All animal rightists and deep ecologists* should oppose the industrialized, nonsubsistence exploitation of wildlife because it is a violation of animals' rights (they are not ours to exploit in the first place) and is fundamentally unsound ecologically, because by favoring some species over others, population imbalances and extinction of undesired species would be inevitable.

_____

*Deep ecologists support the philosophy of preserving the natural abundance and diversity of plants and animals in natural ecosystems.

If the alternative to raising wildlife humanely in captivity for commercial purposes is transgressing their rights, then can it ever be justified? How valid is the argument that raising wild animals in captivity is an act of conservation because it would help reduce pressures of exploitation on wild populations and also provide captive-bred stock for release and repopulation? It is invalid and ethically untenable, I believe, to put any wild animal in captivity if such treatment does not benefit the species and its environment in the long term. If the primary short- and long-term benefits are for humans, then such treatment violates animals' rights.

Encouraging native peoples to raise suitable wildlife humanely for commercial purposes (the former headhunters of New Guinea are now raising exotic butterflies for export to collectors) may be justified if it helps protect species in the wild (they will not be hunted) and gives local communities "cottage industries" that are sustainable and not environmentally destructive.

Some people today with a wildlife management orientation who do not question the ethics of exploiting animals on a sustainable basis have a worldview that is the antithesis of those who oppose the killing of any wildlife. This preservationist view, which is endorsed by many animal rightists, stands in opposition to the conservationist's recognition of the need to monitor wildlife populations and, at times, violate the rights of individual animals by killing or relocating them in order to maintain the integrity of their habitat-sanctuary, not for the benefit of humans but for the benefit of all species and individual animals therein. This is very different from the management mentality where species and ecosystems are manipulated and exploited primarily for human gain. Sometimes the line between such human-centered management practices and conservation for the sake of the animals is unclear. Hence, animal rightists may misjudge conservationists dedicated to protecting wildlife as being on the side of wildlife management, placing human interests before those of the animals. Likewise, animal rightists may be misjudged as being unrealistic, anthropocentric, and ignorant, especially when they fear, for example, that to condone the killing of wild animals could lead to a kind of "ecological fascism," where conservationists play God, violate the rights of animals, and do not let nature take care of things. But while nature knows best, many wildlife habitats and sanctuaries are no longer natural because of human interference, ranging from adjacent farming, forestry, dam construction, acid rain, and so on. Thus responsible stewardship encompasses monitoring ecosystems and all species therein.

Humane ethics—animal welfare—and animal rights are not incompatible with ecologically sound wildlife stewardship. They are an integral part of such stewardship, which includes treating wildlife necessary for research purposes humanely, and finding humane ways to control the populations of species that are out of balance with the ecosystem. That mistakes may be made in stewardship-management policies is inevitable. It is, for instance, difficult to know if the sudden abundance of one or more species and the dwindling of others is part of the natural process of succession and should be allowed to continue, or if these changes are abnormal and should be corrected. Perhaps the best that can be done with our present knowledge and expertise is to "freeze" many wildlife sanctuaries by endeavoring to maintain optimal species diversity and numbers. Clearly, in any of our actions, we should take the conservative, cautious approach so that if we err we can make corrections before irreparable harm is done. Wildlife ecologist-conservationists and deep ecologists who are insensitive to legitimate animal rights and welfare concerns need to be confronted. So must those animal liberationists who take animal rights philosophy too far and lose sight of the ecological principles of sound stewardship and of the the rights and interests and subsistence needs of indigenous peoples.

Some animal rightists contend that farm animals have a right not to be eaten. This does smack of anthropomorphism and alienates deep ecologists and conservationists who see predation as natural and farm animals as prey species. Unless deep ecologists see humanitarian animal rightists' concerns as trivial sentimentality and of lesser priority than more global ecological concerns, this difference should cause a problem. The abusive treatment of animals is no different from abusive treatment of nature: Both are symptoms of a lack of reverence for the sanctity and dignity of the life of the individual and of life as a whole.

Hence I see animal rights philosophy and "ecosophy," the philosophy of deep ecology, as two sides of the same coin of a new currency: a new dialectic where the dualities of individualism and holism—specifically concern for the rights of the individual and for the integrity of the biospheric whole—are reconciled.

In their book entitled *Deep Ecology: Living as If Nature Mattered*, authors Bill Devall and George Sessions uncritically cite deep ecologist John Rodman who concludes that the animal rights movement "while holding out promise of transcending the homocentric perspective of modern culture, subtly fulfills and legitimizes the basic project of modernity—the total conquest of nature by man." Then they take to task animal rights philosopher Tom Regan, who with others of like mind has "expressed concern that a holistic ecological ethic . . . results in a kind of totalitarianism or ecological fascism."

It disturbs me that this otherwise excellent book has taken such a negative attitude toward animal rights philosophy. In an appendix, however, George Sessions does suggest that philosophers need to work toward nontotalitarian solutions to environmental problems and that "in all likelihood, this will require some kind of holistic ecological ethic in which the integrity of all individuals (human and non-human) is respected." I interpret "integrity" as rights and sanctity.

Ironically, while the authors are so critical of the animal rights movement, they quote Arne Naess (who coined the terms ecosophy and deep ecology and is arguably the founder of the deep ecology movement), who expresses many of the views of the animal rights movement. For instance, Naess[2] states, "The intuition of biocentric equality is that all things in the biosphere have an equal right to live and blossom and to reach their own forms of unfolding and self-realization. . . ." He also observes that "with maturity, human beings will experience joy when other life forms experience joy and sorrow when other life forms experience sorrow. Not only will we feel sad when our brother or a dog or a cat feels sad, but we will grieve when living beings, including landscapes, are destroyed. . . . Only a very narrow range of feelings have interested most human beings until now."

The depth of feeling and empathetic awareness for other living things that Naess sees us acquiring "with maturity" is expressed in these words of Australian aborigine Bill Neidjie[3]: "Feeling all these trees, all this country: When this wind blow you can feel it. Same for country . . . you feel it. You can look, but feeling . . . that make you.

If you feel sore . . . headache, sore body; that mean somebody killing tree or grass. You feel because your body [is] in that tree or earth. Nobody can tell you, you got to feel it yourself."

This "primitive" aboriginal's "maturity," relatively speaking, suggests a regressive or retarded condition of ego development in contemporary industrial society.

Lack of feeling—empathy and compassion—for animals and other living things on the one hand and for the integrity of biospheric ecosystems (nature) on the other are two sides of the same coin. Their currency is the root and source of the holocaust of the animal kingdom and of the "progressively" destructive transformation of nature into an industralized wasteland.

As Chief Seattle said over a century ago, "This we know —the earth does not belong to man, man belongs to the earth. All things are connected like the blood which unites one family. Whatever befalls the earth befalls the sons of the earth. Man did not weave the web of life; he is merely a strand in it. Whatever he does to the web, he does to himself."

More recently, the Six Nations of American Indians in a proclamation made in Geneva entitled *A Basic Call to Consciousness*, stated, "The people who are living on this planet need to break with the narrow concept of human liberation, and begin to see liberation as something which needs to be extended to the whole of the Natural World. What is needed is the liberation of all the things that support life—the air, the water, the trees —all the things which support the sacred web of life." Linked with nature liberation philosophy is an emerging *creation-centered spirituality*[4] that emphasizes man's creative participation and role as a responsible planetary steward.

A decade ago Charles Birch observed in an address in Nairobi before the World Council of Churches that

> . . . It is a cockeyed view that regards ecological liberation as a distraction from the task of liberation of the poor. One cannot be done without the other. It is time to recognize that the liberation movement is finally one movement . . . all creatures are fellow creatures and human responsibility extends infinitely to the whole of creation . . . if we are to continue to inhabit the earth, there has to be a revolution in the relationship of human beings to the earth and . . . to each other.

The accelerating rate of extinction of unique plant and animal species of diverse ecosystems and of human societies that have lived for generations in a relatively stable if not creative harmony with nature, attests to the fact that the fate of the Earth, of the animal kingdom, and of humankind are inseparably interconnected.

The principles and goals of the animal liberation, conservation, and deep ecology movements are fundamentally complementary. From different perspectives—concern for individuals, species, and whole ecosystems—they converge upon the political and socioeconomic realities of the times but are as yet not consonant with the dominant worldview of industralized technocracies. Differences aside, the supreme task of these movements is to transform the prevailing worldviews of all nation-states to one of enlightened planetary stewardship and respect for all living things.

CHAPTER 10

The Greenhouse Effect and the

Animal Kingdom

We are committing matricide, killing the Earth, Mother of us all.

Scientists are reaching unanimity over the potentially devasting social, economic, and health consequences of the intensifying global greenhouse effect caused by an increase in carbon dioxide, methane, nitrous oxide, and chlorofluorocarbons in the atmosphere. A variety of factors, ranging from the burning of fossil fuels to the destruction of forests that naturally help remove excess carbon dioxide from the atmosphere, is contributing to global warming. Serious droughts, crop losses, and severe storms and floods are predicted consequences of this process. And as the ozone layer is destroyed by various chemicals, particularly chlorofluorocarbons, this natural filter of ultraviolet rays will no longer protect us from harmful solar radiation. Ultraviolet rays weaken the immune system, increasing the body's susceptibility to disease and the susceptibility of animal and human populations to disease epidemics.

The greenhouse phenomenon, caused by the accumulation of excessive and unbalanced quantities of gases, especially carbon dioxide, that trap solar heat is predicted to double by the middle of the next century. According to current reports, the 20 percent reduction in carbon dioxide (CO_2) emissions by the year 2000 proposed by several European governments and some U.S. legislators will not prevent continued warming.[1] Most climate models agree that global average temperatures will increase by as much as 8 to 10 degrees Fahrenheit.

In testimony before the Senate Committee on Agriculture, Nutrition and Forestry on December 1, 1988, Dr. John Firor of the National Center for Atmospheric Research in Boulder, Colorado, emphasized that the climate is warming and that major problems for agriculture and unmanaged forests will result. Emissions of heat-trapping gases, especially carbon dioxide, should be reduced quickly.

Firor also stated that "One effect that will be truly global will be the rise in sea level . . . averaging two inches or more per decade."

In his review of major contributing factors to the greenhouse problem, Firor said that the second most important gas causing a problem is methane, most of which comes from dumps, rice paddies, and—while it may sound humorous—cattle and termite intestines.

From a clinical perspective, the planet's metabolism has been accelerated to a potentially irreversible state by various human activities, especially the burning of fossil fuels. (Nuclear power is neither a cost-effective nor environmentally acceptable alternative.) Such activities must be curtailed. The natural, self-regulatory processes of the biosphere that maintain the health and stability of the atmosphere and the entire planetary ecosystem are becoming dysfunctional. The planet can no longer adjust to our harmful influences or continue to sustain those demands and activities that are destroying its life-support systems.

The greenhouse effect and destruction of the ozone layer are not isolated problems. Others include the pollution of water, oceans, air, and the food chain with agricultural chemicals and industrial wastes; the destruction of forests and lakes and acidification of soil by acid rain; the spread of deserts; and the extinction of both wildlife and natural habitats especially by the livestock industry and other ecologically unsound farming practices. Together these problems are responsible for the deterioration of the quality of all life on Earth.

For the animal kingdom, the global greenhouse effect spells suffering, death, and extinction as a consequence of climatic changes and extreme aberrations that destroy vegetation and food sources. Unable to reach greener pastures and cool, clear waters, animals will roast inside their fur coats, broil in their burrows, and suffocate in lakes and oceans. Only a few species will be able to migrate to less inhospitable habitats, and the competition for such places would be intense and probably result in rapid habitat degradation. The majority of aquatic and terrestrial species will face the chaotic and desperate conditions of a dysfunctional planet, as will billions of people. Competiton will be intensified by the mass migration of people dislocated by floods, droughts, crop failures, and widespread famine and disease to more hospitable latitudes. People and animals will thus be thrown into more direct competition than ever before. The anticipated doubling of the human population within the next forty years will compound the problem.

Even a slight increase in ambient temperature can trigger changes in animals' physiology and behavior that, if not linked with natural seasonal cycles (which would be disrupted by the greenhouse effect) could have devasting consequences. These include aberrations in development and insect metamorphosis; in reproduction and breeding cycles; and in such activities as hibernation and migration. Some species might flourish and become overabundant while others will decline or become extinct. Population instabilities would disrupt the interdependent food web, causing further extreme oscillations in the number and diversity of species. Opportunist species may take over some habitats, becoming serious "pests," displacing others and causing further ecological perturbations.

These problems will be compounded by increasing ultraviolet radiation, which will affect the growth of plants and aquatic microorganisms, especially phytoplankton, the basis of the food chain for all ocean life. Such radiation will also increase animals, as well as humans' susceptibility to disease, because high levels impair the immune system and are thought to increase the incidence of some infectious diseases. Climatic changes will also favor the spread of a host of tropical and other diseases to regions where indigenous life forms have no natural immunity.

Changing rainfall patterns causing floods and droughts and destruction of vegetation will cause additional animal suffering. Many ecosystems, already highly toxic with agrichemical and industrial pollutants, will quickly cease to function. Those animals high in the food chain would, predictably, be the first to become extinct, because the life-forms they consume will be contaminated, these toxins becoming even more concentrated in creatures higher up the food chain.

Some ecologists believe that the predicted rise in sea level could prove to be the most serious impact of the greenhouse effect on wildlife in the United States. The worst-case scenario must include the additional impact of acid rain, agrichemical, industrial pollutants, human sewage, and farm animal wastes. As the natural detoxifying and life-sustaining processes within the soil and aquatic ecosystems become increasingly dysfunctional due to the greenhouse effect and intensified ultraviolet radiation, pollutants will become more of a problem.

Nitrate fertilizers and acid rain also contribute to the greenhouse crisis by interfering with the ability of soil microbes to remove methane from the atmosphere.[2]

While there is more CO_2 than methane in the atmosphere because of automobiles and other fossil fuel sources of CO_2, methane is of concern because it traps heat some twenty times more than CO_2.

Agriculture's significant contribution to the greenhouse crisis is being hotly debated and discounted by many. However, the Environmental Protection Agency[3] reports that livestock and animal waste account for 18 percent of methane's sources. Clearly, a reduction in methane-producing livestock and better animal waste management would be prudent. (Note: as global warming increases, more hectares of frozen tundra will thaw to release more methane into the atmosphere, thus quickening the global warming process.) In *The New York Times* review of this EPA study, Dr. Ralph Cicerone, head of geosciences at the University of California at Irvine, is quoted as saying, "When you look at the cattle source, it's got to be 80 or 100 million tons a year. Then you know cattle are a big part of the answer."

And, I would add, so are pigs, whose wastes are now a major cause of excessive soil, groundwater and coastal nitrification, which, as shown earlier, fuel the greenhouse effect.

Research in the United Kingdom and Holland[4] has linked the dairy and beef cattle industries with acid rain. The liquid slurry excrement of cattle (as distinct from composted manure), stored in lagoons and later sprayed on fields, releases ammonia into the atmosphere. This interacts with sulfur dioxide (an industrial pollutant, especially from power plants burning fossil fuels), increasing the rate of oxidation of sulfur dioxide and the formation of ammonium sulfate on plant foliage, which results in the death of trees and acidification of soils and surface waters.

Acid rain contributes to the greenhouse phenomenon by killing trees among other things, which normally remove carbon dioxide. (Trees also gradually return CO_2 back into the earth as carbon, carbon soil deficiency being, as yet, a little researched issue.)

We cannot reverse the greenhouse phenomenon. At best, we may stablize the planet at a slightly higher temperature, perhaps not unlike the climate and atmospheric conditions prior to the extinction of the dinosaurs.

Some feel that this living planet will be destroyed anyway when the sun burns out. But that will be billions of years from now. What a waste of wonder and potential, beauty and splendor for us to destroy the natural world now and put our faith in technology to develop artificial life-support systems, when we are still in our infancy according to sun-time. The dreams of the nuclear power and agribiotechonology industries are of a utopian wonderworld, while the emerging reality is the antithesis: a poisoned "wasteworld," as Father Thomas Berry foresees in his seminal text, *The Dream of the Earth*.[5] According to conventional aboriginal wisdom, animals and nature are part of the Dream that is dreaming us: When we harm and destroy them, we harm and destroy the Dream and thus, inevitably, ourselves also.

The greenhouse effect caused by industries and our life-styles is an ominous foreboding of worse things to come if we do not heed and green the Earth and heal ourselves by resanctifying the Earth Mother of us all. Otherwise, the fate of the dinosaurs may well be ours also.

In many ways, the large multinational corporate oligopolies are analogous to the dinosaurs of old. Corporate anarchy by the petrochemical and related argichemical and pharmaceutical industries (and related consumer dependency) is now intensifying the greenhouse effect. Most of their products—from jet planes and fast cars and drugs to make ever more corn and beef, along with the energy-consumptive entertainments of the consumer society: from high-speed motorboat and stock-car races to late-night football and baseball games—exacerbate the greenhouse effect. They also contribute to ozone pollution, acid rain that kills lakes and forests, and so on, and have made our water unfit to drink, poisoned the air, and exhausted (demineralized and "de-humusified") the soils.

It is ironic, and a point of concern, that as we strive to improve the human condition, as by raising more cattle so more people can eat meat regularly and maintain it as a dietary staple, the condition of the planet deteriorates. And as a consequence, the human condition deteriorates further. We cannot profit at nature's expense. Nature's economy dictates a sustainable human economy. Any human economy that destroys nature's economy by disrupting the ecology, accelerating the rate of entropy, and reducing biodiversity ultimately harms itself and the climate. The greenhouse phenomenon is evidence of the global ramifications of such imprudence. And the dire economic conditions of half the world's human population attests to this. Conditions will only worsen if ecologically disruptive and environmentally harmful economic solutions are initiated.

In sum, while the greenhouse effect is a product of industrialism, attempts to alleviate this problem should not be perceived as being antiindustry. An enlightened industrialism surely will realize the limitless profits of environmentally appropriate and socially just biotechnologies and other industries.

CHAPTER 11

The Zoo: A Cruel and Outmoded Institution?

Zoos have been with us for a long time. The Romans brought many varieties of wild animals back from military expeditions and kept them on display until they were slaughtered in public arenas as entertainment. Thousands of African mammals were killed until a Christian, Telemachus, threw himself into the arena as a protest against such inhumanity, an act that purportedly put an end to these atrocious public spectacles. Since the Middle Ages, public zoos have been popular urban entertainment centers. In the wealthy metropolitan centers of industrial Europe, zoo menageries with specimens collected from all over the world became symbolic of colonial imperialism and national pride.

Gilles Ailland in an essay entitled "Why Look at Animals" states that public zoos came into existence just as animals began disappearing from daily life.[1] "The zoo to which people go to meet animals, to observe them, is, in fact, a monument to the impossibility of such encounters. Modern zoos are an epitaph to a relationship which was as old as man."

Private zoos and menageries of emperors and kings were displays of power, wealth, and prestige. The public zoos of the nineteenth century endorsed modern colonial imperialism. "Explorers proved their patriotism by sending home a tiger or an elephant. The gift of an exotic animal to the metropolitan zoo became a token in subservient diplomatic relations."

To claim a civic function independent of imperialism, zoos emphasized the science of zoology to educate the public and advance knowledge. With the high-tech innovations of operant training devices, behavioral monitoring, ova transplantation, and genetic engineering, the contemporary zoo is fast becoming an endorsement of capitalist industrial technocracy.

Today's zoos and wildlife safari parks are radically different from the early iron and concrete zoos. It takes money to run a modern zoo, and zoo directors realize that they must compete with a wide variety of leisure-time activities. Concession stands, miniature railroads, and other carnival amusements, as well as dubious circuslike shows with performing chimps or big cats, lure many visitors to some of our large zoos and wildlife parks. What tricks and obedience the animals display are more a reflection of the power of human control than of the animals' natural behavior. Performing apes, elephants, bears, big cats, dolphins, and "killer" whales especially draw the crowds. Man's mastery over the powerful beast and willful control over its wild instincts is a parody of the repression and sublimation of human nature and personal freedom.

As we demean animals in making them perform unnatural acts, so we demean ourselves. The training, which is often brutal, and the socialization to the trainer, which is unnatural, in the course of subordinating performing animals to the will of the trainer is like a ritual enactment of humanity's control over the forces of nature. Public spectacles of performing animals thus serve to perpetuate the righteousness of humankind's domination over animals and nature as well as the myth of human superiority.

Even if the trainer or animal handler loves the animals, as soon as they begin to perform, what is manifested is not love but domination. Domination—the need to have power and control over other beings—comes not from love but from fear. Most fundamentally, performing animals, therefore, are an expression not of human love and understanding but of fear, ignorance, and the desire for power and control.

The more people begin to empathize with animals that are forced to perform, the less they will be entertained, and the more they will be repulsed by the dark side of human nature that enjoys making and seeing animals perform upon command.

Some zoo visitors show little respect for the animals they have come to see. They flaunt the rules by feeding the animals, and in some cases they inflict deliberate injury. In contrast with such "zoopaths," some zoophilic visitors, in misguided efforts to establish a closer rapport with the animals, have been injured or killed by reaching into a cage to feed or pet an animal.

THE CAPTIVE PANTHER

Some experiences can be so painfully intense that they are soon forgotten. Amnesia protects the psyche. Then again, in anticipation of vicarious suffering, we may simply tune out certain experiences altogether. Other times, perhaps for good reason, the psyche is not so protected. It is as if the soul—the observing, feeling self—is actually burned by certain experiences. The imprint is branded so indelibly that we can go back and review every detail so completely that the experience is actually relived. I had just such an experience with a panther in a zoo many years ago.

The first time that I ever really _saw_ an animal in a cage was in a small zoo at the Jardin des Plantes, a natural history museum in Paris. I entered a large, ornate Victorian rotunda that housed a few animals in small wrought-iron cages. I now recall seeing only one animal there. At first it appeared not to see me even though I stood beside its cage for a long time.

Time did end that day as a part of me separated and was incorporated as part of the creature in the cage.

In retrospect, I was probably mesmerized by what at first appeared to be a shiny black serpent in constant motion. Its liquid form brushed across the front of the cage. After insinuating itself around some artificial rocks and a body-polished tree stump toward the back of the enclosure, it ricocheted off a ceramic-tiled wall to again caress the front of the cage. Form and motion were so unified and the pattern of movement within the confines of the cage so repetitive that at first encounter the creature was barely recognizable as a panther, or black leopard. Her movements were executed with such precision—even to the point of always touching the tree trunk with her left hip and the same ceramic tile with her right front paw—that she was more like a perpetual motion machine than a sentient being.

And then I saw the blood—a streak of blood down her left thigh, draining from an open sore that would never heal until the cat was freed from the hypnotic lines she traced and was so inexorably bound to execute. Each scraping turn around the tree trunk kept the sore open, like a broken heart bleeding for the loss of all that was wild and free.

I wondered if she felt any pain. Her yellow-green eyes were like cold glass, with neither fire nor luster. Perhaps this was a slow ritual form of suicide, gradually grinding and rubbing and shredding the body to pieces to free the wild spirit within. I saw the glint of white bone—or was it tendon—through the cat's thigh muscles winking as she turned and paced before me. And there was no pad left on the right front paw that struck the tile wall polished ocher with the patina of dried blood and serum. Yet still the crippled creature continued her measured minuet.

The panther body, denied freedom of expression and fulfillment of purpose, had become a prison for the creature spirit within. Following and anticipating every movement she made, I began to breathe in rhythm with the cat. I felt part of myself entering her cage while the rotunda started to revolve faster and faster around that part of my consciousness that remained in my body outside of the cage. Then when I entered the prison of her body the other visitors strolling around the rotunda became ephemeral shadow-beings, as if they were part of a dream and the only thing that was real was the measured universe of the tortured panther.

Confined in such limited space, how else could this bound-less spirit of the jungle respond? Her rhythmic, trancelike ac-tions were more than thwarted attempts to escape. Was her compulsive animation designed simply to help her cope with the emptiness of existing in body without any purpose for the spirit, a kind of living death?

When I looked out from her body I saw that the pellucid people, cage walls, and bars were suffused by a warm pure white light that was without apparent beginning or end. The panther was abiding in this numinous dimension, held by the merest thread to the body that paced and turned and paced and turned in the finite dimension of its cage.

A sudden, intense wave of nausea brought me back to where I was leaning against an ornamental palm tree beside her cage. I slowly looked around at the people in the rotunda. They were no longer dreamlike but palpably real. I felt a deep sense of bars that would not be there if we could empathize fully with captive creatures and see the bars through their eyes. Then we might rage against the dying of the light and not rationalize in the name of conservation, research, and public education that the keeping of animals in zoos is for their own good and is therefore ethically acceptable.

Loren Eisley wrote, "One does not meet oneself until one catches the reflection from an eye other than human." If this be true, then it perhaps explains why the people at the zoo seemed so unaware of the panther and the plight of the animal in their midst was neither seen nor felt. They did not see them-selves through the panther's eyes, the windows of its soul. I would rather think that they did not dare than not even care.

The cage may be the last refuge for many endangered spe-cies, but such "protective custody" is a sad reflection indeed of how far we have desecrated nature's creation. Zoos have been as slow to address the psychological needs of the animals they keep as they have to question their own purpose. But times are changing; more and more people have begun to feel and see the world through the eyes of the animals. The cage bars are dis-appearing as we begin to empathize and come to realize that the fate of the animal kingdom is inextricably linked with the fate of humanity. The black panther in the cage is a mirror reflecting our own condition. And we are not helpless to do something about both.

But when we reach into the cage with our hearts, we may feel very differently about keeping animals in zoos or ever visiting a zoo again.

While I do not believe my experience was unique, it would be interesting to make a study of zoo visitors and their responses to the animals. My own observations have led me to the conclusion that people unconsciously tend to reflect upon themselves when they visit a zoo. Anthropomorphism is a natural product of human thinking and perceiving in relation to animals. Although on the surface it may be based on misconceptions, it is more deeply rooted in the psyche of our being as a vague awareness that humans and animals are one. Only our heightened ego has created the illusion of human and nonhuman animals as being separate entities. Yet a deep-seated collective unconscious recognizes our essential kinship with all of creation. But because zoos separate the observer from the observed, they preserve and enhance the false duality between the human and the nonhuman. The human is the visitor, the voyeur, and no longer a participant. And the animal is a displaced refugee existing in a kind of alien and unnatural limbo.

Can we justify the existence of any but the best of modern zoos? What do these zoos do to warrant any justification?

The best zoos claim to be advanced in conservation, in research into wildlife diseases, surgery, and reproduction. And in educating the public. But could they not educate the public just as well, if not even better, with documentary films? A polar bear or a fish in a zoo or aquarium does not show people—and cannot—the chemical and radiation pollution in its body. No zoo exhibits fish from the Great Lakes exploding and eroding from cancer. Yet these fish are plentiful.

Do zoos educate the public adquately to political action and compassionate concern for the plight of wildlife and nature? Are they not too tame, sanitized, and beautified? They are becoming facsimiles of how animals once were in the wild. Some zoo safari parks are run for profit and secondarily for entertainment. And zoos are also an illusion, a false assurance to the public that lions and cheetahs and tigers and elephants are plentiful and lead free and easy lives. Some amusement parks even have safari zoos purely for public entertainment. This is surely an unethical exploitation of wildlife.

Even the best of zoos cannot justify their existence if they do not sufficiently inform and even shock the public into compassionate concern and political action. I know of no zoo that exhibits crippled but otherwise healthy animals that have been maimed by trappers and hunters.

Regarding the claim that the best zoos are helping save species from extinction by breeding them in captivity, it may be best to let them become extinct if there is no place for them in the wild. Life in captivity can never fulfill any species or individual, because the animal *is* its natural environment, and no species lives in isolation from others. Certainly the better zoos have seminatural environments—miniswamps, artificial rivers, climatrons, and mixed-species exhibits. But to what end? For exhibition. They are not conserving nature by creating high-tech facsimiles thereof. And even if such artificial environments enhance the overall welfare and reproductivity of endangered species, where are their offspring to go? To other zoo collections.

In fact, a disturbing by-product of breeding exotic wildlife in captivity has been the advent of the game ranch. For a fee, hunters can bag a trophy animal from Africa and South America without having to leave the United States. Such lucrative ranches are numerous in Texas, and *zoos* actually provide the stock for the trophy hunters' pleasure.

Ethologists have studied the behavior of many captive species and have documented a wide variety of behavioral abnormalities, including neurotically repetitive compulsions known as stereotypes. These take the form of rhythmic pacing, head-twisting, circling, weaving, mouthing, vomiting, licking, and grooming (which often lead to self-mutilation). More recent research has shown that such actions result in the production of natural opiates in the brain (endorphins and enkephalins) as a way of coping with a stressful environment. These abnormal behaviors, which are especially common in captive carnivores and primates, are not a sign of adaptation but of frustration and distress.

Another disabling syndrome called learned helplessness also afflicts captive animals that have no control over (and especially escape from) their immediate environment. This syndrome is linked with lethargy, depression, and increased susceptibility to disease because the immune system is impaired.

Inbreeding is another problem that results in lower viability and genetic disorders. Zoo biologists are beginning to rectify some of these problems, but no matter how well the animals' environments and gene pools are enriched to enhance their survival and adaptability, such endeavors do not atone for our collective inability to preserve viable populations and whole ecosystems in the wild. While these problems have stimulated much dedicated research by biologists and veterinarians, I consider such work to be if not misguided, at least unwise, for it transfers resources and talent from making real inroads in conserving animals in the wild. We should work to develop appropriate agricultural and industrial technologies and human population control. Radical changes should be made in the dietary and overall consumer habits of the more affluent nations, whose populace contributes to the worldwide destruction of habitat and extinction of terrestrial and aquatic fauna.

Zoos must be closely linked with conservation efforts not only of captive species but of their wild habitats. High-tech facsimiles that do not enhance animals' welfare and reproductivity are a waste of good resources. For example, the high-tech Baltimore Aquarium should be abolished as it makes no attempt to engender public outrage at what is happening to the oceans and all that live therein. Even the dolphins which were used purely as a public attraction, have expired from stress-related diseases.

I believe that even the best zoos and aquaria in the world are not doing an adequate job of nature conservation. They have taken more species from the wild than they have ever put back, and until this situation is dramatically reversed, zoos cannot make any claim to effective nature conservation. Breeding endangered species in captivity is animal preservation, not conservation, and animals preserved forever in a cage or synthetic habitat are at best unreal.

As for zoos' often high-blown research into exotic animal diseases, nutrition, and reproduction, all of this would be unnecessary if we had just left wildlife alone and respected their rights and protected their habitats.

Until recently, zoos played a significant role in the decline of wild species, since most of their collections of animals were wild-caught and not captive-bred. It may be reasoned that animals in the better zoos fare better than in the wild, have all their needs catered for, don't have to hunt or be preyed upon, live longer, receive veterinary care, and do not miss being in the wild. Such reasoning is flawed because "the wild" and the animal are not separate and discrete entities.

Animals are an integral part of the interrelated web of life. To put animals on exhibit as "specimens" and "social groups," torn from the very fabric of their ecosystems wherein they evolved and have existed as an inseparable part of the seamless web of creation, violates the biological and spiritual unity of all life. It is a reflection of our own dualistic worldview where we see ourselves as individuals and not as an interdependent part of the unified field of life. We are, but we think and act otherwise, to the detriment of the rest of creation and of the creative process itself.

We must now monitor wildlife species and populations and acquire the knowledge to define optimal environments and population densities, and help control diseases and understand the effects of industrial pollution, agriculture, fishing, and other human interferences. Right or wrong and for better or for worse, we have put ourselves in this managerial role. Zoos thus have an important part to play in the basic and applied research of wildlife husbandry and conservation.

Are zoos a necessary evil? Wildlife's last refuge? Sometimes I think so. Sometimes I think not. I respect the many people who are dedicated to good zoo management, research, species preservation, and veterinary medicine. But all this dedication may be seriously misplaced if we lose sight of the fact that the problems of zoo animals and the crisis of wildlife's threatened annihilation are primarily man-made.

Building better zoos at the expense of efforts to conserve nature is wrong. We should need no zoos and we are misguided if we do not work toward this end, however far into the future it might be. Zoos are not so much a necessary evil as they are a tragic mirror of an evil for which we may yet atone.

As it is estimated that at the current rate of habitat destruction, some 500,000 to 2 million plant and animal (including insect) species will be extinct by the year 2000, obviously captive breeding in zoos is not the answer. Habitat protection is the only solution, and all nations and peoples must be prepared to make the necessary adjustments and sacrifices if the health and vitality of the Earth is to be preserved.

One of the best exhibits in any zoo that I have ever visited was a large mirror behind bars. The caption read: _Homo sapiens_, a dangerous, predatorial tool and weapon-making primate. Status: endangered by its own doing.

There can be no communion with our animal kin when they are held captive, no matter what the justifications may be for their "protective custody." The zoo is a trick mirror that can delude us into believing that we love and respect animals and are helping to preserve them. And like the animal circus, the zoo can have a pernicious influence on children's attitutes toward wild creatures. We cannot recognize or celebrate the sanctity and dignity of nonhuman life under such conditions. There can be no communion: only amusement, curiosity, amazement, and perhaps sympathy. The deprivation of these creatures and the loss of wildness and wilderness are ours also. When we fail collectively to feel these things, and in the process come to accept and patronize the zoo as some cultural norm, we lose something of our own humanity—that intuitive wisdom and a sense of reverence for all life that are the hallmarks of a truly civilized society.

CHAPTER 12

Our Inhumane Pet Society

Many people overlook the multibillion-dollar-a-year pet industry, which is another aspect of the holocaust of the animal kingdom. After all, pets surely must enjoy pampered lives. Yet even for the most pampered of pets, purebred "pedigree" dogs and cats, all is not well.

"DESIGNER" ANIMALS: BUILT-IN CRUELTY

While some animal liberationists contend that animals should not be kept as "pets"—as emotional slaves and status symbols—a more reasonable view is to accept that there can be reciprocal benefits to people and their animal companions when there is love, understanding, and responsible care. Aside from the widespread problem of irresponsible ownership (which many humane societies are rectifying through local animal control law enforcement and humane education programs in schools and in published materials for pet owners), purebred cats and dogs have fundamental genetic defects. These defects can result in lifelong suffering, sickness, and physical handicaps—what I have termed domestogenic diseases, or diseases inflicted upon animals by humans.

Certain handicaps may be *deliberately created* by selective breeding and become breed "standards" in purebred cats and dogs. The pushed-in (brachycephalic) face of the bulldog and Persian cat are dramatic examples. This deformity makes it extremely difficult for the animals to breathe normally. Their protruding eyes and facial skin folds easily become infected. The bulldog's disproportionately large soft palate sets up a negative pressure so that the animal's windpipe may actually constrict, or sometimes even collapse, and the dog is either partially and chronically or suddenly completely asphyxiated. Because of the standard for large heads and narrow hips in these two breeds, many cannot give birth normally—caesarian sections become routine. Breeders like to play God, but what they create can be a demeaning reflection of human insensibility and demigod egotism.

An extreme example of deliberate genetic manipulation is the creation and propagation of the pathetic hairless disease-prone mutant "sphynx" cat. Other genetic defects are inadvertently introduced by _selective breeding_ for certain traits. Sloping hindquarters of the German shepherd and other breeds are linked with hip dysplasia, a crippling disease. Extremely pendulous ears in cocker spaniels are linked with distressing and lifelong ear infections.

Inbreeding also contributes to an increased incidence of heritable disorders in purebred pets. Because of their narrow genetic base—many originate from a handful of often closely related parent stock—breeding sisters and brothers or half sisters and half brothers results in more and more genetic defects.

This inbreeding problem is further compounded by what I call _overbreeding_ where certain breeds, once they become popular, are mass-produced for the wholesale-retail pet market without any "quality control." Quality control entails progeny evaluation (seeing how the pups or kittens turn out) so that breeders can be sure that they are not breeding from stock that are transmitting heritable disorders on to their offspring. "Puppy mill" factory operators cannot perform because the breeders never contact the puppies' buyers. Little wonder then that owners of puppy millbred animals are at a loss when their six-month old Samoyed turns out to be crippled with hip dysplasia, or their beloved cocker spaniel is blind by one year of age.

Consider the following abbreviated list of genetic defects in purebred dogs. Over *two hundred* inherited disorders have been identified in purebred dogs.

PREVALENCE OF SOME COMMON GENETIC DEFECTS IN PUREBRED DOGS

Defect	Number of breeds affected
Cardiovascular disorders	26
Cataracts	16
Cleft palate	19
Deafness	14
Ectropion (turning outward of lower eyelid)	10
Entropion (turning inward of eyelashes)	24
Epilepsy	17
Female reproductive dysfunctions	15
Glaucoma	9
Hemophilia	25
Hip dysplasia	35
Progressive retinal atrophy	28

Because these animals are purebred, "pedigree" registration papers can be obtained from the American Kennel Club (AKC). This gives prospective owners of puppy mill dogs and of pups from ignorant and unethical hobby breeders a false sense of security. In truth, the registration papers are no guarantee of an animal's physical or psychological soundness and stability. While profiting greatly from its registration business, the AKC has done nothing to prevent the registration of genetically defective animals. Concerned owners and breeders of purebred dogs are trying to save their breeds from genetic disintegration by setting up standards of soundness and their own registries. The real problem lies with the commercial puppy mill industry, which continues to mass-produce highly inbred pups.

Some of the genetic problems in purebred dogs include dwarfism, giantism, epilepsy, deafness, cataracts, glaucoma, progressive blindness, "slipped" disks, patellar (knee-cap) dislocation, progressive muscular weakness, progressive renal disease, increased incidence of various forms of cancer and brain tumors, dental problems (especially in brachycephalic breeds), arthritis and lameness (especially in dwarfed breeds with shortened legs like the bassett hound), hemophilia, hip dysplasia, hysteria, extreme fearfulness, hyperactivity, auto immune diseases, and reduced resistance to infection and disease.

Some of these genetic disorders are used as research "models" and are deliberately propagated to find ways to treat similar problems in humans, such as hemophilia.

Some purebreds also must undergo ear and tail cropping, an unnecessary and painful operation as part of the breed standard, which should be eliminated.

Cats have only recently been subjected to the kind of intensive inbreeding and selective breeding that has been going on for generations in dogs. Hence they have fewer genetic problems, but these are likely to increase as purebred cats gain in popularity. Aside from the squint and related abnormal visual pathways in Siamese cats, other defects in purebred cats with a probable genetic base include progressive blindness (retinal degeneration), skeletal abnormalities linked with folded ears, spina bifida in tailless Manx cats, extreme shyness, and reduced immunity to disease.

Because many of the genetic disorders of purebred cats and dogs have been created by a combination of human ignorance, egotistical self-indulgence, and commercial greed, it is clear that animals' rights are being violated. Until breeders clean up their act and the AKC takes a more responsible and responsive position, the ethics of buying a purebred dog or cat should be questioned. Certainly there are some responsible breeders, but faced with the wholesale commercial exploitation of purebred cats and dogs, they are fighting a losing battle.

I consider it "radical chic" for those who find nothing wrong with having one or more companion animals (the word "pet" *is* demeaning) to choose a "mongrel" or mixed breed over a purebred cat or dog. And ideally they choose it from the local animal shelter. Because of what is termed hybrid vigor, these animals are generally healthier and have far fewer genetic defects than purebred ones.

Because of this hybrid vigor phenomenon, there is an incentive to breed first-generation hybrids, as between a golden retriever and a pointer, or a German shepherd and a collie. Some mixes, like the cockapoo (cocker spaniel and poodle) and pulipoo (puli and poodle) and shitpoo (!) (shitzu and poodle) are quite popular and generally healthier than their purebred parents.

Another genetically related problem, which is also a violation of animal rights, is where people get the wrong breed and temperament for their life-styles. An active working breed like a malamute or border collie does not adapt well to a sedentary suburban existence or to being left alone all day in an apartment. Regardless of breed, many other dogs also suffer from confinement, boredom, and separation from their human companions who are away at work all day.

Aside from the pros and cons of our presumed right to keep animals as pets, problems of bad breeding practices and commercialized exploitation of purebred cats and dogs demand our attention. The rights of these animals are being violated. To uphold the rights of companion animals (especially the right not to be born with a crippling heritable disease), it is essential that those people who are considering buying or adopting a cat or dog have some understanding of the pitfalls of obtaining a purebred animal rather than a "mongrel" or mixed breed. In all fairness, many breeders are concerned and are making concerted efforts to eliminate hereditary diseases in their animals.

Some breeders contend that it is an "act of conservation" to preserve the traits and characteristics of their own favored breeds. But when such "conservation" efforts result in the perpetuation and dissemination of inherited abnormalities, the genetic integrity of purebred animals is threatened.

The rights of purebred cats and dogs are being violated today, and many breeds are becoming endangered, such that their genetic integrity may never be restored. The answers lie not simply in the stars, studbooks, and more scientific research, but in the sterilization of all genetically impaired animals, in breeders changing show standards that favor extreme traits that are linked with health and behavior problems, and in people favoring mixed-breed "mongrel" cats and dogs over purebreds. Those who insist on owning purebred animals should steer away from pet stores. With a little effort, reputable and responsible breeders can be found who are aware of their responsibilities.

Many breeders and owners of purebred cats and dogs will be offended by what I have said against the propagation of genetically anomalous creatures, especially because they claim to "love" their animals. That most veterinarians have remained silent and neither voice concern nor condemn unsound breeding practices and the propagation of deformed, unhealthy purebred animals makes mine sound like a lone, hertical voice in the wilderness. But I would appeal to all who do take offense at my statements to read Professor Yi-Fu Tuan's book, *Dominance and Affection: The Making of Pets*,[1] for a penetrating and sensitive historical account of how, under the guise of affection, we too often exploit living things for our own selfish emotional gratification, at their expense.

PRESERVATION AND IMPROVEMENT OF PUREBRED DOGS: A MODEST PROPOSAL

Many of the more popular purebreds are, I believe, becoming endangered species. Inbreeding has been blamed for many problems, but I believe selective breeding (for extremes in size, conformation, etc.) and overbreeding are more insidious. I see pint-sized English setters; skinny Irish setters that even get lost on the end of the leash; hyperactive poodles and retrievers; Great Danes and other breeds that are too crippled even to walk normally, never mind run.

These are man-made, domestogenic problems, and they are increasing in variety and frequency. Purebred dogs are surely endangered. But aside from the conservation ethic, there is also the humane ethic to consider. Many of these inbred and overbred animals with physical and psychological abnormalities cannot live normal lives. They suffer. They are victims of human exploitation, indifference, greed, and ignorance.

Some breeders might claim that once the breed loses its popularity, everything will self-correct. There is no evidence to support this optimistic, laissez-faire view. On the contrary, the genetic base or gene pool of many purebreeds may be irreparably damaged already. We need more genetic counseling, test mating, and progeny testing. But such efforts will be futile if no temperament tests are given that are tailored for each breed. And these tests would be useless if overbreeding continues, if a major percentage of purebred animals are produced by unethical and ignorant breeders. So what is the first solution here, the first essential step as I see it, to save endangered breeds? Education and legislation? Education helps, but legislation is not feasible.

The solution that I offer is for all purebreed clubs to arrange with the American Kennel Club to have two registries for purebreeds. One would be for the registration of all purebred dogs, as is the present situation. The second would be a first-class or breed-stock registry for dogs that have show points and veterinary certification of soundness (both in temperament and physique). The registry computer service would be programmed to permit progeny testing, advice on test matings, and optimal matching of bitches with available studs or decreased but desirable studs whose sperm has been preserved.

Such a registry might also give municipalities that endeavor to regulate the pet overpopulation problem a means by which to persuade owners of purebred dogs not in the first-class or breed-stock registry to have their dogs neutered. This would not only help reduce the pet population problem, it would also help dry off the influx of "purebred dogs with papers" that are saturating the market.

Knowledgeable and ethical breeders may claim that the current system in their own clubs guarantees that breed quality will be preserved and that there is no need to bother with non-club members who breed inferior animals. I find this attitude not only lazy but reprehensible. Dog lovers surely should care for the welfare of all dogs, and those who favor a certain breed must surely care for the well-being of members of that breed and for the future of the breed. If breeders do not become more politically active and work to develop a breed preservation and improvement program, then the purebred dog world will surely have gone to the proverbial dogs. The only recourse then will be to breed healthy mongrel dogs (thank Dog for hybrid vigor!), or to let all purebred dogs loose on a large island and come back after twenty-five years and collect the fittest who survived.

THE NATURAL DOG: THE SUPERMUTT

What is the best dog in the world? Most veterinarians and dog experts who don't have a bias for any particular breed will respond without hesitation: It's the mongrel or mixed breed.

If we were to take all the various breeds of dog and let them loose on an island with a plentiful supply of food and came back a hundred years later, we would probably have the best dog imaginable. It would probably resemble the so-called pariah dog so common in the villages of Southeast Asia.

Pariah dogs are "supermutts" and the most natural dogs around. They have never been subjected to artificial selective breeding to create local breeds with various unique traits.

Thanks to minimal genetic interference by man, the pariah dog has been subjected to the most rigorous selection and survival pressures of nature. Only the fittest survive. As a consequence, the average pariah dog is a highly intelligent, agile, and beautifully proportioned animal, resistent to many endemic parasites and other diseases and well able to fend for itself without food or shelter from humans. The Australian dingo is a somewhat larger type of pariah dog that has become feral (that is, gone wild). The African Basenji is one example of a local type of pariah dog that has been subjected to selective breeding to "fix" and exaggerate certain traits, such as the curled tail and wrinkled forehead.

The pariah dogs I studied in India are essentially a regional variety of what one might call the *natural dog*. This prototype dog of dogs is best regarded as an "all-breed" rather than as a "pure breed." Nor is it simply a "mixed breed" with an ancestry of two or more pure breeds. However, the more the various pure breeds are mixed together by cross-breeding, the more the offspring come to resemble this prototypical dog of dogs. In every animal shelter from Detroit to Dehli and from London to Rome we can find dogs that are almost identical, yet they are not of any particular purebred lineage. Often demeaned as "mongrels" and "bastard" dogs, they are regional replicas of the Asiatic pariah dogs—the natural dog. They are highly intelligent and adaptable, physically and mentally capable of living independent of man, but sufficiently domesticated to make life-long companions and loyal and affectionate members of a human family.

The natural dog possesses the following basic characteristics: medium build (35 to 55 pounds), a long, slightly upcurled tail, and long, straight legs. The head, body, and limbs are beautifully proportioned and aligned; the ears are erect or semierect; the muzzle is of moderate length; and the eyes are oval or almond shaped. The coat is short and may vary in color from black to white and piebald to brindle, the most common being basically light fawn or a darker reddish brown. With proper care these dogs can live well into their mid and late teens and are virtually free of diseases of herditary origin that are so prevalent in pure breeds.

* * *

After having spent some time studying in southwest India the village pariah dogs that live by their wits, scrounging food wherever they can, I became increasingly disturbed by the contrast between these superb survivors and the relatively sickly and often deformed purebred dogs of the western industrial world.

Veterinarian Wayne H. Riser, who has studied health problems that result from human interference with the genetic integrity of the dog, explains why the pariah dog is so healthy.[2]

> Dogs that have the same skeletal proportions, slow maturity rate, and comparable muscle mass and development as the ancestral dog have few orthopaedic diseases. The incidence of orthopaedic abnormalities increases as the dog's characteristics vary from ancestral type. . . . The dog with a well-balanced length of legs, nose and tail, who matures slowly, and stays within one standard deviation of the mean . . . is seldom out of biomechanical balance and, therefore, infrequently develops orthopaedic diseases. This disease incidence increases as the boundaries of one standard deviation are approached, or if weight and height of the dog exceed the capacity of the musculoskeletal system to support the body mass. Those breeds within two to three standard deviations pay severe penalties in the form of orthopaedic diseases for maintaining their existence.

In sum, even seemingly minor changes in body size can have a profound effect on a dog's overall health and well-being. Such changes, often compounded with others, such as the length of the back, legs, and head, and the depth of the chest, can result in a variety of health problems in purebred dogs, and thus an increased probable risk of suffering some time during their lives.

Many purebred dogs are so deformed and dependent on human care and veterinary attention that I consider them wolf-bonzais: like crippled trees, dwarfed and deformed, often so delicately that we even find them appealing.

Yet our nurturing and loving them is not humane when we also intend to propagate them. Those who really love such creatures (which are not products of our own creation but rather of our own *deformation*) cannot condone their propagation.

To continue to breed structurally and functionally abnormal purebred dogs is surely an ethically reprehensible and selfish activity. Even if advances in veterinary science may help alleviate the suffering of dogs afflicted with inherited and developmental disorders, this treatment approach is bad, albeit profitable medicine. All medicine should aim at prevention. And the best way to prevent the harm and suffering of those breeds of dogs afflicted with heritable and developmental disorders is for people to stop breeding them. All achondroplastic dwarfs with backs that are selectively bred to be too long (dachshund), toy and miniature breeds (poodles), brachycephalic dogs (pugs and bulldog-faced breeds), acromegalic giants (Irish wolfhound and St. Bernard), and mutants like the Shar-pei with its infection-prone and eye-damaging skin folds should be phased out of existence if they cannot be genetically improved. Ear cropping and tail docking of all breeds should also be prohibited. The body confirmation and structure of most breeds need to be drastically improved, and prevalent inherited disorders, such as hip dysplasia, retinal degeneration, and hemophilia, should be eliminated through selective breeding.

As Dr. Riser emphasizes, selective breeding to make dogs abnormally large or small results in disturbances in body metabolism and heat regulation. Because of their light body mass to surface area, toy breeds such as the poodle are very susceptible to the cold, often shiver, and are susceptible to hypoglycemia and tend toward hyperactivity. In contrast, giant breeds such as the St. Bernard, with its large body mass in proportion to body surface area, tend toward hypoactivity, often pant continuously, have poor exercise tolerance especially in hot and humid weather, and are susceptible to heat stroke.

People who genuinely care for dogs will not find my suggestions offensive. Those who do take offense are not offended by the sight of a sickly bulldog or fragile "toy" poodle. Yet such dogs offend me. Because I love animals, I firmly believe that the propagation of these mutants should be questioned and that firm steps be taken to eliminate extreme deformities by phasing out some breeds simply by neutering all of them. Through selective breeding, the structure and overall health of other breeds can be improved.

Many show points of conformation (such as narrow and long or blunt muzzles, deep chests, narrow hips, and long or short backs or legs) need to be revised. All genetically unsound purebred dogs that are sold as "pets" should be neutered. And all breeders should, through their breed clubs and associations, work closely with veterinary and medical genetic consultants to restore the natural beauty and vitality of the dog within a framework that preserves the diversity of various breeds without jeopardizing the health of any individual animal.

Another reason for not breeding purebred dogs is that it is surely wrong to deliberately breed any dog when there are so many homeless ones in the shelters in need of a good home, waiting to be adopted. But that is almost like telling people not to have children! However, those who breed dogs for show always have a surplus since only a few pups in a litter turn out to be of show potential.

My advice to anyone who is looking for a good dog and can't go to Southeast Asia to adopt one of the millions of homeless pariah dogs is to visit the local animal shelter. With a mental image of what a natural dog looks like and knowing they all have good temperaments if they have been socialized and never abused, I will guarantee that there will be at least one waiting to be adopted into a good home. And with a little expertise or advice, it is not difficult to pick out an adult one or a puppy with the characteristics and potentialities of this all-breed and best-of-all-breeds natural dog.

SHOULD PEOPLE KEEP COMPANION ANIMALS?

Some animal rightists believe that it is morally wrong to make animals into "pets." One point of argument is that the benefits to people far outweigh the benefits to animals. Thus the owner-pet relationship is unbalanced, and in the absence of any significant reciprocal benefits to the animal, it is exploitive. Little wonder that those people who dare to criticize the cultural tradition of breeding and keeping animals as companion animals are dismissed as not being animal lovers. Yet too often they see these animals neglected, mistreated, overindulged and kept as status objects, animate toys for children. Is it right to make animals slaves to the emotional whims of owners who crave control over another's life and love animals conditionally in terms of how appealing, overdependent, and obedient they are—or how rare and expensive?

Certainly, many dogs, cats, and other companion animals receive some veterinary care when they are sick. Wild animals don't get that. And companion animals have protection from predators and the elements. Thus it can be reasoned that they live a better and longer life and suffer less than wild animals.

However, many of their diseases are man-made, a result of improper breeding, rearing, feeding, and general treatment and "life-style." Much veterinary treatment would be unnecessary if these problems were corrected. Relatively speaking, wild animals are generally much healthier than highly inbred, overfed, overindulged, and sedentary cats and dogs. Thus, I believe it is an exaggeration to claim that one of the great benefits humans give to animals in "exchange" for their companionship is veterinary treatment when they are sick. (This is analogous to claiming that wild animals are better off in the zoo than in the wild.)

While one of the basic rights of companion animals is the right to receive veterinary treatment when needed, many animals do not receive adequate care. The following list from a 1983 survey conducted for the American Veterinary Medical

Association by Charles, Charles and Associates, Market Management Consultants, reveals some disturbing facts.

Of all species, dogs received more veterinary attention than any other companion or farm animal. While it could be argued that dogs suffer more health problems than these other species, it should be emphasized that the figures include not only treatment for health problems, but also for examinations, vaccinations, and neutering. The lack of veterinary care for these other species is probably a result of a combination of factors—cost (of treatment and of the animal), emotional investment, home doctoring, and inability to recognize when an animal is in need of medical attention. It is worth noting also that 46 percent of dog owners took their animals for an annual veterinary examination, while only 29 percent of cat owners did so.

In the majority of households in the United States, cage birds, cage pets such as hamsters, guinea pigs, and gerbils, and fish never receive any veterinary care.

It could be claimed that a gerbil or guinea pig is a wonderful learning experience for children. But is encouraging children to keep an animal incarcerated in a cage, too often deprived of company of its own kind and of anything natural in its environment, an appropriate learning experience? Children can learn far more about animals under natural conditions. Indeed, keeping animals as pets in cages could give children a wholly erroneous view of the nature and role of animals. They were not created for our own exclusive use and enjoyment.

Studies of the human–companion animal bond have emphasized the positive benefits to humans of keeping animals, which range from using trained monkeys to help quadriplegics, to people having less depression and fewer heart attacks if they have an animal to pet. Prison inmates, the chronically hospitalized, and the elderly in retirement homes have all been shown to derive significant benefit from keeping companion animals.

Only one study has demonstrated any significant benefits for the animals. This benefit is that in some programs, the cats and dogs that are used (and properly cared for) are adopted from animal shelters. Since 12 to 14 million homeless and unwanted cats and dogs are destroyed every year in the United States, it is ethically questionable for people to deliberately breed cats and dogs when there is already plentiful supply of cats and dogs waiting to be adopted. I believe there is a world of a difference between adopting an abandoned cat or dog and buying an expensive purebred one from a pet store or catalog—as much difference as raising orphaned wild animals for release in the wild and providing a good home for those injured ones that can never be released, and breeding, raising, and even importing wildlife species for the pet trade.

I am not wholly against people keeping animals as companions. But I am opposed to the exploitation of animals, especially purebreds afflicted with genetic disorders and wild, "exotic" species that don't do well in captivity, by the pet industry. We do need to reevaluate the morality and ethics of keeping animals as "pets." It entails not only love but also respect and understanding. Animals should be given equal and fair consideration. They were not created for our own exclusive enjoyment; rather they have interests and a life of their own.

It can be argued that many companion animals could never survive in nature. That we have created animals that cannot exist independent of us is no reason to justify their continued propagation and existence.

I do not mean to offend those who create such animals or to demean or doubt the genuineness of the love many people extend to their animals. But this affection is often conditional on the animal's compliance —docility (lack of spirit), obedience (lack of independence), and appealing demeanor. Does not selfish sentimental attachment, quite distinct from empathy and unconditional respect and love, underlie much of the suffering of animals kept as pets? Animals should be free to be themselves, to express their own nature, their independent and mature spirits. Is it right for us to control, manipulate, and direct an animal's intrinsic nature to satisfy our own exclusive ends? Is it not a form of slavery? Scientists involved in genetic engineering, who create transgenic animals, such as pigs and mice that have human genes, see nothing wrong in what they do.

Likewise, people who create bonsais, deformed bulldogs, Persian cats, and overdependent "doglets"—perpetual puppy "toy" breeds—see nothing wrong in what they do. But isn't it time we asked whether it is right to treat other living beings in such ways? And is it not time that we extended the Golden Rule—to treat others as we would have them treat us—to the rest of creation?

RESPONSIBLE CARE OF COMPANION ANIMALS

Responsible care of companion animals entails four basic principles, which are also wisdom's "four pillars" of veterinary preventive and holistic medicine: right understanding, right rearing and environment, right breeding, and right feeding. These may also be recognized as the basic rights of all domesticated and captive wild animals.

Right Understanding

Right understanding involves knowing the animals' behavioral repertoire of body language signals that express its needs and intentions. Without such knowledge, a close empathetic relationship with animals is impossible. Animals are then likely to be anthropomorphized, misunderstood, wrongly disciplined, and improperly responded to. They will not be appreciated in their own right.

For these reasons, I have always felt it of paramount importance to educate people about the whys and ways of animal behavior (ethology) and psychology.[4] With right understanding, training and handling are greatly facilitated, and the clarity and depth of the human–companion animal bond are enhanced. This is of especial value to children, whose intuitive understanding of animal behavior can be enhanced through objective observation, which leads to empathetic appreciation and an enduring respect—the basic ingredients of humane education.

Furthermore, right understanding helps ensure that the animal's needs are satisfied and not frustrated, which can cause stress and distress. Also, people attuned to the animal's behavior and routines can more easily recognize early signs of sickness, which can greatly facilitate prompt veterinary treatment and eliminate suffering.

Right Rearing and Environment

Right rearing and environment are essential for the overall well-being, adaptability, and sociability of companion animals. Right rearing entails socialization with human beings during the critical period early in life—in the dog and cat, this is between four and ten weeks of age. It is advisable to handle puppies and kittens frequently soon after birth and to maintain frequent human contact through the weaning period. Animals deprived of human contact until after ten to twelve weeks of age tend to be shy and difficult to handle and train. It is during this critical period that animals develop a close emotional bond with humans, transferring their earlier attachment to their mothers and littermates to their human caretakers and families after they have been weaned. Delayed socialization disrupts this transference of attachment. Animals so deprived, especially if they are innately fearful or aggressive, rarely make satisfactory companions, develop behavior problems (such as fear biting and avoidance of strangers), and are frequently abandoned, euthanized, or even abused with inappropriate and ineffective discipline.

With proper socialization, the dog comes to regard the human companion as parent and pack leader. This is the optimal relationship; otherwise the dog may attempt to assert dominance over his or her master and other humans. This problem is exacerbated by permissive and overindulgent rearing, which can also result in social maladjustment and overdependence, the so-called perpetual puppy syndrome. In sum, proper socialization helps ensure that the animal will mature to be socially and emotionally well adjusted.

Socialization is part of the animal's environment. Other environmental factors are also an integral aspect of responsible care and right rearing. These include providing the animals with the company of at least one of their own kind whenever possible. Two cats are generally happier and healthier than one. The same is true for dogs, especially if they are left alone all day when their human companions are away at work. With the exception of hamsters, all cage pets—gerbils, guinea pigs, rabbits, and so on—and most species of cage birds and tropical fish benefit from the company of related species.

Additional environmental provisions include regular periods of grooming and play for cats and dogs, which have a bonding effect, and outdoor exercise for dogs. Cats also enjoy an outdoor enclosure or sunporch. Like dogs, they should never be allowed to roam free. Indoors, cats need scratching posts and enjoy carpeted climbing posts with shelves.

Right environment entails providing animals with those conditions conducive to the normal development, expression, and satisfaction of their basic physical and psychological needs so that their adaptivity to domesticity is not jeopardized.

It is not uncommon for puppies and kittens to be confined in a cage or kennel during the first three or four months of life. This extreme environmental deprivation can result in neophobia—fear of unfamiliar things—later in life, especially in those animals that are innately shy and timid. This problem is quite common in cats that have been raised indoors. Such animals respond well when treated with Valium when they are moved to unfamiliar surroundings, such as a new home or boarding kennel. To avoid this kind of shyness in dogs, it is important that their owners do not keep them confined to a pen, kennel, or enclosed yard, especially when they are around eight to twelve weeks of age. The more varied places animals visit and experience during these formative weeks, the more environmentally adaptable they will be later in life. The increasing practice of keeping dogs in holding crates in the house when they are left alone is to be questioned on humane grounds. If pet owners recognize the importance of right rearing and environment, they can avoid much unnecessary suffering and stress susceptibility.

Right Breeding

The next important principle of responsible care is right breeding. For their own well-being, cats and dogs should be selectively bred to be healthy and to have stable temperaments. A host of inherited structural and physiological abnormalities cause much needless suffering in "purebred"-"pedigreed" companion animals. It is surely a basic right of any domesticated animal not to be born with a heritable disorder that might cause suffering or increased susceptibility to disease later in life.

Right breeding therefore entails careful attention to the elimination of inherited disorders that arise as a result of inbreeding and selection for abnormal traits in purebred cats and dogs. An alternative is to promote the ownership of "mongrel" or mixed-breed cats and dogs that have a significantly lower incidence of such anomalies.

Right Nutrition

Right feeding entails providing companion animals with a wholesome, balanced diet. This will vary according to the breed, size, temperament, and age of the animal, as it does also when the animal is growing, pregnant, lactating, or convalescent.

Good nutrition is the final principle of responsible animal care and the cornerstone of animal health care maintenance. Much of this responsibility is now in the hands of commercial pet food manufacturers, some of whom are guilty of selling poor-quality products formulated on the basis of least cost in order to maximize profits in a highly competitive market. Such practices, more common in some countries than in others, is clearly unethical.

These four principles of responsible companion animal care, which comprise the four pillars of veterinary preventive and holistic medicine, are mutually supportive, interdependent, and synergistic. A weakness or deficiency in any one of these may be compensated to some degree by the others. The probability of disease and suffering increases in proportion to the degree of weakness or deficiency in any one of these four pillars, and also insofar as there is a lack of synergy between them. For example, without right understanding, the problems inherent in a dog or cat afflicted with an unstable temperament (which could be a product of wrong rearing and breeding) can be exacerbated. Likewise, with wrong feeding, the health problems of companion animals that are linked with a genetic predisposition to metabolic or endocrine disorders can be aggravated.

There are three corollaries to these principles of responsible companion animal care. The first is to have the animal *neutered*. This makes both cats and dogs more adaptable and generally healthier and longer lived. It is also one of the best ways of dealing with the almost worldwide problem of cat and dog overpopulation.

And the second is to guarantee that the companion animal receives a *regular* (at least annual) *veterinary health care checkup* including examination for parasites, protective vaccinations, and so on.*

The last principle is to ensure that when the time comes for a companion animal to be *euthanized*, it is done so humanely and *with dignity and respect*.

WILD ANIMALS AS "PETS"

Clearly, if we are to accept these four principles as the rights of companion animals and the ethics of responsible care, then it is irresponsible and unethical for wild/exotic animals to be exploited as pets. They have not been bred to adapt to the conditions and demands of being domesticated. When kept as pets, such animals often do not receive proper nutrition or the

_____

*I regard such treatments as *protective* as distinct from *preventive* medicine because they are interventive procedures that can have harmful side effects. The four Rs of preventive/holistic medicine—right understanding, rearing/environment, right breeding, and right feeding—have no such harmful consequences.

right social and environmental conditions, because both the expertise and the proper facilities are lacking. And few people, except for a handful of veterinarians, ethologists, and animal care technicians, have the right understanding to help ensure that such animals thrive in captivity. Human health risks arise from a variety of zoonotic diseases that these animals may transmit, including rabies, salmonellosis, tularemia, toxoplasmosis, psittacosis, plague, dermatophytosis, Shigella enteritis, hepatitis, and tuberculosis. With many species there is also the added risk of human injury. In addition, wild/exotic species are either taken from the wild, which can have an adverse impact on wild populations, or are bred in captivity, often under conditions that are not conducive to their overall well-being. And if some exotics escape or are deliberately released and become feral, they may compete with and displace indigenous species and cause irreparable harm to natural ecosystems.

Despite these problems, many people are attracted to the idea of keeping wild and exotic animals as pets. Prospective owners need to know something about the hazards to themselves and to their families. Over the past couple of years in the United States, pet wolves and wolf-dog hybrids have killed or severely mauled young children, as have pet lions, tigers, and cougars. They have also caused serious injury to other people when they have escaped from often grossly inadequate and poorly constructed facilities. Problems of this nature have become so common that the city of San Francisco has passed an ordinance banning the ownership of all wild and exotic animals.

An increasing number of states, including California, Connecticut, Louisiana, and Washington, now have legislation preventing the interstate shipment of wildlife species and of keeping them as pets.

A pet raccoon attacked and severely mutilated a ten-month-old girl, and a ten-foot-long python strangled an eleven-month-old boy in his crib. Many injuries and health threats attributed to wild and exotic animals kept as pets are not officially reported.

Rabies is a major problem with wild animals kept as pets.

Of six other attacks by pet raccoons, one animal was rabies positive and one killed a baby girl. Seventeen of twenty-one skunks that attacked people were rabid.

These accounts are not intended to imply that wild animals are inherently vicious but rather to emphasize that they don't make good pets.

The National Animal Control Association[6] has officially gone on record as stating that

> it is opposed to the keeping and sale of wildlife as pets. Once an owner of a wild animal is no longer willing to care for it, the animal is usually unable to re-adapt to a wild environment if released. With very few exceptions, formerly-owned wildlife must be destroyed because of the lack of appropriate facilities to maintain them. For these reasons, N.A.C.A. urges animal control agencies to take steps to make the selling or keeping of wild animals as prohibitive as possible.

The American Veterinary Medical Association[5] has also endorsed the following resolution: "The American Veterinary Medical Association strongly opposes the keeping of wild and exotic species of animals as pets and believes that all commercial traffic of these animals for such purposes should be prohibited."

The high mortality rate of captive wild animals in zoos even where experienced veterinary care is available has been well documented. Presumably the mortality rates of wild and exotic animals kept as pets by people without any professional expertise is even higher—as is the associated suffering prior to death. For these reasons alone, the keeping of such animals as pets should be discouraged.

No statistics are available on the mortality rates of the common domesticated cage pets (rabbits, gerbils, parakeets, and so on), but as 80 to 90 percent of these animals in the United States never receive veterinary care, at least the ethics of keeping them should be questioned. The extreme social and environmental deprivation of these animals is also a point of major concern.

* * *

In conclusion, if people decide to keep one or more animals as companions, they should regard it more as a responsibility and a sacred trust than as an unqualified right based on superiority and dominion over the animal kingdom.

By encouraging, through education and legislation, public recognition of the four Rs of responsible pet ownership—right understanding, right rearing/environment, right breeding, and right feeding—a greater respect for all creatures and recognition of their inherent value and rights will arise spontaneously. As the four Rs are also basic principles of veterinary preventive and holistic medicine and of animal welfare and rights philosophy, they help forge a common bond between the veterinary profession and the animal protection movement.

There is one area of gross cruelty involving dogs that should not be overlooked. This area includes such "spectator" sports as pitbull dog fights; "baiting" or setting dogs onto wild creatures like badgers, boars, and bears; "coursing," sending hounds off to chase and tear down hare, deer, coyotes, and other creatures; fox hunting with horses and hounds. Popular in the U.S. and the U.K., these cruel "blood sports," many of which are still not illegal, reveal a pervasive lack of respect and reverence for nonhuman life that is not limited by class, creed, or culture.

CHAPTER 13

Animals and Genetic Engineering

Although genetic engineering biotechnology has been applied to animals only relatively recently, there is already cause for concern. Aside from the ethics of transgenic manipulations (inserting one or more genes of one species into another), this new research field needs careful monitoring and regulatory guidelines in order to prevent animal suffering.

A few proponents of genetic engineering have implied that the new technology may help save endangered species and also be used to help animals adapt better to such natural conditions as drought or unnatural conditions as we see in intensive livestock and poultry factory farming. Certain inherited disorders in companion animals might even be corrected through appropriate genetic engineering. However, because of the costs involved, it is unlikely that animals will benefit significantly from genetic engineering at least in the immediate future. This technology will be applied first and foremost to make animals even more useful. Farm animals will be genetically manipulated and hyperstimulated (as with genetically engineered bovine growth hormone) to grow faster, produce more milk, and so on. This will result in stress and an increased incidence of production-related diseases already caused by intensive husbandry practices. The additional application of biotechnolgy will simply aggravate and compound the severity of disorders that already affect farm animals today. While biotechnologists claim that farm animals' health and well-being will be enhanced because of new vaccines and drugs produced through genetic engineering, it is well documented that such "biologics" are needed because the animals are in an unbalanced environmental situation, under stress and are highly susceptible to infections and contagious diseases. New vaccines and drugs will help stop them from becoming sick but will do nothing to alleviate those conditions that cause stress, suffering, and increased susceptibility to disease on the factory farm. Thus animals' welfare will not be improved or their suffering significantly alleviated even though the incidence of actual disease may be reduced.

There are other welfare concerns related to the application of biotechnology in biomedical, military, and agricultural (pesticide) research. Animals will be subjected to toxicity and other tests of genetically engineered microorganisms created for military and agricultural purposes. And they will be genetically manipulated to create "models" of human diseases of hereditary origin, which may cause the animals great stress and suffering. Furthermore, animals could be subjected to genetic engineering designed to modify their physiology and biochemistry so that they produce abnormal quantities of various medically and commercially valuable biochemical compounds—hormones, enzymes, and so on—for commercial extraction (from their blood, sera). They would be turned into "chemical factories." While they may not actually suffer, the ethics of such exploitation needs to be seriously questioned.

Certainly many benefits could arise, especially in the fields of human and veterinary medicine and agriculture, from the *appropriate* use of genetic engineering biotechnology. Yet the public must be made aware of some very real concerns in order to help ensure that the future of biotechnology has no detrimental impact on the rights and interests of the people, on the welfare of animals, or on the environment.

In 1984, the Board of Directors of The Humane Society of the United States passed a resolution regarding the threats inherent in genetic engineering biotechnology. Recognizing that there had been a marked increase in actual and proposed experimentation in genetic engineering and that the long-term consequences on humans, other animals, plants, and the entire biosphere are largely unknown and unpredicable, The Humane Society urged that "the critical nature of these concerns be recognized and that those persons in government and private industry involved in genetic engineering act to preclude animal suffering and negative ecological consequences."

ANIMAL SUFFERING

Since animal suffering has resulted from genetic engineering, and acknowledging the fact that as more animals are subjected to transgenic intervention (or reprogramming) the probability of animal suffering increases, we should specify what types and sources of suffering we are dealing with. These types are as follows.

Developmental Abnormalities

Following gene insertion into embryos, the embryos often fail to develop and are aborted, because gene-insertion techniques are still far from perfect and are often "hit and miss." Spliced genes often finish up in the wrong organs of the body and don't always get into the right cells to be passed on to transgenic offspring. Some may develop abnormally and die *in utero* and be aborted or resorbed, or be born with a variety of developmental defects, some of which are attributable to so-called insertional mutations; or be infertile. Health problems may not be manifested until later in life, hence there can be no accurate prediction as to whether or not engineered animals are going to suffer. Lacking the controls of other "regulator" genes, some foreign genes produce too much of a certain protein, such as insulin or growth hormone, causing animal sickness and even death. Because of the nature of some form of genetic reprogramming there can be no safeguards to prevent animal suffering in the first place. These problems are to be expected in the initial phase of creating transgenic animals and in other genetic manipulations.

Deleterious Pleiotropic Effects

Once the anticipated genetic changes have been accomplished and the new animal prototypes developed as foundation breeding stock, additional problems are to be anticipated. These deleterious pleiotropic effects have been shown to occur in transgenic animals. This term refers to multiple harmful effects by one or more genes on the animal's phenotype. And the phenotype is the entire physical, biochemical and physiological makeup of an individual. One example is the many health problems of the USDA's transgenic pigs that carry the human growth gene. These were unexpected, since mice and rabbits reprogrammed with this same gene did not manifest deleterious pleiotropic effects to anywhere near the same degree. These pigs were arthritic, lethargic, had defective vision arising from abnormal skull growth: and they did not grow twice as big twice as fast as was anticipated on the basis of the effects of the human growth gene in mice. These pigs had high mortality rates and were especially prone to gastric ulcers and to pneumonia, the conclusion being that the genetic change had seriously impaired their immune systems.

This illustrates that pervasive suffering can arise from genetic engineering. It also demonstrates another principle: that a genetic change in one species may cause little apparent sickness and suffering as in the cases of transgenic mice, but this does not mean that the same genetic change in another species will have the same consequences. In other words, predictions and assurances as to the safety and humaneness of genetic engineering cannot always be generalized from one animal species to other species.

New Health Problems

As the biotechnologists themselves have shown, new health problems following genetic reprogramming can arise, resulting in animal sickness and death. Pigs given somatotropin growth hormone require more lysine and possibly other essential amino acids in their diets. What this research indicates is that special diets and other health-corrective treatments will be needed following some forms of genetic reprogramming. And veterinary medical knowledge will be inadequate to deal with the special requirements of animals subjected to genetic reprogramming, additional research being needed to correct health problems and associated suffering.

Furthermore, growth hormone–treated pigs have little protective back fat, which means they must stay confined in buildings. Likewise, dairy cows treated with growth hormone to boost milk production cannot be let out to graze, because they need special high-energy diets. This means a life in confinement for them as well.

Disease Resistance and Animal Suffering

Biotechnologists contend that through genetic engineering, animals can be made disease resistant, and this will help reduce animal suffering. However, the notion that genetically engineered disease resistance will reduce animal suffering is scientifically naive. It is naive because it reflects a single cause (bacteria/virus) approach to disease. Simply endowing an animal with resistance to a particular disease will not protect it from the stress factors and contingent suffering that make it susceptible to disease in the first place, such as overcrowding and stress in confinement "factory" farm buildings. These are in themselves pathogenic—stressful and disease enhancing.

Genetically Engineered "Bio-boosters"

It is unlikely that new transgenic varieties of farm animals will become part of the food production system within the next 5 to 10 years, with the exception of genetically engineered fish, such as salmon and catfish. Instead, genetically engineered bacteria are being utilized for the cloning and mass production of injectable "bio-boosters" designed to increase disease resistance, growth rate, milk production, leanness of carcass, and fertility and fecundity.

Genetically engineered vaccines to block cholecystokinin, developed to make swine eat more (by blocking their sense of satiety), and antisomatostasin in sheep to deregulate growth inhibition, follow the same logic as using anabolic steroids and genetically engineered growth hormones to make livestock more productive. The overall direction of the nonveterinary use of these drugs in farm animals is ethically questionable; altering animals' autonomic tuning and overall homeostasis and overcompartmentalizing or partitioning their metabolic resources for growth and productivity places in jeopardy their immune systems and overall well-being.

The animal welfare implications of improper use as well as the social, economic and ecological consequences of these biologics being adopted by farmers is being hotly debated. Also their desirability is being questioned in these times of overproduction and serious problems of meat and dairy surpluses in the United States and Europe, which cost the public billions of dollars in storage costs, and which, coupled with the price subsidies to other sectors of the livestock industry cast a dark shadow over these innovations that some believe now threaten the structure and future of agriculture. Suffice it to say that agribiotechnology will fail in the long-term if it is not integrated with a sustainable, regenerative agriculture and is instead used to boost what is fundamentally an ecologically and economically unsound meat-based agricultural system.

Productivity and Suffering

Using genetic engineering biotechnology to increase the productivity and "efficiency" of farm animals (their growth rates, milk or egg yield, etc.) kept under current intensive husbandry conditions will increase the severity and incidence of animal suffering and sickness. It is already extensively documented that farm animals raised under intensive confinement husbandry systems in order to maximize production and efficiency suffer from a variety of so-called production-related diseases. The argument that if animals are suffering they won't be productive and farmers won't profit is demolished by the fact that animal scientists, in using the term "production-related diseases" acknowledge that animal sickness and suffering are an unavoidable and integral aspect of modern livestock and poultry farming. Using biotechnology to make animals even more productive and efficient under these conditions as many animal production technologists are proposing, will place their overall welfare in greater jeopardy than ever, because the severity and incidence of production-related diseases will be increased if animals are kept under the same conditions as they are today.

Erroneous "Benefits" to Animals

There are other erroneous claims of the potential benefits of biotechnology to the animals themselves. It has been claimed that genetic engineering could be used to help cure animals of genetic disorders. Over 200 diseases of genetic origin, like hip dysplasia, have been identified in highly inbred "purebred" dogs, and there are dozens that afflict other domesticated species. Aside from the fact that it would be a poor investment to correct germ-line defects since disease termination in this way is not profitable (and this point is also relevant to corporate investment and involvement in human medicine), simply stopping the practice of inbreeding and the breeding of defective animals is the best prevention.

On closer examination, it is not mere animal rights sentiment or some spiritual or religious belief that lead to the conclusion that it is wrong to alter an animal's intrinsic nature (*telos*) by genetically altering its germ line. Beyond the moralist polemics of right and wrong, there is the cold fact that regardless of any purported benefits to animals from such genetic engineering, there are safer, less invasive and more practical alternatives such as changing husbandry practices and mutations and other inherited anomalies in domestic animals. Thus from a purely utilitarian perspective, the animal's *telos* need not be altered. The only grounds for doing so are at best a "last resort" to save some endangered species whose gene pool is contaminated by a lethal gene. In sum, the sanctity of being and the inviolability of the *telos* of animals are ethical principles that need not be dismissed for quasi eugenics reasons that favor genetic engineering because there are many alternatives to enhancing the welfare and overall well-being of animals without having to resort to genetic engineering biotechnology. And it would be bad medicine to resort to the latter without a thorough consideration of viable alternatives that uphold the above ethical principles.

Future Concerns

The genetic engineering of animals and other biotechnologies, such as embryo transplantation, cloning, and the creation of chimeras like the "geep"—a sheep with a goat's head—are relatively recent developments. This means that at present, there is a total lack of evidence that the welfare of animals subjected to these manipulations can be guaranteed and that coincidental and contingent suffering to these animals will be avoided. It is wrong to presume or promise that animals' welfare will not be placed in jeopardy and that "unnecessary" suffering can be avoided.

We already have clear evidence of suffering in genetically engineered animals whose welfare has been jeopardized by this new biotechnology. Transgenic engineering of animals has already caused animals to suffer and sometimes this was anticipated, as in causing birth defects and cancer. Other times this was not anticipated by the researchers. Diabetic mice, for example, temporarily cured by insertion of human insulin genes, died later from excess insulin production. Federal animal welfare regulations contain no reference to genetically engineered animals and have to do with the care of animals: they have nothing to do with the prevention and alleviation of animal suffering following genetic reprogramming. Basic guidelines are needed, as for example to avoid unnecessary suffering in transgenic animals from induced diseases by killing them as soon as possible. Furthermore, the Federal Animal Welfare Act excludes from protection most species used in transgenic research, namely, mice and farm animals, a situation demanding immediate attention.

Genetic Parasitism?

Transgenic mice have been bioengineered to secrete human tissue plasminogen activator in their milk, which helps remove blood clots from heart attack victims. Cows and sheep may be next, producing many useful pharmaceuticals in their milk, such as human blood clotting Factor 9 for hemophiliacs and alpha-1-antitrypsin for emphysema victims. If there is no animal suffering following certain genetic changes, then it is difficult to argue against such molecular farming, where animals are used as "protein factories." After all, they have been long exploited for products far less vital to human health, namely, meat, hides, milk and eggs. Yet does a history of exploitation establish an ethically valid precedent for continued and intensified exploitation? Cows may be made to manufacture drugs that are more effective and cheaper than from genetically engineered bacteria. Such developments should be accepted only on the condition that the animals are kept under the most humane husbandry conditions that fully satisfy their behavioral and social needs. In providing us with life-saving pharmaceuticals, we would surely owe them no less. The fact that these animals will be so valuable will help ensure that they will be well cared for. But rather than keeping them under sterile conditions, their environments should provide for their social and behavioral requirements.

However, this incorporation of human genes into nonhuman beings for human benefit could be seen as a form of parasitism. Molecular farming, an example of genetic parasitism, is as abhorrent to some people as the practice of grafting pigs' livers and chimpanzee hearts into humans. And it is difficult for others who do not share such feelings to go on and discover the intuitive wisdom behind this emotional response. For example, it is self-evident that the genetic deterioration of *Homo sapiens* will continue and increase in severity if the major focus of biomedical research in not on prevention but on developing ways of identifying defective genes, deficient proteins—enzymes, hormones, etc.—and in isolating those genes that produce these proteins so that they can be cloned by bacteria or spliced into the genomes of farm animals for them to manufacture these proteins for us. In sum, molecular farming profits could indirectly contribute to genetic deterioration, if not to medical nemesis per se. Such genetic parasitism should be beneath our dignity, but after all, we eat pigs and graft their organs into our own bodies.

THE PATENTING OF ANIMALS: SCIENTIFIC AND ETHICAL IMPLICATIONS

According to *Science* magazine[1], "A ruling by Board of Patent Appeals and Interferences of the United States Patent and Trademark Office (on April 3, 1987) appears to have cleared the way for the patenting of animals with unique, man-made characteristics that do not occur in nature. . . . Until now, the patents have been granted to plants and microorganisms, but not to higher life forms."

The board thus broadened the interpretation of the 1980 Supreme Court decision in *Diamond* vs. *Chakrabarty* (which ruled that genetically modified microorganisms can be patented) to include all life forms. But can the U.S. Patent and Trademark Office actually grant and protect the exclusive right to produce and/or sell a particular kind of animal—one that has been genetically altered?

Domesticated animals have been subjected to genetic alteration for thousands of years. Contrast the structure and physiology of a Holstein cow and a Hereford steer or a St. Bernard dog and a Mexican Chihuahua. To now permit the patenting of animals subjected to genetic alteration, principally via the new biotechnology commonly termed genetic engineering, could have several adverse consequences. From a scientific perspective, these include the following concerns.

1. Once genetic engineering research on animals is patent-protected, there will be a dramatic increase in animal experimentation for agricultural, biomedical, and other industrial purposes, which cannot be effectively regulated. Regulation is impossible because the outcome of many genetic experiments

cannot be predicted in relation to the animals' health and welfare and in relation to their long-term social, economic, and environmental impact. Furthermore, in many instances animals will be abnormal at birth, and generations will suffer until techniques are perfected and accidents prevented.

2. Animals subjected to genetic alteration for purely utilitarian reasons (such as to increase growth rate or milk production) will be at increased risk of suffering and related health problems.

3. Because some genetic alterations will affect animals' structure and physiology, new health problems will arise. More research will be needed to correct or treat these man-made disorders, and animals will suffer in the interim. Veterinary medicine will never be able to keep up with these problems and practice the "first" medicine—prevention. The costs of correcting certain genetic changes harmful to the animal, but profitable to the patent holders, could be a major deterrent to alleviating animal sickness and suffering. This probably would be rationalized as economically justifiable (as is the case with intensive livestock and poultry farming practices, including selective breeding for high "performance and productivity" today).

4. Patenting could result in monopoly of genetic stock and predominance of certain genetic lines of animals. Thus there may ultimately be a loss of genetic diversity within species. This could have a significant impact on agriculture, as well as adverse social, economic, and ecological consequences.

From an ethical perspective, the patenting of animals reflects a cultural attitude toward other living creatures that is contrary to the evolving concept of the sanctity of being and the recognition of the interconnectedness of all life. The patenting of life fails to recognize living beings' inherent nature.

In other words, if we do not oppose the patenting of animals, the wholesale exploitation of the animal kingdom for purely human ends will be endorsed. Yet are not other animals ends in themselves? As humans are also animals, then logically there should be no legal constraints to prevent the patenting of techniques to genetically alter human beings, if not of human beings per se, for the benefit of society. But there are ethical constraints to protect the sanctity and dignity of human life. To permit the patenting of animals will effectively eliminate ethical constraints over genetically altering them for the purported benefit of society. Such a utilitarian "commoditizing" attitude toward nonhuman life reflects the ethical blindness of the times and indicates a purely human–centered worldview.

This worldview is in part responsible for the continuing destruction of the environment and the extinction of plant and animal species (which, ironically, some biotechnologists believe could actually be corrected via genetic engineering!).

In conclusion, if the patenting of genetically altered animals is permitted, the wholesale industrialized exploitation of the animal kingdom will be sanctioned, protected, and intensified. Our control and transformation of life and of the creative process to serve purely human ends will accelerate, and, the end of the natural world, as many see it, will result.

In order to see how this may come about, we must not look at genetic engineering in isolation or try to reduce the issue to a simplistic right-or-wrong, for-or-against question. This industrialized commercial exploitation of life must be seen and felt in a much broader context of what we are doing to the natural world and to the created order. The Earth is being turned into a desecrated and polluted wasteland through the synergism of the desperate poverty of the many and the insatiable greed of the few.

Currently many people view the whole of creation as made for humanity's own exclusive use. With this mind-set, the application of genetic engineering biotechnology will accelerate the now-unnatural pace and direction of evolution of life on this planet and guarantee the end of the natural world.

In creating genetically altered life forms, the bioengineer plays God. A society that would accept the patenting of genetically altered animals and a government agency that would regard such creatures as "new" life forms assumes dominion over God. The Greeks recognized this as a cardinal sin, which they called *hubris*: arrogance.

I believe it is the height of human arrogance to regard genetically modified animals as patentable by their "creator-owners." They are not "new" life forms, because no scientist has yet been able to create life. They are simply modifications of existing life forms, whose future is imperiled now on many fronts.

Proponents of genetic engineering and of the patenting of genetically altered animals are quick to state that humans have been altering animals genetically, through the relatively slow process of selective breeding and cross-breeding, for thousands of years. Yet ethically and scientifically speaking, this is not a valid historical precedent. Genetic engineering is of a wholly different order of magnitude. In traditional breeding practices, genes cannot be exchanged between unrelated species, as is the case with so-called transgenic manipulations. Furthermore, genetic changes can be wrought very rapidly through genetic engineering, while in selective breeding changes take much time and many generations of animals.

Yet it is significant that proponents of genetic engineering and of the patenting of animals use the example of selective and cross-breeding in the earlier domestication of animals to support their case. The term domestication means "to tame, to accustom to home life." Such domestication of animals, through selective breeding and socialization to humans in early life, is very different from their wholesale industrial exploitation through genetic engineering and patenting.

Biotechnology has placed us on the threshold of gaining absolute control over the life process itself. It is as imprudent to assume that all technology is bad and vainly seek the total prohibition of the inevitable as it is to become entranced by the utopian promises of biotechnology and oppose any questioning and public debate on this issue. The scientific "priesthood" of the technocracy is neither evil nor infallible. But what is urgently needed is a more open public form on this issue, even while the biotechnology industry and government work to create "an environment of public acceptance" (to paraphrase a recent symposium held at the National Academy of Sciences in Washington, D.C.!). We also need legislation to prohibit the patenting of all life until scientific serendipity, the profit motive, and the ethical sensibility of our common senses are considered.

It has been said that where there is no vision, the people shall perish, just as shall those who forget their history. Those who envision some future utopia through genetic engineering —and there are many who do so, this is the most outstanding growth and investment industry of the 1980s—may well be suffering from what Father Thomas Berry calls "technological entrancement." As he sees it, rather than "reinventing" ourselves to assume a more creative planetary role, this entrancement leads us to re-create the world in our own image to serve all our needs, no matter how spurious. As history teaches us, the consequences have been highly destructive and even injurious to ourselves. Hence the importance of ethical sensibility—"the final choice between suicide or adoration," according to Jesuit priest and theologian Pierre Teilhard de Chardin.

While some may not see the advent of genetic engineering and the patenting of life as apocalyptic, or even as heralding a future utopia, it would be wise for all of us to find the middle way between the extremes of probability and delusion. And that middle way is not simply to condone and regulate all genetic engineering research on living beings, but to consider each project on a case-by-case basis. The patenting of animals would impair this reasoned and sensible approach because proprietary interests would prohibit outside oversight and censorship.

The principles and percepts of democracy are at odds with members of the technocracy who have claimed both economic necessity and divine sanction to justify "scientific freedom" and no oversight or regulation of genetic engineering. Recently the biotechnology industry has flagrantly and repeatedly violated government regulations (which are minimal at best and poorly enforced) controlling the release of genetically engineered living organisms into the environment. This cavalier attitude is reflected in the remarks to me by one member of the National Institutes of Health Recombinant DNA Advisory Committee: "No regulatory guidelines are needed for the biotech industry since, after all, we haven't had any major ecological or public health catastrophe in the last five or ten years."

This same committee endorsed the view that animals have no inherent nature (which is an aspect of their "beingness," that Aristotle called their *telos*). Instead they insisted that *telos* means death or extinction. And logically, therefore, because the fate of animals is death or extinction (and because they have no inherent nature, or soul, but are basically similar chemical-genetic processes expressed in diverse forms and functions), there is nothing morally wrong with genetic engineering. Thus from this mechanistic and simplistic perspective supporters reason that the genetic engineering of animals is not an ethical issue.

It is frightening to realize that the nation's main scientific intelligensia shared, without a dissenting voice, this utilitarian attitude toward nonhuman life.

If we allow this attitude to prevail and do not confront it publicly, the end of the natural world will ensue. The public is confused and propagandized, if not hypnotized, by the hype of high-tech genetic engineering. Promises of unlimited food for all, freedom from all diseases, and perhaps even immortality have dazzled uninformed citizens.

This kind of hype panders to the fears of people who fear death and disease and promises great revenues for those who would invest in this new industry.

We should also reflect on the fact that there is a strong connection between the rise in birth defects and genetic disorders in all industrial societies and the presence of teratogenic and mutagenic agrichemicals and industrial pollutants in our air, food, and water. Applying genetic engineering to humans to correct these health problems in the future would be bad, albeit profitable, medicine. As I've stated many times, the "first" medicine is prevention. We should therefore begin to clean up our environment and the food chain. If medical genetic engineering is accepted as a panacea, it will become a flourishing new industry that will be utilized by a sickened populace in order to adapt to an increasingly poisoned and uninhabitable planet.

The biomedical industry will play upon public fear to block all attempts to prohibit the patenting of animals. Yet medical advances have been made in the past without animal models and genetic engineering techniques. In fact, patenting in this area could actually inhibit medical progress because, for proprietary reasons, research findings between privately funded laboratories and university research institutions would not be shared. Considerable unnecessary and costly duplication of research would result in this competitive rather than collaborative research atmosphere.

If we do not exercise this newly acquired power over the genes of life with the wisdom that comes from humility and compassion for all living beings and respect for the ecological interdependence and interconnectedness of all of life, the costs to all will far outweigh the benefits to the few.

I believe congressional legislation should prohibit the privatization of genetic engineering of animals through the patent process. The greater good can only be assured if we, as a society, continue to hold to the principles of democracy. In the context of genetic engineering, this amounts to a *transspecies* democracy. We must respect the rights and sanctity of all sentient beings who are part of the same creation and ecological community as we. By logical extension, they are therefore part of the same community of moral consideration and ethical concern as we, and they are thus entitled to equal and fair consideration.

NATURE-CONSERVATION AND BIOTECHNOLOGY

If congressional legislation does not rescind the ruling of the U.S. Patent and Trademark Office that all genetically engineered animal species can be patented, the indirect impact on wildlife worldwide will be devastating. The patenting of genetically modified animals will accelerate the rate of destruction of wildlife habitats. Through biotechnology, farm animals will be modified genetically so that they will be able to adapt to and expand into currently unsuitable tropical, arid, and swamp habitats. And they will be endowed with resistance to such diseases as trypanosomiasis and Rift Valley fever.

This final transformation of remaining wilderness areas (followed by the rising wave of human overpopulation) will be intensified further by the global agribusiness system. Its patented, genetically engineered plants and world monopoly of seed stock and control over who will grow what for export will take over. Cash crops for export are of little benefit to the farmers of multinational corporate colonial agriculture. These once-self-sufficient peasant farmers now use dangerous pesticides, many of which are so harmful that they are banned for use in their countries of origin. Soon they will be using bacterial pesticides that petrochemical companies are developing as a substitute because fossil fuel reserves are dwindling. Petroleum is used in the manufacture of poisonous pesticides (which were developed from World War II poison-gas warfare) and also ozone-layer-destroying nitrogenous fertilizers that intensify global warming. The petrochemical companies are only now begrudgingly acknowledging that pesticides devastate wildlife populations and threaten all terrestrial and aquatic ecosystems worldwide. We now have pesticide rain and fog, pesticide drinking water, and pesticide mother's milk. The entire food chain and chain of life has been contaminated. And the soils are disappearing, losing their nutrients, eroding as the deserts expand and the icecaps melt from global warming, into the dying oceans.

The new pesticides and fertilizers from genetically engineered bacteria, along with herbicide- and disease-resistant seeds and feed-efficient, disease-resistant livestock will mean the genetic contamination and mass annihilation of nondomesticated-plant and animal life.

Wild "stock"—genetic reserves of plants and animals, seeds, sperm, and ova—will be preserved: We already have our zoos, herbaria, aquariums, and wildlife sanctuaries and "critical bioregions." Genetic engineering laboratories have spread hopes around the world of more profits, more food, more children, and less sickness and death.

These are *false* hopes. The human species cannot be healthy or fulfilled in a totally transformed, unnatural, and thus dehumanizing world, one that is also poisoned and exhausted. We do not need to eat meat, or at least as much as the people in the overdeveloped nations of the industrial world feel is desirable. Nor do we need to empty the seas to feed ourselves or to fatten our livestock. Nor do we need to impoverish other countries by having them raise crops for export instead of to feed themselves.

If animal patenting results in the predicted "bioexplosion" of meat-based agriculture, we may never arrest the degradation and final transformation of nature into an industrialized wasteland.

The few tropical and deciduous forests that remain will soon become genetic "banks" for the pharmaceutical and chemical industries—those remnants, that is, that are saved from the loggers, dam builders, monoculture foresters, and cattle and sheep ranchers. Beware of biotechnologists who speak of conservation. They will soon have native peoples raising selective species of wildlife and natural forest products for export. The last of the wilderness will be a "resource" for the biotech industry.

Likewise zoo animals will be (indeed they are *now* being) genetically screened, experimented on, cloned, gene-spliced, and artifically reproduced, and their germ plasm (sperm, ova, and embryos) is stored for future use—all in the name of conservation. But the funding comes primarily from those industries that now place the future of nature in grave jeopardy by having so profoundly defiled its very integrity.

Those who are actively involved in the conservation of domestic varieties of seed stock and various breeds of domesticated animals should also see the biotech industry as a major threat. The patenting of genetically engineered animals will herald the end of traditional animal breeds. New varieties of greater utility for use primarily on factory farms will result in the grad-

ual extinction of existing animal breeds and thus a further reduction in genetic biodiversity.

The biotechnology industry is potentially one of the most
serious threats to the biodiversity of planet Earth. It is a matter
of great urgency for all concerned citizens—and especially conservationists, humanitarians, real farmers, gardeners, nature lovers, ecologists, and religious people—to decry the patenting of
animals and guide the biotech industry to act responsibly for the
sake of all life on Earth.

CHAPTER 14

Reflections of a Veterinary Heretic

I decided to become a veterinarian at an early age to help alleviate and prevent animal suffering. I empathically identifed with animals' vulnerability and mortality. The death of various pets and caring for sick and injured animals and orphaned wildlife, which my parents encouraged, certainly helped strengthen my motivations to become an animal doctor.

But when I did so, I soon realized that the degree to which I could help alleviate animal sickness and suffering was limited less by my lack of skills than by the stark economic realities of veterinary practice. I was first interested in specializing in sheep that roamed the wild and beautiful moors of Derbyshire,* my home county in the United Kingdom. But economically it was prohibitive to give reasonable veterinary treatment to animals on an individual basis.

For several years I studied animal behavior, partly to avoid these hard realities of general practice and partly to satisfy my curiosity and understanding of animals.

Today I see the veterinary profession entangled in the economic web of animal exploitation, ranging from the inhumane incarceration of farm animals in industrialized factory farm sys-

---

*I would now opt to have many of them, and domestic cattle, replaced by indigenous and once-indigenous wild species.

tems of food production to the too-often needless suffering and destruction of laboratory animals in biomedical experimentation, teaching, and product safety testing.

In small (companion) animal practice, veterinarians face a relatively affluent pet-owning public that is by and large ignorant of animals' needs and rights. As the ownership of "exotic" pets that are not suited to a domesticated existence increases, so the genetically related domestogenic diseases of highly inbred varieties of cats and dogs have increased over the years since I graduated. Consumer demand for purebred animals and exotic pets has become yet another animal industry, as more people keep "pets" and more are raised on factory puppy farms and used for research purposes.

I feel that I and the profession have failed to alleviate, to any significant degree, the suffering of animals under humanity's dominion. Admittedly, advances have been made in veterinary preventive and diagnostic medicine, in surgery and therapy, but these advances have not kept up with the increasing numbers of animals subjected to stress, suffering, and disease. The veterinarian's major role today is to serve the interests of society and its ever-expanding animal industries. Economics dictate that concern for the rights, interests, and well-being of animals must take second place to the interests of the animal industries themselves.

In order to reestablish the veterinary profession's dignity and what I believe to be its primary responsibility for animals' health and well-being, all members of the profession need to take a much more radical and affirmative stance in support of animals' welfare and rights. To continue to remain silent, or to give lip-service to humane ethics while supporting inhumane animal industries (notably factory farming, horse racing, animal research and the wholesale-retail pet trade) is surely a transgression of professional ethics, unless of course the veterinarian believes that his/her primary obligation is not toward the alleviation of animal suffering, but to society. At this time, the profession seems divided on this issue as to which comes first, humans or animals. To give both equal and fair consideration is not easy.

There are some promising signs of a transformation within the profession, with the establishment of such associations as the American Association of Veterinarians for Animal Rights (AAVAR), the American Veterinary Holistic Medical Association, American Society of Veterinary Ethology, and the Animal Welfare Committee within the more conservative American Veterinary Medical Association.* Courses in veterinary schools on animal behavior, welfare science, humane ethics and animal rights philosophy, along with student associations concerned with animal welfare and rights, are auspicious beginnings. And there are many veterinarians actively participating in local and national humane society work, ranging from spay-neuter programs to humane education, legislation, and wildlife rehabilitation. Many state and federal veterinarians whose task it is to see that the Animal Welfare Act is properly enforced, although generally overworked and under-staffed, are clearly dedicated to improving the welfare of animals in society today.

In spite of these promising signs of increasing concern within the veterinary profession for the welfare and rights of animals, animal cruelty and suffering are increasing as the major animal industries have expanded over the past twenty years. Working to make these industries more humane has its own limitations, because of custom, convenience, and costs. A _reduction_ in the numbers of animals being exploited for various purposes would help reduce their overall suffering. But this would perhaps adversely affect the economic livelihood of the veterinary profession, which in many regions has too many practitioners already.

These conflicts of interest, as between economic livelihood, the needs of society, and concern for the well-being of animals, are something that each veterinarian must work out for him- or herself. They need not be mutually exclusive, although today

---

*However, the AVMA took a backward step for political if not ideological reasons when they eliminated representation by AAVAR on their Animal Welfare Committee.

they generally are. It is ultimately enlightened self-interest for society to have a reverence for all life and to treat animals with respect and compassion. And it is a challenge to the veterinary profession to resolve the moral dilemmas and conflicts of interest that stand in the way of society accepting the supreme ethic of reverence for all creatures. Idealistic, utopian, and unattainable as this ethical goal may seem, we should surely strive toward it, because ultimately it is the way by which human attitudes toward animals will be transformed and the socially accepted, institutionalized cruelty and suffering of animals will become a thing of the past. As a veterinarian, I believe this is the goal my fellow animal doctors should take, if they are truly committed to the prevention of animal suffering under humankind's dominion.

VETERINARIANS AND ANIMAL RIGHTS

Upon graduation from veterinary school, American veterinarians are usually sworn to adhere to the veterinarian's oath (as printed and distributed by the American Veterinary Medical Association [AVMA]), the first part of which reads as follows: "Being admitted to the profession of veterinary medicine, I solemnly swear to use my scientific knowledge and skills for the benefit of society through the protection of animal health, the relief of animal suffering, the conservation of livestock resources, the promotion of public health, and the advancement of medical knowledge. . . ."

This oath thus places the veterinarian's obligation toward society first—"to use my scientific knowledge for the benefit of society." In swearing to uphold such an oath, one is bound to render one's services first and foremost for the benefit not of animals but of society. The veterinarian's allegiance, concern, and priorities are thus determined by societal (and client) demands, and by the industrial and politicoeconomic imperatives of the times, rather than being linked primarily with the welfare, physical, and psychological well-being of animals. For example, if a client demands the veterinarian must crop a dog's ears or give an analgesic to a lame horse (rather than just prescribing rest) so that it can be raced, the veterinarian is obliged to consider the "rights" of the client above the "rights" of the animal. Ethically this is clearly unacceptable. The financial incentive of operating a "client-first" rather than "animal-first" business is no justification for unethical professional behavior.

Increasingly veterinarians are being called upon to make ethical, as distinct from purely professional, decisions concerning the welfare and "rights" of animals. However, it is difficult to reconcile the industrialized exploitation of animals (by the biomedical, agricultural, and fur industries especially) with the basic tenets of humane ethics. Statements made by the AVMA's Animal Welfare Committee, for example, recognize the need for humane standards in the treatment of animals, yet industrialized exploitation is regarded uncritically as an unavoidable and justifiable social necessity. This committee reflects the prevailing view that if animals are to be exploited for the benefit of society, then they should be treated as humanely as economic constraints may allow. No attention is paid to the question of societal benefit; the means do not always justify the ends, as when animals are killed or made to suffer for reasons that do not contribute significantly to the greater good, even though they are justified economically. The fur industry is a prime example.

Today there is consensus acceptance (primarily by those groups with vested interest) in the continuous tethering or close confinement of breeding sows, close confinement of laying hens in poorly designed battery cages, raising of veal calves in narrow crates, and housing of socially deprived laboratory primates in tiny cages. And because there are purported societal benefits from such practices, economic values and priorities take precedence over ethics, over humane concerns for the welfare, intrinsic worth, and rights of animals. Veterinarians and others are beginning to challenge many socially accepted forms of animal exploitation, including trapping, whaling, horse-race "doping"; certain intensive livestock and poultry husbandry practices; and the care and treatment of laboratory animals and their widespread use in testing nonessential consumables, in teaching demonstrations, and in research projects that have either little or no relevance or entail so much suffering or privation that the ends do not justify the means. The ethical costs to society in accepting unconditionally the wholesale exploitation of animals may in the long run be far greater than short-term, immediate gains, be they financial or scientific.

Yet in questioning such societal benefits, veterinarians are clearly acting contrary to their oath. Some veterinarians interpret my criticisms politically, contending that in a free-enterprise system, the only realities are utility and economics. But the sheer utility of animal exploitation and the economic incentives must be balanced by ethical considerations. Respect for animals' intrinsic worth and interests, as distinct from the extrinsic worth the market economy places upon them, requires that we treat all animals humanely. Veterinarians are in a unique position; because of their training, they are able to speak out for animals, to articulate what interests and needs—physical and psychological—animals have and which should be provided for, in order to eliminate unnecessary suffering and deprivation and to ensure their overall well-being.

The philosophies and ethics of humaneness, reverence for life, and animal rights are by and large still incompatible with the realities of our industrial society. Human rights were likewise once considered inconceivable and incompatible with the greater good, because many societies were economically dependent on slavery and other forms of human exploitation. By the same token, the wholesale exploitation of animals for the greater good is still justified on the grounds of necessity. Accepting the reality of this should not cause us to conclude that such animal exploitation is in all cases justifiable and unavoidable. Rather it should engender a deep sense of obligation, gratitude, and a commitment by individuals and society as a whole to make those personal and public sacrifices, economic and otherwise, to improve the well-being of animals under our stewardship. We should also pledge to develop alternatives to reduce drastically the magnitude of suffering, death, and destruction that we wreak on the animal kingdom.

As veterinarians, we are able to play a significant role in bringing about such a societal transformation. The first part of our oath might be rephrased: "Being admitted to the veterinary profession, I solemnly swear to use my scientific knowledge and skills for the benefit of *animals through relief of suffering*, to benefit society through the protection of animal health, the conservation of livestock *and wildlife* resources, the promotion of public health, *responsible animal care and humane ethics*, and the advancement of medical knowledge . . ."

VETERINARY ETHICS—FROM ANIMAL RIGHTS TO DEEP ECOLOGY

The question of animal rights has generated considerable debate within the veterinary profession over the past half decade or so. But animal and human interests and rights need to be seen in a broader, ecological framework, because what we do to the environment can have a significant impact on animal and human health and on the survival of animal populations and entire species. A deep ecology movement has now surfaced that as environmentalist Bill Devall describes is philosophically and politically far more radical and holistic than the traditional conservation movement.[1]

Some of the concerns and questions raised from the deep ecology perspective are relevant to veterinary ethics and practice. A major issue is the international promotion of livestock production, which is resulting in widespread deforestation, overgrazing, soil erosion, drought, and the displacement, reduction, and extinction of wildlife. It has been estimated that within the next forty years, the human and livestock biomass is likely to represent 40 percent of the total animal biomass on earth, "all of this being at the inevitable expense of more than an equivalent biomass of wildlife" according to Professor A. H. Westing.[2]

Deforestation in Australia and South and Central America, to provide land to raise beef for the U.S. fast-food industry, could have long-term adverse affects on the world's climate. The United Nations Environmental Council now recognizes veterinary services as a major contributing factor to the problem of worldwide desertification.

Erecting hundreds of miles of fences to separate wild animals from livestock in Botswana in attempts to control foot and mouth disease in the cattle industry (beef is exported to serve Europe's growing fast-food market) has resulted in the death of millions of wildebeest and other wildlife whose traditional migration routes have been blocked.[3]

Would a well-organized vaccination program be the best solution? What of the long-term impact upon wildlife and the environment of developing a vaccine to protect livestock from trypanosomiasis (to which indigenous wildlife are naturally immune)? What we regard as progress in the short term could have serious long-term consequences, not the least of which is the unabated expansion of human and livestock populations and of deforestation, extinction of nondomesticated animals and plants, overgrazing, and desertification.

While it may be misguided altruism for the veterinary profession to help increase the world's livestock biomass, it is surely imprudent to use nonrenewable resources and most available arable land to raise foodstuffs for livestock and not primarily for human consumption, as is occurring in the case of the United States.

Critics have also voiced concern over the increasing numbers of carnivorous companion animals in more affluent countries. Regardless of the fact that cats and dogs are fed "efficiently" on many by-products of the agribusiness food industry, they do require some quality animal protein, the costs of which are becoming increasingly prohibitive. As a consequence, more veterinarians are exploring the connection between pet health problems and diet.

THE PURPOSE AND FUTURE
OF VETERINARY SCHOOLS

From an animal rights perspective, it may be reasoned that veterinary schools ought not to exist—or at least not function as they do today, turning out graduates to serve the industries of animal exploitation.

It is surely unethical to make animals suffer and turn them into test substitutes to advance our technological prowess in developing ever more lethal weapons of self-destruction. And we should likewise question the ethics and morality of those who test new poisons, pesticides, predaticides, traps, and even cosmetics and nonessential household consumables on laboratory animals. Yet perhaps it is better that veterinarians do this and supervise laboratory animal care than leave it to wildlife biologists, animal and human medical scientists, technicians, and animal psychologists, who are generally untrained in veterinary medicine, surgery, and proper animal care.

Then there are veterinarians—and a dwindling number at that—who are involved in farm animal practice. For economic reasons they focus primarily on enhancing animal productivity rather than overall animal health and welfare. If they did not, then they would have long ago opposed the trend toward factory farming. And perhaps more would be in business today because there would be fewer superfarms and more midsized family farms. With more and smaller farms, more veterinarians would be needed. Yet the profession as a whole has not questioned the development of superfarms and inhumane intensive husbandry practices that are linked with the bankruptcy of the family farm and the economic crisis of U.S. agribusiness—witness the advertising in the *Journal of the American Veterinary Medical Association* by drug companies that promote animal farm-factories.

Certainly, veterinarians should treat animal diseases, alleviate their suffering, and as my Royal Veterinary College of London motto urges: *Veniente occurite morbo* (Go to meet disease as it comes).

But should not veterinarians serve animals first and help

prevent disease before it comes? To serve society first, by treating the domestogenic diseases and suffering rather than focusing on their prevention, is in accord with the self-serving oath of the AVMA to serve society first. Little wonder that animal rightists and many humanitarian animal lovers see veterinarians as the mercenaries and "pimps" of the animal industries—of the pet trade, the biomedical industry, agribusiness, and so on.

How accurate indeed is this perception? Committee reports and various other publications document the lamentable response of both the British and American Veterinary Medical associations to the well-documented abuses and suffering of factory farm animals and their essentially uncritical and unconditional endorsement of vivisection and other types of animal exploitation. This worldview does not serve the veterinary profession well, not simply because it is unethical, anthropocentric, and utilitarian, but because it makes many veterinarians place the interests of those who own and otherwise exploit animals for emotional and economic purposes above those of their animal patients.

A 1980 survey of veterinarians' views on a number of animal welfare and rights-related topics, conducted by the College of Veterinary Medicine, Michigan State University, has revealed some rather interesting insights. Of the more than 450 veterinarians who responded to the questionnaire, 65 percent worked primarily with small animals. There was a strong overall agreement that veterinarians have a duty to promote pet sterilization. However, a significant majority of veterinarians surveyed believed that humane societies should *not* be allowed to operate low-cost spay-neuter clinics. Furthermore, a significant majority believed that economic considerations can properly outweigh humane considerations in treatment decisions and that a veterinarian's primary responsibility is to the client, and not to the patient. The majority of veterinarians did not agree that human beings do not need to kill animals to obtain proper nutrition. (Although ironically they did agree that it is wrong to destroy the habitat of wild species.) Clearly, few respondents seemed to realize that in raising livestock for human consumption and in using land to raise feed grains, we are destroying wild species' habitats.

It was encouraging to note that only 7 percent of the veterinarians surveyed did not agree that an animal's ability to feel pain makes it worthy of moral consideration. Also a significant majority of veterinarians believed that some research using animals is unjustified and that farm animal husbandry practices that improve animals' productivity are not always in the animals' best interest. Most veterinarians felt that the confinement of wild animals in zoos for educational and scientific purposes was justified. However, they were divided in opinion over whether or not some species of animals have rights. Twenty percent agreed very strongly, 19 percent agreed strongly, 17 percent agreed somewhat, 14 percent agreed slightly, and 30 percent did not agree at all that some animal species have rights. Most veterinarians surveyed believed that it is all right to euthanize a companion animal for nonmedical reasons and that using anesthetized live animals for teaching surgery to students is essential for training veterinarians. The majority also felt that hunting wild animals is a legitimate means of managing wild populations.

As a veterinarian, I find these responses from my colleagues both encouraging and disheartening. In some areas there is considerable ignorance, as in the belief that it is necessary to kill animals to obtain proper nutrition; in other areas, such as recognizing that animals have rights, the profession is clearly divided. To be charitable, I would say that while the results of this survey do not cast any doubts on the profession's technical ability to deal with animal health problems, it does reveal certain inconsistencies in the profession's ability or readiness to take a strong and united position on many of the ethical issues concerning animal welfare and the exploitation of animals in society today.

As a whole, the veterinary profession seems divided on whether its allegiance is first for the animals or first for society. If allegiance to society becomes the consensus over the next decade, *veterinarians should perhaps drop the title of veterinary doctor* (in the United States) and surgeon (in the United Kingdom) and call themselves animal health and production maintenance technicians. To some this may be offensive. However, as a member of the British and American Veterinary Medical associations, I am offended by how these organizations—the voices of the profession—condone animal exploitation in all its diverse forms for the benefit of society without question, while merely giving lip service to what I regard as veterinarians' prime obligation: to alleviate unnecessary and otherwise avoidable animal suffering. We do not need factory farms—they are not efficient. Meat is not an essential dietary staple for humans. Nor do we need or can we justify the continuing propagation of purebred animals with genetic defects. People do not need to kill wildlife for pleasure and profit. As outlined elsewhere, much animal research is scientifically invalid and ethically untenable. We should also question the ethics of making healthy laboratory animals sick in order to find cures for animal and human diseases. Should we not learn simply from treating the sick and injured?

Is it right to make one or a few suffer for the benefit of many? Is not the life of one healthy dog of equal worth to the lives of many dogs? If the ethic of reverence for life is to ever become a reality, then we must discard the utilily of making healthy animals sick for the benefit of many.

Those veterinarians who see humans and other animals as coequal, morally equivalent, and who endorse the extension of the Golden Rule to include how we treat other nonhuman beings are growing in number. This is enlightened self-interest and will help save and resurrect the profession to its original purpose: to heal animals and to alleviate animal suffering.

In veterinary schools more courses on animal awareness, animal welfare science and rights, deep ecology and moral philosophy are needed. But these will not transform the veterinary profession until there is a more general societal change in attitude toward animals. They were not created for our own exclusive use. They have feelings, interests, and lives of their own.

As long as animals are exploited for various purposes, their health and welfare need to be assured. The veterinary profession has played an important role here, but it has failed to challenge some forms of questionably unethical exploitation. And in placing the interests of client owners and the animal industries before those of their animal patients, the profession as a whole falls short in its conflict of interest of being what it could be: a voice for animals, dedicated to the alleviation of animal suffering under humankind's too often inhumane dominion.

It would seem that the primary purpose of veterinary schools is to produce graduate animal technicians to serve society and the animal industries. This is implicit in the AVMA's Veterinary Oath. But from the aforementioned survey, it is apparent that the profession is somewhat divided over which comes first—the interests and rights of the animals or the interests of society.

One could argue that it is not an "either/or" situation and that compromises can be made. However, I believe that organized veterinary medicine has compromised itself too far. As a consequence, the well-being and rights of millions of animals in society are placed in jeopardy.

Little wonder then that organized veterinary medicine views the economic and political ramifications of the animal rights and liberation movement as a threat. This is unfortunate but understandable. And as the movement grows, polarization intensifies. In fact, the dean of at least one veterinary school has threatened a professor who invited me to speak by saying that students would not receive any grade for their course if I were to come.

With growing public knowledge and concern over what amounts to a holocaust of the animal kingdom, the schools of veterinary medicine that endeavor to maintain and justify the status quo of the animal industries will be subject to increasing censure. And the status and dignity of the profession will be ridiculed if it continues to compromise itself by placing the interests of people before those of their animal patients and the economic interests of society before the rights of animals.

* * *

As a veterinarian, ethologist, and concerned humanitarian, I believe people should not keep animals as pets unless they know how to feed and care for them properly and provide them with veterinary care when needed, as well as routinely, for preventive medical purposes.

- I favor people keeping cats and dogs adopted from animal shelters either as adults or as kittens and puppies.

- I am in favor of knowledgeable people keeping various native species of orphaned and injured wildlife that cannot be set free, rather than keeping wild animals that have been deliberately caught, bred, or even imported for sale as pets.

- I am in favor of vegetarianism and organic farming, because of the inherent suffering and sickness of animals raised on factory farms and related harm to the environment.

- I am in favor, for scientific and human health reasons, of the phasing out of animal experimentation for human medical and other commercial-industrial military purposes. I consider it unethical for veterinary and other students to make healthy animals suffer as part of their education.

- I am in favor of the kind of stewardship of wildlife and of endangered species in captivity that is aimed at the protection and restoration of natural ecosystems rather than their "management" primarily for commercial and recreational purposes, notably monoculture forestry, hunting, and trapping.

- I am in favor of the development of appropriate and sustainable technologies, industries, and food-

production systems consonant with the principle of
humane planetary stewardship that recognizes the
right of all living things to a whole and healthy environment and the right of each living thing to equal
and fair consideration.

Animals need to be liberated from all forms of human domination and exploitation, from horsebreaking and dog fighting,
to vivisection and hunting. They are not commodities, nor were
they created for our own use and unjust dominion. Rather they
are entrusted to us. We demean our own humanity when we
fail to give them equal and fair consideration. Humility and
compassionate reverence for all life are essential aspects of a wise
and enlightened planetary stewardship. If we do not stop the
poisoning and destruction of nature and the holocaust of the
animal kingdom and show reverence to all life, no matter what
economic or other justification we may have to the contrary,
their fate will be ours also.

CHAPTER 15

Toward a Recognition of Animal

Rights

While it may be ethical and/or ecologically sound to exploit certain animal species, the extent of their commercial exploitation has become incompatible with their overall welfare. The reasons are many and have already been documented in this book. The industrial system is driven by an ideology that has come to place economic interests and the iron law of supply and demand over the autonomy, intrinsic value, and interests of the individual, be it human or animal. This ideology purports to serve the "greater good" of society as a whole, which historically and in contemporary technocratic societies has led to the justification of human oppression and the violation of individual rights. It is also the rationalization that is used to justify any form of animal exploitation for the benefit of society. For example, while it is recognized that modern intensive farm animal husbandry systems designed to maximize production efficiencies do not maximize the well-being of individual animals, supposedly such ethical and health costs are offset by the gains from economies of scale and are justified to provide society with a relatively cheap and plentiful supply of farm-animal products. Such an attitude toward animals and nature is biological fascism.

In the human sphere, we are burdened with the consequences of this ideology. The symptoms include poverty, unemployment, environmental degradation, pollution, increasing human sickness, and spiraling inflation. In the animal domain, we find suffering, disease, habitat destruction, and accelerating extinction of species, all portents of a global crisis. Examples of major commercial animal industries include factory farming; fur ranching; "managing" wildlife for trapping and hunter recreation; the exotic pet trade; sealing, whaling, and fishing; horse racing; rodeos; biomedical research and the testing of new drugs, consumer products, agrichemicals, and other hazardous industrial chemicals and pollutants; and the most recently developed industry, puppy mills for the mass production of purebred dogs. As the scale of any of these enterprises is directly proportional to the magnitude of capital investment, so the size of each industry is correlated with a quantitative increase in potential and actual animal suffering. This can be attributed in part to the fact that the intrinsic value and interests of animals as individuals are secondary to the economic necessity of maximizing returns on investments (euphemistically termed "efficiency" in the livestock industry) and to the ideology of some societal benefit (furs to wear, meat to eat, deer to shoot, "safe" levels of pesticides and radiation to absorb after toxicity tests on animals, and so on).

Veterinarians, wildlife biologists, and farm-animal scientists are in a paradoxical position. Many are concerned about animal health and welfare if not rights, yet at the same time they are economically dependent on, if not also ideologically aligned with, those industries whose commercial exploitation may jeopardize animals' overall welfare. This paradoxical position is evident in the attitudes and policies of those professional organizations that are aligned with the major animal industries. As discussed in the last chapter, the U.S. Veterinarian's Oath clearly states that veterinarians are obligated to use their skills for the "benefit of society" first and foremost. But what veterinarian or scientist can morally defend puppy mills, indiscriminate predator control, overcrowded battery-caged laying hens, and socially deprived, environmentally impoverished laboratory primates? Economic justifications can be easily made, but they neither answer nor reconcile the ethical question.

In some instances this contradiction can be reconciled by applying the utilitarian philosophical principle of whether or not a given act (or way of treating animals) contributes to the greater good. Some animal industries most certainly do not, especially fur ranching and trapping, hunting, sealing, whaling, puppy mills, and exotic pet establishments, horse racing, rodeos, roadside zoos, and so on. This leaves us with three areas of animal exploitation to analyze: fishing, animal research, and factory farming.

The plight of the dolphin is but the tip of the commercial fishing iceberg, because the dolphin is threatened (like all ocean species) by yet another industry: tuna fishing. And the entire ocean ecosystem is endangered by pollution (from agrichemicals, industrial wastes, and excess raw sewage) and overfishing.

The plight of laboratory animals is only the tip of yet another industrial iceberg, wherein animals are used to test nonessential consumables. They are also employed to test what are often redundant—or ineffective and frequently harmful—human (and animal) drugs and vaccines (that are nonetheless profitable) and also to test dangerous agrichemicals and industrial pollutants (the more serious findings about these agents are often suppressed). As animal "models," they are used to develop new and often very elaborate, and therefore costly, therapies and diagnostic procedures that only the rich (and well insured) can afford. (Insurance rates are increasing markedly at present.) And they are also utilized in trivial and irrelevant experiments that are often performed under atrocious conditions, especially in small colleges and private institutions.

The plight of farm animals represents another burgeoning nightmare that is part of the industrial revolution of animal exploitation. Hog confinement operations are so disease-making that farm workers, who spend but a fraction of their time (compared with their pigs) in overstocked and so-called environmentally controlled buildings, can suffer acute and potentially serious respiratory problems. Due to economic pressures, even humane farmers are forced to adopt inhumane methods of production, such as placing too many animals in one pen or cage. The enclosures themselves are highly unnatural, impoverished environments (no matter how clean or filthy they may be). This creates health risks, which mandate more costly environmental engineering and more intense drug use, but more profits for the drug and other industries that vigorously defend factory farming methods. Many farmers (especially those who have been forced out of business) do not endorse such methods; they generally regard them as inhumane.

Do the justifications that fall under the rubric of utility negate all moral arguments and ethical concerns over these kinds of wholesale animal exploitation? In the law courts, the answer is still yes. Animals are conceptualized as blacks, women, and children once were, as having no rights. They are merely "things," objects of personal or collective property, mere commodities.

But we need to recognize animals' rights for the same reason society now recognizes the rights of other minorities. And in so doing, we will become more human and will better comply with the Judeo-Christian injunctions of charity, respect for life, and benevolent self-sacrifice. As Albert Schweitzer wrote in _The Teachings of Reverence for Life_[1]: "Whenever animals are impressed into the service of man, everyone of us should be mindful of the toll we are exacting. We cannot stand idly by and see animals subjected to unnecessary harshness or deliberate mistreatment. We cannot say it is not our business to interfere. On the contrary, it is our duty to intervene in the animals' behalf."

When we step back and look at all the profitable major animal industries, we discover a common thread: increasingly intensive exploitation and degradation of animal life, which thereby increases the rates of turnover of life and of entropy (the rate of destruction and consumption of nonrenewable resources, notably fossil fuels, fresh water, and topsoil). At the same time, a rapid reduction in biological diversity is occurring in both plant and animal species. This latter problem will be soon "fixed," in a very narrow sense, by the new technological wonder of biotechnology (which allows us to create new life forms). Jeremy Rifkin terms this process "algeny, which is the extension of medieval alchemy into modern times."[2] We already have a rapidly growing genetic engineering industry, with its crowd of patents and lawyers. An increasingly industrialized monopoly and a further concentration of control over life will result, leading ultimately not to human well-being and an eventual relinquishing of the need to control, but rather to an ever-worsening vicious cycle in which everything must be controlled and monitored in order to ensure the survival of a global technocratic empire. And for the privilege of survival, each life form will pay more in suffering. Even more artificial and ecologically unsound or inhumane sets of needs, primarily for personal profit, will be created, and an even more artificially controlled and unhealthy environment for us to live in and to adapt ourselves to will arise.

Agriculture and medicine, like other industrial systems, such as wildlife "management," profit from *inappropriate* and *improperly applied* technological control over life. Linked with this treadmill of increasing dependence on such controls, we find such rationalizations as deer need to be shot, bobcats trapped, and coyotes poisoned to control their numbers; confined swine need air conditioning and more drugs and vaccines to maintain health, and so on.

Blaming science and technology for these problems is as wrong as believing that we will find all the answers in science and technology. In fact, the problems and their answers lie within the same bedrock of ethical values from which all religious and political ideologies are born and from which personal responsibility, expressed as empathetic concern and compassion, can be awakened. Responsibility depends on a sense of obligation and indebtedness (to nature and all creation). But when we control nature and manipulate life forms, whether through selective breeding (domestication) or genetic engineering (biotechnology), we come to regard life as our own creation and property. There is only one way to pay back such an enormous debt to nature. In order for nature—and with it, the future—to be secure once more, we must relinquish many of our consumptive habits and demands. Rifkin urges that we make ourselves more vulnerable in order that the rest of existence can become more secure. We should choose to serve nature, even though we are able to dominate and extract what we need from her.

This is easier said than done. We are so comfortably blinded by our own rationalizations, denials, and self-limiting ideologies that we do not recognize that we are, as a self-determining species, as much responsible for our own destiny as we are the source of our own suffering. A first step might be admitting that we do cause unnecessary destruction and suffering in the animal kingdom. A self-redeeming sacrifice is necessary to restore balance and harmony among us, nature, and the rest of creation. The quality of human life, if not our future survival, entails recognizing how the "animal connection" relates to our own well-being and acknowledging that this connection should be one of empathy and responsible compassion, rather than one-sided exploitation and control.

The sacrifices that we must make in our dealings with animals necessitate the application of the ethical principles of animal rights developed in this book. Basically, it is morally wrong to kill animals or to subject them to suffering and/or privation for trivial purposes. Application of this principle would virtually eliminate many animal industries, such as trophy hunting, trapping, and the sale and ownership of exotic pets. It also would mandate a radical reassessment of the rightness, and real benefit to society, of much biomedical research on animals and also of the use of animals for teaching and testing purposes. Likewise, our dietary habits need to be reevaluated in terms of health, environmental impact, use of resources, and economic considerations, because these are the primary rationalizations for keeping farm animals under unacceptable conditions. One of our highest national priorities should be a reduction in the production and average per-capita consumption of meat and of all other farm-animal products.

One virtue in the being anthropomorphic serves to mitigate

all its limitations. This virtue is a correct recognition that all living things share the will to live and common events, such as birth, sickness, and death. These shared events give us a mortal sense of affinity and of a vulnerability to forces that are still beyond our comprehension, but which science is quickly de-mystifying and technology is destructively endeavoring to control. Because of our anxiety and inadequate way of coping with mortal fears, we cannot "let live and die." The recognition of the shared will to live engenders understanding, humility, and compassion. When we cease to recognize this attribute in other living beings, the problems of inhumanity arise, for we become indifferent to them and have no empathetic connection. Life then ceases to have meaning; its only significance diminishes to thoughts about how we might best exploit and control it for our own ends, regardless of the consequences.

Feeling connected with nature and the community of animals can give us a deep sense of security and belonging. This sense of security has a profound influence on our attitude toward our own death and thus on our perceptions of and attitude toward nature and animals, because through such connectedness we may know immortality. Our disconnectedness from nature increases our alienation from the world and thus increases our sense of aloneness, vulnerability, anxiety, and the need for more power and control. We then become alienated from nature, God, and reality.

THE QUESTION OF ANIMAL RIGHTS

The logic of animal rights philosophy, as I see it, is based on the emotive (sympathetic and empathetic) and intuitive appreciation of the beingness of animals. It is anathema to the emotionally closed-off, rational egotism and scientific imperialism of these times that undergird the politics of biological fascism. When we seek to profit at the expense of others' natural rights to be, this political power hierarchy opposes entelechy and the telic completion, self-realization, and fulfillment of other living things. For human beings, this culminates in self- or God realization. Such growth takes more than courage to be; it also takes love, and this is what my emotivist philosophy of animal rights and deep ecology recognizes and exalts: love of our fellow creatures, who like we "have groaneth and travaileth until now," as St. Paul observed.

And what is this "now" but the realization that, as the philosopher Krishnamurti observed, "What _is_, is sacred." This is why animals, by virtue of their existence and of their beingness (rather than "thing"ness) have natural rights. Realization of the significance of animals having inherent and inalienable rights opens the door to a transspecies democracy. Only in such a society can humanity realize its humanity. It is a society of compassion; of enlightened self-interest; of economic stability, freedom, and unlimited potential. It is a paradisical ectopia (where human and nonhuman, wild and domestic, plant and animal communities live in the harmony of nature's dynamic equilibrium), not some human-centered technocratic utopia of global power and control. There is no hierarchical principle, which, in its insecurity and ignorance—and above all, its _emotional insensitivity_—causes so much suffering to those in the weaker strata of human society and to the animal kingdom.

To deny animals rights but to say we have certain obligations or duties toward them (such as to treat them humanely) is patronizing and contradictory. If animals are entitled to be treated humanely, then is not such an entitlement the animal's right? Natural and customary rights are based on social (rather than legal) recognition of animals' entitlement: It is one of our moral obligations (a derivative of natural law, following Hobbes and Locke), hence it is a "moral right." It is not a duty only if we are going to exploit animals (that is, a kind of exchange or implicit contract) but an obligation quite independent of what extrinsic value we may place upon them. Whether we exploit animals or not, it is logically consistent and emotionally satisfying to respect their rights. The self-serving and intellectually and emotionally impoverished arguments used to deny animal rights and to give lip service to humaneness and animal welfare codes is the height of hubris and hypocrisy.

Many people feel that animals cannot have rights and that it is better to speak of human obligations toward animals, because only humans can claim rights. However, the concept of animal rights focuses attention on animals. Aside from its political overtones, it forces us to change our perspective from a human-centered one to one that considers the needs, wants, interests, and intrinsic value of other animals. Philosopher Peter Singer in *Animal Liberation* states: "The capacity for suffering and enjoyment is a prerequisite for having interests at all."[3] His utilitarian hierarchy of subjective capacities is limited, though valuable, in breaking down the species barrier between humans and other animals. What is also needed in animal rights philosophy is reference to kinship, animals' intrinsic value, and concern for the environment. The Golden Rule that we should treat others as we would have them treat us is enlightened self-interest. In truth, there are no morally valid reasons why we should treat animals in ways that we would not have them treat us. Though some things may cause them to suffer more or less than we, suffering is suffering. Thus animals should be given equal and fair consideration, which is their right and our obligation. Without such egalitarianism, how can we claim any rights over them? As animal rights philosopher professor Bernard Rollin insists, Might does not make right.

ANIMAL RIGHTS: LEGAL OR NATURAL?

Critics of the concept of animals having rights tend to think only in terms of legal rights. However, there is another category of rights termed *natural rights*, which (according to Webster's Third New International Dictionary) would hold in the absence of organized government (and therefore of legal rights per se). Significantly, under the many different meanings of rights listed in Webster's, a right can mean "a power, privilege, or immunity vested in an animal or a group of animals (as by custom): (grazing rights of a herd of antelope)."

It is important therefore not to condemn the concept of animal rights by perceiving them only in a legalistic framework.

Animals also have (or should have) natural rights that we, as a matter of *custom*, respect and uphold as unwritten law.

Seen this way, animal rights are mainly moral injunctions that constitute a humane, and hopefully also an ecologically sound, ethic. So it can be argued that while a pig may have no right, legal or natural, not to be eaten, it does have a legal right under the Humane Slaughter Act to be killed humanely. While there is no law that also stipulates that pigs should be raised humanely,* it is as much their natural right to be treated humanely as it is also a tradition or custom of sound animal husbandry. We therefore have a moral, rather than legal, obligation to ensure that their right to humane treatment is upheld. If a pig, or any other animal, had no needs and could neither suffer nor feel pain, it would have no interests, and therefore no rights. But clearly pigs and other creatures do have interests. When we have control over some or all of those interests, (as farmers, hunters, and so on), we must pay the price, so to speak, of such dominion, by accepting that we do have both moral and legal obligations toward these animals. We would not have these obligations if animals had neither natural nor legal rights, or if animals had no interests or intrinsic worth, or if they had no extrinsic worth to us and we did not need them for anything and simply let them be. But society is dependent on animals in many ways. For this reason, society as a whole must recognize that animals do indeed have rights that should be upheld and respected by all.

In many countries people have a legal obligation to uphold certain animal rights, such as the right to life of endangered species and the right to humane treatment of laboratory and companion animals (under the Endangered Species and Animal Welfare Acts).

The law thus recognizes that other entities have various interests or rights (such as not to suffer), which we, as stewards, guardians or trustees, have a moral and legal obligation to re-

---

*Although there are state laws that stipulate animals should *not* be treated cruelly, no laws specify how they *should* be raised and treated.

spect. However, the law does not yet recognize that animals have legal rights, because they are not regarded as persons entitled to legal standing. This outmoded view needs to be challenged in the courts and changed, as there are countless legal and ethical inconsistencies (see chapter 1).

The law regards animals more as objects of property than as "legal persons" entitled to certain "rights." The law goes so far as to recognize that animals, like any other property, can be *harmed*; that it is morally wrong to harm an animal (to be cruel to it); that some animals have a legal entitlement to life (endangered species) or to a humane death (domestic animals). But as *objects of property* the legal standing of animals is still higher than their legal standing as *subjects of moral concern*. Also in animal research (where animal suffering is justified), animals are more often regarded as *objects of utility* (delicate biomachinery for study) than as subjects warranting moral concern first and foremost. While the law does not yet recognize that animals should be regarded first as subjects of moral concern and only secondarily as objects of property/utility, there is a deep cultural recognition that animals have intrinsic worth and natural rights. This provides the ethical basis for reversing the priority of legally recognizing animals as mere objects of utility/property and as subjects of moral concern.

It also creates a legal and ethical conundrum when concerned individuals "take the law into their own hands" to protect the natural rights of animals through acts of civil disobedience or commit a felony by stealing such animals. As there are legal grounds for justifiable homicide (in self-defense), so too should there be legal grounds for such ethically justifiable acts of "animal liberation." As the law makes provision for citizen's arrest, so too should the law consider fairly the well-intended interventions of those who believe animals are being mistreated and take the law into their own hands. It would be unjust to prosecute such persons for having committed felonies. Christopher Stone has offered a similar argument to change the legal standing of trees, lakes, wilderness, and other natural "objects," which, although they may not suffer, can indeed be harmed and have, like sentient animals, their own intrinsic worth.[6]

In sum, as Professor Bernard Rollin[8] has stated:

> The animal rights advocate argues as follows: "If the concept of rights is embodied in our legal system as a protection for the individual human being on the basis of his or her being a moral object, then some such protection must be granted to animals as well, for we can find no difference between humans and animals that is morally relevant." This is not to say there are no differences between human beings and animals. There are of course myriad such differences. The point is that these have nothing to do with morality; the entire history of our moral and legal systems may be seen as a process of recognizing the irrelevance of such differences.

ANIMAL RIGHTS AND SPECIESISM

Several critics of contemporary animal rights philosophy have attempted to discredit the notion that animals can have rights. They point out that if animals had rights, then they could be put on trial, as occurred in medieval times. Such trials were ridiculous. So, by extension, it is argued that the concept of animals having rights is no less ridiculous.

It is fallacious to say that rights cannot be extended to a class of beings without exacting correlative duties from them (and inflicting punishment for breach of those duties). The legal status of children and mentally incompetent individuals directly contradicts that notion. Similarly, animals are not regarded as moral agents and are deemed incapable of forming the intent to breach duties. Modern law can grant rights, extend protections, and, at the same time, modify the application of criminal and civil liability to all three groups. Thus the approach is not new, and we need not fear a return to primitive medievalism.

While animals are not regarded as legal persons having the

standing to invoke the power of the courts, several laws, such as the Animal Welfare and Endangered Species acts, recognize their interests (to be treated humanely, to not become extinct, and so on). These interests can be interpreted as animals' natural rights, which we are morally and legally bound to respect. In the nonlegal sense, therefore, animals already have rights. That animals could eventually come to have legal standing would not necessarily mean a regression to medieval "animal trials." Agents or guardians could represent animal plaintiffs. Animals cannot speak for themselves and present their case or be expected to owe certain "duties" (as a correlative of having rights); nor can babies, mentally incompetent individuals, or comatose adults. It is only the barrier of speciesism (which is being broken down) that prevents animals from having legal standing today.

I do not claim that animals have equal rights, because many of their needs, wants, and interests are different from ours. They do not need or have any interest in a right to vote or to free speech. Still, their interests should be given equal and fair consideration in relation to our interests in exploiting them for various purposes.

To argue that only humans can have rights is "speciesism"—a term analogous to sexism and racism. There are no logical reasons for denying animals any rights while at the same time claiming rights for ourselves. Philosopher R. G. Frey in his contentious book *Interests and Rights: The Case Against Animals*[4] argues that animals cannot have rights because they cannot have interests. They cannot have interests he argues because they lack emotions and desires. They cannot have emotions and desires because they are not aware and cannot think about what they feel and want. And they cannot think because they cannot talk. Studies of animal behavior, psychology, and brain physiology make Frey's statements clearly prejudicial and ignorant. Yet he follows the tradition of Immanuel Kant who wrote, over a century before him, that "So far as animals are concerned, we have no direct duties. Animals are not self-conscious, and are there merely as a means to an end. The end is man."

Enlightenment thinking, with its emphasis on social contracts, rational consent, legality, and justice, excluded animals from the scope of moral concern, except insofar as recognizing that deliberate mistreatment of animals was a sign of bad character and could lead to inhumanity toward humans (which is true). Others have argued that animals cannot have rights because they cannot establish contracts or be morally responsible agents, but this confuses legal with moral rights. Philosopher Jean-Jacques Rousseau called these *natural rights* and wrote in opposition to Kant's egotistical utilitarian view that

> As they [animals] partake, however, in some measure of our nature, in consequence of the sensibility wherewith they are endowed, they ought to partake of natural right; so that mankind is subject to a kind of obligation even toward the brutes. It appears, in fact, that if I am bound to do injury to my fellow creatures, this is less because they are rational than because they are sentient beings; and this quality, being common to man and beasts, ought to entitle the latter at least to the privilege of not being wantonly ill-treated by the former.

Natural rights are synonymous with what I call moral or inherent rights* for all that is, *is* sacred from the animal and nature/environmental rights perspective. It is through respect and love that we might best begin to redeem ourselves for the "now" to which St. Paul referred is coming: the day of Judgment, ere we will destroy ourselves, "in a bang or a whimper." The first step is to be "born again" with the realization that all that is, *is* sacred and to act accordingly by respecting and upholding the rights of all living things, including our mother Earth. Denial of our duties toward all creation culminates in dominion over God, and the values and rationalizations that

---

*"Moral" implying human duty and "inherent" referring to the inherent divinity in all things.

lead to this pyramid of power with humanity at the top is the biological fascism of the anti-Christ.

FROM ANIMAL SUFFERING TO ANIMAL RIGHTS

Human health is not simply the abolition of disease. It is also the opportunity to maintain physical and mental well-being. Likewise, animal welfare is not simply the abolition of human cruelty. It also entails: (1) the right to receive equal and fair consideration; (2) the right to humane treatment at all times which includes the behavioral freedom necessary to maintain physical and emotional well-being and appropriate veterinary treatment when kept under direct human control as companions or for financial, medical and other purposes.

EQUAL CONSIDERATION AND TREATMENT

The life of an animal is of equal value to that animal, as our life is to ourselves, regardless of what extrinsic value we place on animals. Thus animals should be given equal and fair consideration—but this does not mean equal rights.

Furthermore, animals of obviously similar sentience* should be accorded the right to equal and fair treatment. The moral status of farm animals in society is rife with legal and ethical inconsistencies. A person can be prosecuted for branding a dog with a hot iron, for castrating it without an anesthetic, or for keeping it tethered or confined in a narrow pen for its entire life. But farm animals, in contrast, have no such protection.

Not only should we avoid deliberate cruelty, neglect, and suffering, but animals should be given equal and fair consideration: their basic freedoms should be recognized and provided for; and all animals of similar sentience should be given equal and fair treatment.

_____

*Animals of similar sentience have similar capacities to experience pain, deprivation, frustration, fear, anxiety, and so on.

A RIGHT NOT TO BE KILLED AND EATEN?

To claim that farm animals have a right not to be killed and eaten is surely anthropomorphic. All farm animals are prey species and ultimately will be consumed, just as all living things die and become part of the Earth and of the bodies of other living things. To claim that a person has no right to eat an animal is biologically absurd. An enlightened person, however, eats with conscience. This can be done by eating animal products from animals treated less inhumanely than others (such as broiler chickens over veal calves and eggs from free-range hens over eggs from battery-caged laying hens), and also by eating less or even *no* farm-animal produce. This latter option results from the negative impact on the environment of overproduction and consumption of animal produce under the current ecologically unsound and drug-dependent agribusiness system of food production.

ADDITIONAL CONSIDERATIONS

Animals have additional rights that are worth consideration. First, the benefits derived from our assumed right to exploit animals should be counterbalanced by minimizing the costs to the animals in terms of their lives and suffering or deprivation. Few forms of animal exploitation meet these criteria. Currently only the use of draft animals in labor-intensive agriculture that are properly husbanded and given veterinary care as needed, the keeping of animals as companions, and using animals in essential, preventively oriented biomedical research that benefit animals as much as people would qualify.

In addition to awakening concern and respect for the rights of animals as individuals and as species (reflected in state anti-cruelty laws and the Federal Endangered Species Act), the rights and interests of *social groups* of animals also need consideration. For instance, random killing of whales or wolves will mean that survivors may suffer from the loss of companions and young suffer and die following their parents' deaths. The social group itself may also be so disrupted as to jeopardize its survival.

All wild animals also have the right to sanctuary and to a healthy environment. This right places ethical constraints on agricultural, wildlife management, and other practices, notably overgrazing and predator control on rangeland and hunting, trapping, and other consumptive and destructive human activities in wildlife sanctuaries. Range-raised beef and lamb may violate this right, when livestock take over native wildlife's habitats.

These considerations place the entire issue of animals' rights into an ecological and socioeconomic perspective, which takes us far beyond the simplistic concern of abolishing deliberate animal cruelty. This is the difference between today's animal protection and rights movement and yesterday's humanitarian focus of simply preventing deliberate cruelty toward animals and alleviating suffering. It is a more complex perspective and a more difficult problem to grasp and advocate. But we are more likely to succeed, because this broader vision does not exclude humanitarians from responsibility. We must all learn how our own consumer habits violate animals' rights and learn how hypocritical it is for humanitarians to judge others as being cruel toward animals when they themselves unwittingly support those industries that exploit animals and nature.

In sum, I see the following rights as being *absolute*: (1) the right of all animals as individuals and societies to humane treatment and to equal and fair consideration; (2) the right of endangered species to protection; and (3) the right of all species to a whole and healthy environment (which brings in concern for the rights of plants as living things also).

This ecological ethic takes precedence over an individual's right to life in cases where feral species need to be eliminated or controlled. We must decide, from case to case, where to draw the line in terms of benefiting human interests (short and long term) and those of individual animals, species, and ecosystems. The three absolute rights provide the ethical framework to guide and constrain human actions. As has been demonstrated in this book, such ethical parameters are consonant with the long-term interests of humankind because inhumanity has no boundaries; the animal kingdom was not created exclusively for our use; and the extinction of species—the reduction of biological and genetic diversity—and the destruction of ecosystems reduce the economic and other biopotentials of nonrenewable resources at great cost to future generations.

Politically, animal and environmental rights philosophy is the equivalent of transspecies democracy, which, as has been shown, is enlightened self-interest for humanity to abide by. To violate animals' absolute rights or to deny sentient animals the right to equal and fair treatment for reasons of custom, convenience, or profit such that they suffer physcially and/or psychologically is the political equivalent of biological fascism. The fine line between biological fascism and responsible stewardship is the difference between violating animals' rights for the greater good of society and subordinating the relative rather than absolute right of animals to life (for example, for the greater good of the species or the environment).

Thus the culling of animals on wildlife preserves and zoos can be justified ethically in terms of serving the greater good (of habitat management and species preservation), while the killing of animals or manipulation of habitats for purely gratuitous purposes is ethically untenable. The greater good of society should be consonant with the greater good of all life. Societal good should not be achieved at the expense of the absolute rights of animals and the environment, because the long-term interests of society are too often jeopardized.

BEYOND HUMANENESS: RECIPROCITY AND TRANSSPECIES DEMOCRACY

Every argument offered to support humanity's assumed unconditional and absolute right to exploit animals is based on self-serving, human-centered attitudes and perceptions, such as humankind's superiority and God-given dominion. That some people believe that we have no such right shows that these attitudes and perceptions are not immutable: They are arbitrary and relative rather than absolute.

Some people contend, on the grounds of necessity and of value to society, that it is our right to exploit animals for whatever purpose. Yet there are, in fact, no morally valid grounds for exploiting animals and causing them to suffer or to die, unless we believe that we are superior to them and are thus entitled to use them as we wish, or that they were created primarily for our use.

Is superiority a morally valid and acceptable criterion for denying animals equal and fair consideration and for condoning their suffering and death? If it is, then the distinction between humans and animals is one of speciesism and, like racism and sexism, is based purely on being a member or nonmember of the human species or some select segment thereof. Such a human-centered attitude is biologically absurd because we *are* animals.

As the concept of human superiority is, as Charles Darwin emphasized, logically and ethically untenable, then the only grounds for contending that it is humankind's right to exploit animals are based on custom and utility. Custom—enculturated attitudes and values—can be changed, because they can become outmoded, anachronistic, and contrary to social progress, especially moral progress.

The custom of using animals in biomedical research is increasingly coming to be seen as contrary to social progress and to the advancement of holistic, environmental, and behavioral medicine. Likewise the custom of making meat a dietary staple is becoming seen as contrary to public health and also to the advancement of a sustainable and ecologically sound agriculture, since it wastes nonrenewable resources.

While enlightened change in custom accords with self-interest and social progress, animal rightists, humanitarians, and conservationists view utilitarian rationalizations in support of the continued exploitation of animals as being unenlightened when those who have a vested interest in maintaining the economic status quo ignore the ethical imperative to actively seek alternatives to the use of animals. This results in a polarization, the first stage of social change. The defensive posture of the biomedical research establishment and agribusiness in particular are positive signs that the humane transformation of society is beginning. Such a transformation is enlightened self-interest, for no good can come from the unethical exploitation of non-human life. The long-term costs to society, especially the erosion of empathetic sensitivity and ethical principles, far outweigh whatever short-term benefits people may gain from killing animals and causing them to suffer for reasons of custom, convenience, and personal gain.

What is the basis of our assumed right to experiment on animals to alleviate human suffering? If it is not a theologically based belief in humankind having God-given dominion, and in our superiority over other animals and specialness in the eyes of the Creator, then it is based on sheer utility and power. However, might does not make right, and as some moral philosophers have argued, it is speciesist to not give animals equal and fair consideration, because there are no morally relevant differences between humans and other animals. To condone the wholesale exploitation of animals provided it is done humanely in order to minimize their pain and suffering and not question the ethics and ultimate value of such exploitation is hypocritical patronage.

Fear also underlies the public's acceptance of vivisection, and the scientific priesthood is quick to exploit this by proclaiming that any restrictions on the wholesale use of animals in biomedical research would arrest "progress." They also state that to question the validity and morality of vivisection is to place the interests and rights of animals before those of people. Yet regardless of the promises of scientific "breakthroughs" and the myth of scientific progress toward some future utopia, evidence is mounting that overreliance on vivisection as a way to alleviate human sickness and suffering is actually inhibiting scientific and medical progress. Animal research in the laboratory has little relevance to the environmental, nutritional, genetic, psychological, social, and economic causes of human sickness and suffering. And by condoning animal suffering in vivisection laboratories, our moral as well as medical progress is impaired.

The dialectical tension between utilitarianism and egalitarianism with respect to our assumed right to exploit animals and the ethic of reverence for all life can be reconciled by placing a condition on this assumed right: the condition of *reciprocity*. Any death or suffering of animals for the good of society should also be for the good of the species or of individual animals. For example, a horse or ox that works to plow fields and gather in the harvest has, in return, its basic needs provided for (ample food, shelter, veterinary care, and so on). Similarly, "pets" such as cats and dogs are given affection, understanding, and satisfaction of their basic needs in reciprocation for their companionship and devotion. But when there is no possibility of reciprocity, as when animals are used to test cosmetics (because animals don't use cosmetics), or when the animals' basic needs are not provided for (as in factory farming), such exploitation cannot be considered morally just.

Raising animals for human consumption entails breeding them and thus giving them life. But there is a lack of reciprocity between giving them life and taking their lives when, during their short lifetimes, they are subjected to such deprivation that they cannot express and experience their *telos*, or intrinsic nature. Furthermore, they are not our own original creations: They still have a life and interests of their own.

Likewise the killing and suffering of laboratory animals can be justified only if the research promises to lead to a greater reduction in the death and suffering of other animals at some future time. To derive primarily human benefit from laboratory animal research lacks reciprocity and, as argued earlier, cannot be considered morally just or ethically valid, even if it is done humanely. Benefits to humans derived from experimentation on animals should be a by-product of research done primarily to benefit animals.

This is not a strictly antivivisectionist stance, for the reciprocity can be quite extensive; for example, test animals can be used to evaluate and new potentially beneficial pharmaceuticals. Both humans and animals would benefit from such research. It is utopian idealism to say that such drugs should not be used in the first place.

And it is a rationalization to insist that if one does support the concept of reciprocity with respect to the use of animals in biomedical research, then one should not avail oneself of any medical treatments because animals were probably used in the past to develop such treatments. The past cannot be changed, but the future can be influenced by challenging the rightness and validity of the continued wholesale exploitation of animals by the biomedical industry.

If we are to exercise our dominion over animals in accordance with the ethic of reverence for the sanctity and dignity of all life, we must accept that the only morally valid grounds for us to cause them to suffer or to die should be primarily for their ultimate benefit. And where human benefit may be derived from their suffering, toil, or privation, there should be clear evidence of reciprocal benefits to the animals themselves. The virtue of this principle of reciprocity is that while it is utilitarian, it is not exclusively human-centered.

The principle of reciprocity brings us closer to a relationship with animals based not only on empathy and altruism, but also on respect and recognition of their interests (analogous to filial piety toward our own kind), thus laying the foundation for a transspecies democracy. The rights and interests of humans then would not take precedence over those that our common-sense morality recognizes in animals, nor would their rights and interests take precedence over ours.

If we adhere to this principle of reciprocity, some classes of animal research would be eliminated entirely. These include all forms of military research; cosmetics testing; and toxicity testing of all nonessential food additives, household chemicals, alcohol, tobacco, and other addictive drugs. Likewise, agricultural chemicals such as pesticides and herbicides can be considered nonessential from the perspective of organic or biodynamic farming. Industrial chemicals and pollutants are in a "borderline" category. Their toxicity needs to be known in order to regulate their use and emission for the benefit of humans and animals alike.

Another "borderline" area is research done to improve farm animal health and welfare. Ethical vegetarians, who consider farm-animal produce as nonessential, would oppose all such research. A more reasonable position is to accept that as long as people consume farm animals and their produce, research to improve farm animal health and well-being is ethically acceptable. But wildlife research for fur ranching and increasing the "harvest" of fur-bearing wildlife should be questioned—furs and skins are as nonessential to human health and well-being (commercial interests notwithstanding) as are wildlife trophies. However, this is also somewhat of a borderline area, because without appropriate research and management, exploited species could become extinct.

Research to improve the health and well-being of other exploited animals, such as racehorses and greyhounds, should be questioned, because the degree of benefit to the animals is outweighed by the nature of their exploitation, which is nonessential to human health and well-being. Zoo animals are also in a borderline category; they can benefit their species (as "ambassadors") if their captive presence awakens respect and concern for their conservation in the wild.

Research to improve the health and welfare of companion animals crosses the border into acceptability (even though some animal rightists contend that animals should not be kept as pets or bred to become pets). There is increasing evidence that pet-keeping is not some nonessential bourgeoise luxury. As companion animals can and do enhance people's health and well-being, I would place their exploitation in an "essential" category if the animals are treated with respect and understanding and if their needs are provided for.

But respect and understanding, along with protective legislation and more animal welfare–focused research, are insufficient to justify the continuation of most animal exploitation. The principle of reciprocity may therefore help us decide which forms of animal exploitation are ethically and socially unacceptable.

If we are to exercise our power of dominion over the animal kingdom responsibly, democratically, and compassionately, we should give the rights and interests of animals equal and fair consideration. The principle of reciprocity holds that when necessity dictates that we must violate individual animals' rights and interests, some tangible benefit to animals or to the environment must be evident. This essence of transspecies democracy should be applied on a case-by-case basis to determine which kinds of animal exploitation and human-animal relationships are morally just and ethically acceptable.

Thus the principle of reciprocity does not prohibit the satisfaction of certain human needs and interests at the expense of animals' rights and interests. Rather it helps establish a balance that is neither exclusively human-centered nor animal-centered, because the needs, interests, and rights of both are given equal and fair consideration. And by evaluating case by case each human-animal relationship that entails some degree of animal exploitation and human benefit, the principle of reciprocity will reveal if there is a deficit to the detriment of the animal. An objective basis is thus available to determine whether or not the degree of exploitation is ethically untenable.

An inherent paradox that amounts to an insoluble ethical dilemma lies behind what is often believed to be scientific or medical progress. Personal ethics dictate that we should provide food for the hungry and find cures for disease. Population ethics, in contrast, sees such actions as being contrary to the long-term interests of our species and of unborn generations. Medical advances that reduce human suffering are good and necessary, but should we not question those that reduce human mortality and contribute to our population becoming more out of balance with nature? Altruism toward our own kind is ultimately misguided when it is at the expense of the needs and rights of other species, who are exploited and displaced (as their habitats are destroyed) by an expanding human population, inappropriate technologies (medical, agricultural and industrial), and by a now-global economic system that is eroding its own economic-ecological base.

It may be argued that because animals naturally prey upon and exploit each other and the environment in various ways, then it is natural for us humans to do the same. But because of our numbers and because we have technological and other powers that free us from the same immediate constraints and laws of nature, this argument is invalid. Our condition is fundamentally different, hence the imperative of elaborating ethical constraints as a substitute for nature's constraints and "laws" that we are able to avoid temporarily. I say "temporarily" because no matter how sophisticated and appropriate our technologies may be, they must conform to the constraints and laws of nature; otherwise we will be in a continuous and increasingly critical and vulnerable state of disequilibrium, necessitating more and more costly controls to prevent our own nemesis.

The principle of reciprocity can help resolve such ethical dilemmas. We must, as individuals, be prepared to make certain sacrifices, because we are indebted to others, animals, nature, and life itself, and responsible for the future. The principle of reciprocity is the antithesis of the principle of dominionism, which holds that the world is ours and we owe it nothing. When individuals act in this way, society is destroyed. When we as a species act in this way, the world is destroyed. With democracy, society may be restored. With transspecies democracy, we may save the world and be redeemed.

While some may see animal rights philosophy as moving toward communism, *The British Communist Newsaper* sets the record straight by stating:

> Historically, the progressive evolution from one mode of production to another, higher form of society—e.g. slavery to feudalism to capitalism—has depended upon humanity's increasing ability to master the forces

of nature. Communism will represent man's ultimate control over nature. Animal liberation seeks to free one part of nature from our control. It flows against the tide of history, and we oppose it as a reactionary sentiment.

The obvious lack of respect and empathy for nature and animals in this statement is certainly not unique to communism. That the concept of animal rights is not yet widely accepted in the Western world may be attributed in part to our alienation from nature and our limited ability to empathize with nonhuman beings.

CHAPTER 16

Living Humanely

BEYOND ANIMAL RIGHTS

The concept that animals have rights and should be given equal and fair consideration elicits a predictable reaction from society as a whole. It brings to the surface human fear of hunger, disease, deprivation, and suffering if it means that animals should no longer be exploited for food, fiber, and medical research. Any threat to entitlements as members of a relatively conspicuously consumptive culture evokes the assertion of preeminent human rights: What of *our* rights to health and happiness, which in society today entails the exploitation, suffering and killing of billions of animals every year?

Is it a wise strategy to pit animal rights against human rights? It is confrontational. Confrontation is beneficial when some begin to ponder the concept and question their values and actions, but can evoke guilt and anger in those who eat white veal and wear furs when they feel misjudged as being cruel and insensitive. But it is counterproductive when the case for animal rights is presented judgmentally and without concern for human interests. Then many will either deny any validity in the notion or even resort to lobbying and media campaigns to protect their "rights" and the *status quo*.

I see the issue of animal rights succeeding only if it is cast in a broader framework fostering reverence and respect for the natural world and for all life. This framework includes more than animal rights and welfare concerns because it is concerned about the well-being of not just animals, but also of people, the environment and all of Earth's creation. It is an all-embracing movement that I would simply term the *humane movement*. By linking concern for all life, for the rights of both human and nonhuman animals with concern for the environment and for the sustainability and future of native peoples and industrial society alike, a common ground is established.

How are we to feed a possible 10 billion people, ameliorate global warming, human disease and poverty, animal suffering and extinction, as well as the extinction of wildlands, indigenous peoples and the family farm? These concerns are all interconnected since everything boils down to the common-sense morality and ethical sensibility of being responsible and responsive toward the interests of others and respectful of the sanctity of all life and the sacred unity and interconnectedness of the natural world. Being aware of the needs of the planet and of fellow beings, we bring humility, compassion and social justice into the world and by so doing, realize the wisdom of living by the Golden Rule. And science is not perverted by selfish interest.

The polemics of such concerns as animal rights and human interests, conservation and industrial expansion, environmental protection/restoration and economic growth/employment opportunity, need to be reconciled and transcended. The well-being (and liberation) of humans, animals and nature are mutually interdependent and conditional upon the boundless humane ethic of a reverential and compassionate respect for all life. They cannot be mutually exclusive.

And so we must move beyond the rhetoric of exclusive rights and entitlements, and the narrow fundamentalist ideologies of industrialism, scientism, colonialism, anthropocentrism, patriarchy, and economic determinism that have entailed the violation of human rights, the holocaust of the animal kingdom and the destruction of the natural world. This movement from an inhumane society to a more humane one entails nothing less than putting animals and nature on every agenda of public policy and private action, which until quite recently have failed to even include social justice and human rights within the scope of their concerns. It requires a shift in consciousness, life-styles, institutional structures and social policies to strengthen humane sustainable communities. If we are to ever see a healthier and less troubled world and not lose the hope of world peace, or enjoy the inspiration of nature's eternal presence and the promise of equal opportunity and responsibility for all people, we must extend to all creatures equal consideration and concern.

Anything short of this will be too little too late.

A creation-centered, humane and sustainable culture was intuited by President George Bush, in his pre- and post-election vision and promise of a "kinder, gentler nation." To make this vision and promise come to fruition, we must all recognize our kinship with the animal kingdom. Then the genius of humanity, in the spirit of being humane and living in harmony with earth's creation, may be realized and a gentler and kinder world would evolve. Our only obstacles and adversaries to this possible world are ourselves. But when we are obedient to the Golden Rule, attuning our thought, will and actions to ensure the integrity and future of creation, and not just of some nation, corporate interest or ideology *that is not creation-centered*, the promise, hope, and vision voiced by at least one president of the United States might be realized. But no White House or inspired leader can accomplish this alone. The public must begin to demand less of their political representatives by reducing and eliminating many of their own demands that contribute to the holocaust of the animal kingdom and the death of Nature. Then their representatives, including George Bush, will have more power, support, and freedom to indeed make this world a kinder and gentler place.

But the abuse of power and freedom is still widespread in political, military and corporate circles. Until we all actively care for the animal kingdom and the fate of the natural world and indigenous peoples, such abuse and injustice will continue. So I close this book in a declaration of war against the anti-Christ; against the powers of human evil evident in our corrupt and selfish proclivity to abuse the powers over life we have achieved.

Perhaps these powers have been given to us in sacred trust, and if they are abused they are to destroy us in some Promethean nemesis that casts a shadow of futility upon the entire history, tragedies and aspirations of the human species: or at least of that mutant form that exiled itself from Eden, and found profit and even enjoyment in its exploitive desecration of the natural world. The politics of all nation-states have yet to embrace the egalitarianism of a global democracy that insures equal consideration not only for all races of humankind, but for all plant and animal species and the environment that sustains us all.

So how can we make this world a better place for all creatures? Our task of humane planetary stewardship is indeed almost overwhelming. When we learn about all the suffering and destruction in the world under humankind's too often cruel and unjust dominion, we may feel hopeless and helpless. And our rage against the injustices of the world can impair our effectiveness when we judge others as inhumane and fail to show them by example the way of compassion.

The complexity and magnitude of our collective destructiveness of nature and cruel exploitation of other animals is overwhelming. That the whole of creation "groaneth in its travail until now" is an essential aspect of reality with its floods, droughts, famines, and epidemics of disease and war. But as ecologists and environmentalists are discovering, it is not all nature's doing. Everything is interconnected, for we are all part of the one life. When we harm nature, we ultimately harm ourselves; and when we are not compassionate toward other animals, we harm ourselves, for compassion is boundless or it does not exist. When we destroy the forests and wildlife therein, we cause floods, droughts, and famines. The Earth is our home. When we mistreat it, all who dwell therein are harmed. When we rationalize away the subordination and suffering of animals for the benefit of society, we cause an erosion of the ethical principles and morality that sustain all societies: compassion and respect for others' rights. If we do not live by the Golden Rule, which in all religions embraces all of creation and not just human interests, society suffers. Compassion is total, embracing all living things, otherwise it is a masquerade of sentimentality and patronage.

We can all strive, step by step, to live by the Golden Rule, even at the risk of alienating those who see us as too idealistic or obsessed. When a thousand people make one simple and fundamental change in their life-styles, such as bicycling to work, not wearing furs, or eating no meat, they reduce the rate of entropy—energy consumption, pollution, and animal suffering.

The unnatural, human-caused suffering of the animal kingdom is a symptom of the wrongness of our relationship with the rest of life. The extinction of species is a consequence. We may feel hopeless or powerless about all of this, but we need feel neither. We each have the power to assume greater responsibility for our lives so that the way we live does not harm other living things.

We are not powerless, because we have the power of compassion—what Mahatma Gandhi called *satyagraha*, the power of truth in action. It entails loving thine enemy as thyself. If we would have others treat animals with love and respect, and have reverence for all life, then we must extend respect, if not compassion and humility, toward them. Farmers who run cruel animal factories are not all cruel and ignorant people: they are forced to do so by the competitive economic treadmill of agribusiness, which we should all work to change. Biomedical and other scientists who vivisect animals are not all deliberately cruel persons. Their motives are generally altruistic, if not overly human-centered. We need their collaboration to instigate alternatives and new paradigms that will reduce and someday eliminate the need to make animals suffer in the name of science and progress.

Dealing with institutionalized forms of inhumane animal exploitation takes teamwork and specialist expertise. The Humane Society of the United States employs lobbyists, scientists, attorneys, investigators, humane educators, fund raisers, and support staff in this endeavor. Likewise teamwork and specialist expertise is needed in dealing with such global issues as deforestation, the extinction of endangered species, and acid rain. Without the support of a concerned and informed public, progress would indeed be limited. "Put your money where your heart is" is a relevant cliché; people can financially help make this world a better place for humankind and animalkind alike.

The other cliché, to think globally and act locally, entails more than sending money to a favorite cause or charity. This involves self-scrutiny and assessing how our life-styles and consumer habits may contribute, directly or indirectly, to animal suffering and to the destruction and pollution of the environment. To be a conscientious consumer is to assert our power as individuals: to be the kind of person who can think globally and act responsibly, and locally, as by not wearing furs and exotic animal skins. We should avoid cosmetics that contain ingredients of animal origin and that have been safety-tested on laboratory animals. And we should also buy old brands of various products, not new and improved ones that have probably been tested on animals first.

As conscientious consumers, humanitarians can set the trend of eating no meat that has been inhumanely raised, transported, and slaughtered, or even no farm-animal products if they feel that no method of livestock treatment can be fully humane or that the production of meat is a waste of nonrenewable resources.

To maintain a diet and life-style that is conducive to our overall physical and psychological health and well-being helps reduce our dependence on the drugs, surgery, and other costly and often harmful ministrations of the medical-industrial complex, most of which were devised and developed on laboratory animals.

Organized medicine has opposed many nontraditional

medical practices, such as homeopathy, herbal medicine, chiropracty, nutritional therapy, and until recently even counseling psychology, acupuncture, and meditation. All these therapeutic approaches, which have not entailed animal research and testing, are valid alternatives to modern allopathic medicine and are part of the new holistic, or mind–body, medicine that many human and animal doctors are beginning to integrate into their practice.

Conscientious consumers are also mindful of the following concerns. They can help steer society toward a more responsible and humane way of life and, in the process, support those industries and entrepreneurs whose products and services are more ethical—humane and ecologically sound.

1. Agribusiness-processed food products are laced with preservatives and other chemicals that have been safety-tested on laboratory animals. Many of these chemicals are widely used even though animal tests indicate they are hazardous to our health. These chemicals, such as fungicides in bread, are deemed essential to prevent spoilage. But they are a product of a monopolistic overcentralization of food distribution. Find and support your local baker or food co-op. Agribusiness also uses pesticides, other agripoisons, antibiotics, and other drugs on farm animals that are hazardous to wildlife, the environment, and consumers alike, supposedly because this is the only way to produce food efficiently and thus at lowest cost to consumers. The alternatives are to cook "from scratch" and to select organically raised produce primarily of vegetable origin from local farmers' markets, food co-ops, and health stores.

It is wise to avoid eating imported fruits and vegetables out of season, in part because these crops rarely provide any cash returns to the native peoples and in part because of the wholesale and unregulated use of agrichemicals that contaminate these foods. Pesticides and other agripoisons banned for use in the United States are exported and eventually come back to our tables in these imports. Furthermore, the impact on the environment and wildlife in United States agribusiness colonies necessitates that we eat selectively, and frugally. The destruction of tropical rain forest in South and Central America for the U.S.

beef and fast-food hamburger markets and the destruction of sustainable peasant farms to make way for corporate pineapple, banana, coffee, and soybean plantations are well-documented atrocities.

2. Around the home and garden, we can all avoid the use of pesticides, detergents, and other chemicals that have been tested on laboratory animals and that are a hazard to our families, animal companions, and wildlife. "Pest" problems, from fleas and cockroaches to rats and termites, can be dealt with by more humane, integrated pest-management programs. Putting a flea collar on a pet, using weed killer on the lawn, and having a blue-light electric bug zapper on a patio are thoughtless practices that should be abandoned.

Wildlife (including insects) can be encouraged to come into our gardens by planting wildflowers, grasses, trees, and shrubs. Large lawns and formal gardens are good for nothing and require regular watering, mowing, and application of weed killer. A wild garden needs no pesticides or weed killers, and conserves resources since regular watering and mowing is unnecessary.

3. The humane homemaker can set the trend to conserve resources and energy by properly insulating the house and restoring an old house rather than having a new one built. Resource conservation even includes buying and refinishing old furniture and not purchasing new furniture, especially that made from exotic imported woods from rapidly disappearing tropical forests; and recycling all possible materials, from old clothes and newspapers, to bottles, jars, cans, and even food (which can be turned into garden compost).

4. Likewise, conscientious consumers purchase clothing from natural materials, which are healthier to wear than synthetics that are wasteful of fossil fuels in their manufacture. While some concerned consumers even buy recycled clothing, all certainly avoid wearing the furs of live-trapped and ranch-raised animals, and question the wearing of wool products because of inhumane methods of sheep husbandry and predator control.

5. Every action, from flushing the toilet to using disposable

plates and Styrofoam cups and not purchasing anything that cannot be recycled, entails an ethical choice. To act with conscience necessitates both knowledge and sensitivity. Parents and educators alike need to inform and sensitize children to adopt appropriate values and life-styles that do not violate others' rights or support those industries and institutions that are ethically unsound in terms of their environmental impact and undemocratic with respect to the public good and rights of animals. Responsible, humane planetary citizenship and stewardship may then be more than some impossible dream.

6. Another aspect of living conscientiously is investing with conscience. Individuals and organizations must research those corporations in which they have invested, to be sure corporate values jibe with their own. Sometimes, but rarely, shareholders can bring about reforms in corporate policy and ethics.

It is through these small acts of commitment to the humane ethic that significant progress can be made. Citizen-consumers have great power, which they can wield to make this world a better place for all. There is our hope. Most people do care, once they are informed, have viable choices, and do not feel judged by humane crusaders for being insensitive and ignorant. Indeed such judgments are in themselves insensitive and ignorant of the inherent goodness and potential for compassion in the hearts of most people.

This is not to imply that people never treat animals indifferently and even cruelly, or each other. Ethical blindness, erroneous beliefs (such as that animals do not have emotions) and a host of rationalizations (such as economic necessity and medical progress) help those who exploit animals ease their consciences. When empathy—the bridge of compassion—is cut, others' suffering is objectified and is no longer felt. But it is still there and it cannot be denied. The humanitarian can appeal to reason and objectively prove that animals suffer, but the greatest challenge is to help others open their hearts and *feel* the animals' suffering. People do not want to suffer in this way, but it is the only way to awaken compassion.

We need a new measure for what we call our standard of

living. This is not so much a function of the gross national product (GNP) and of available goods, services, and jobs as it is determined by the quality of our relationships with each other, animals, and the environment. As Mahatma Gandhi observed, the greatness of a nation and its moral progress can be determined by the way in which people treat animals. Animals, like people and nature, are treated as resources by this and other technocratic nations, which see economic determinism as the supreme ethic and the GNP as the definitive measure of the nation's well-being. But how can they be, when the quality of the environment is declining; when our relationship with the animal kingdom reflects a lack of respect and compassion; and when the basic rights of human and nonhuman beings alike are sacrificed to these materialistic ends?

The values of contemporary society are derived in part from the sanctified belief in humankind's unconditional dominion over the rest of God's creation; that only humans have rights; and that animals and nature were created primarily for our own exclusive use. These self-serving beliefs are reinforced by an attitude toward animals that denies them feelings, interests, rights, and souls, or inherent divinity. With this worldview, we cannot see or feel the inherent divinity in nature and all living things and experience kinship with all life. It gives rise to a political attitude toward nonhuman life that I call biological fascism. It results in the violation of animals' rights, the desacralization of life, and the destruction of the natural world. Life is desacralized when it is controlled and exploited exclusively for the benefit of humans.

If we are to survive as humane beings and not lose those attributes of the higher self that we know as humility, compassion, and empathy toward all life, then we must now follow a different evolutionary path. Pure economic determinism and utilitarian materialism are self-limiting and ultimately destructive of both self and the world. These values must become balanced by the emerging libertarian spiritualism of the deep ecology and animal rights movements, which are becoming an integral part of school and college curricula.

To paraphrase Albert Schweitzer and Sioux medicine man Black Elk, we shall never know world peace until we learn to live in harmony with the power of the world as it lives and moves and does its work, and until we embrace all creatures in the same circle of compassion as we now embrace our own kith and kin.

The humane, ecologically conscientious citizen-consumer endeavors to live in harmony with this power, with the laws of nature, and with respect for the rights of fellow Earth citizens, human and nonhuman alike. The supreme ethic of compassion as respect and reverence for all life is a matter of perception, of how we see the world and relate to other living beings. The very existence of other beings, miraculous and mysterious as it is, is surely evidence enough that they are worthy of our moral concern and respect for their inherent nature or beingness.

Sensing, feeling, and acknowledging the inherent divinity in all things is the essence of panentheism. It is not a philosophy or a theology so much as it is a condition of perception, awareness, and of relationship with other beings from which the ethics and morality—of what Buddhists call right heart, right mind, and right action—arise spontaneously.

Panentheism is thus not a theology but a way of life. As the American Indian Rolling Thunder[1] declared:

> Understanding begins with love and respect. It begins with respect for the Great Spirit, and the Great Spirit is the life that is in all things—all creatures and plants and even the rocks and the minerals. All things—and I mean *all* things—have their own will and their own way and their own purpose; this is to be respected. Such respect is not a feeling or an attitude only. It's a way of life. Such respect means that we never stop realizing and never neglect to carry out our obligations to our selves and our environment.

Over thirty years ago Robert J. Chenoweth, chairman of the board of The Humane Society, expressed the religious nature of the humane movement: "Our creed is that love and compassion are due from the strong to the weak—I might say that man is to live by the Golden Rule, with the rule extending to the lowest of earth's creatures. If we hold this creed, then we are morally bound to be teachers and preachers and evangelists." Thus the religious nature of the animal protection and rights movement has been long recognized. What of the theology of the movement? Animal rights philosophy is the stepping-stone to this next level of concern and consideration and is not an end in itself. Animal rights philosophy has helped free the humane movement from the patronizing and judgmental morality of its Victorian heritage. And with this heritage we have moved from the idea of treating animals kindly and killing them humanely to considering their interests and inherent value and rights, and ultimately to recognizing their inherent divinity.

If we accept that religion is a major determinant of morality, then it would be prudent to examine the role that religion plays in influencing peoples' attitudes toward and treatment of animals and nature. When there is devotion or reverence, the humane and deep ecology movements, along with animal rights philosophy, become transformed into a religion. The devotional inspiration of recognizing the sacredness of the world, of nature and all living things leads us to virtue and to a morality of compassion that gives equal and fair consideration to all of creation.

Panentheism as reverence for the sacredness of the Earth and for the inherent divinity of animals and all living things is not pagan, animistic idolatry. It is a view shared by many religions: in Hinduism in the proclamation "We bow to all beings with great reverence in the thought and knowledge that God enters into them through fractioning Himself as living creatures" (*The Bhagavad Gita*) and in Christianity when St. Paul speaks of "one God who is Father of all, over all through all and *within* all" (Ephesians 4:6).

The suffering of the world can draw us closer in kinship with all life. Endeavoring to live humanely—with conscience, so as to help minimize our impact upon wildlife and nature, and curtail our support as consumers of inhumane animal industries—is a great challenge. Humanitarians can rise to this challenge and by example help others practice what they preach.

Governments and corporations can no longer ignore the serious environmental impact of ecologically unsound technologies and industries. These corporations cannot fail to realize that they are acting unethically if they violate the rights of people and animals alike to a whole and healthy environment. Private interest and the public good need to be wedded in a concerted cooperative effort of global conservation and humane planetary stewardship. In the long term, corporate self-interest and enlightened self-interest are one and the same. Capitalistic technocracy and democracy are not mutually exclusive. But when the principles of democracy are ignored (and these include respect for the rights of the public, of native peoples, and of wild and domesticated animals), capitalism becomes fascist imperialism, whether it is under the flag of private free enterprise or communism.

These political, social, economic, and ecological concerns are all relevant to the work of the humane/animal protection movement and to those of us who are seeking ways to live more humanely—with conscience. The more we as consumers can minimize our negative impact on the environment and the animal kingdom, the more we as humanitarians will be able to help others practice what we preach.

The starvation of millions of people today, wars, extinction of species, cruel exploitation of animals, and poisoning of the environment and of our own bodies are all interconnected with the way in which we choose to live, impose our will and power of dominion over others, and to the circumstances and conditions that result therefrom. These are passed on from one generation and civilization to the next, for better or for worse.

We have, I believe, a moment's grace to preserve what is left of the Earth by discovering that which is sacred within ourselves and within all things. This supreme goal is surely as much a revolutionary and survival imperative as it is an evolutionary spiritual one. To live compassionately and with conscience, in reverence of all life, is the spiritual transformation that the humane, animal rights, and deep ecology movements are helping bring about. Making compassion an integral part of the life-style of the 1990s is an auspicious beginning for the millennium to come.

Notes

CHAPTER 2

1. Upton Sinclair, *The Jungle* (Modern Classics Series) (New York: Penguin, 1980).
2. Steve Turner, *New England Farm Bulletin* 150 (March 1982).
3. Michael W. Fox, *Farm Animals: Husbandry, Behavior, Veterinary Practice: Viewpoints of a Critic* (Baltimore, MD: University Park Press, 1983).
4. Wendell Berry, *The Unsettling of America, Agriculture and Culture* (San Francisco, CA: Sierra Club Books, 1977).
5. Mark Kramer, *Three Farms: Making Milk, Meat, and Money from the American Soil* (Boston, MA: Atlantic, Little Brown, 1980).
6. Ivan Illich, *Medical Nemesis: The Expropriation of Health* (New York: Bantam, 1977).
7. D. Carpenter (ed.), *Animals and Ethics* (London: Watkins, 1980).
8. U.S. Department of Agriculture, *Report and Recommendations on Organic Farming* (Washington, D.C.: U.S. Government Printing Office, 1980).
9. National Research Council, *Alternative Agriculture* (Washington, D.C.: National Academy Press, 1989).
10. See Fox, *Farm Animals.*
11. Tanya Roberts, "Human Illness Costs of Foodborne Bacteria," *American Journal of Agricultural Economics* 71 (1989) 468–74.

CHAPTER 3

1. Wendell Berry, *The Unsettling of America* (San Francisco, CA: Sierra Books, 1977).
2. Lao Tzu, *Tao Te Ching* (New York: Knopf, 1972).
3. See Michael W. Fox, *The New Eden* (Santa Fe, NM: Lotus Press, 1989).
4. M. Scott Peck, *The Road Less Traveled* (New York: Touchstone, 1980).
5. Masanobu Fuknoka, *The One Straw Revolution* (Emmaus, PA: Rodale Press, 1978).
6. Michael W. Fox, *Agricide: The Hidden Crisis that Affects Us All* (New York: Schocken, 1986).

CHAPTER 4

1. Michael W. Fox, *Laboratory Animal Husbandry: Ethology, Welfare and Experimental Variables* (Albany, NY: State University of New York Press, 1986).
2. F. L. Marcuse and J. J. Pear, *Ethics and Animal Experimentation: Personal Views*, in J. D. Keehn (ed.) *Psychopathology in Animals* (New York: Academic Press, 1979), pp. 305–29.
3. Abraham Maslow, *The Psychology of Science: A Reconnaissance* (New York: Regnery-Gateway, 1966).
4. D. Carpenter (ed.), *Animals and Ethics* (London: Watkins, 1980).
5. Jean L. Marx, The Immune System Belongs in the Body. *Science* 227 (1985): 1190–1192.
6. Rudolph Bahro, *Building the Green Movement* (Philadelphia, PA: New Society Publishers, 1986).

CHAPTER 5

1. Paul Starr, *The Social Transformation of American Medicine* (New York: Basic Books, 1982).
2. Stanley Wohl, *The Medical Industrial Complex* (New York: Harmony, 1984).

3. A. R. Feinstein, D. M. Sosin, and C. K. Wells, "The Will Rogers Phenomenon: Stage Migration and New Diagnostic Techniques as a Source of Misleading Statistics for Survival in Cancer," *New England Journal of Medicine* 312 (1985): 1604–1608.

4. John Cairns, "The Treatment of Diseases and the War Against Cancer," *Scientific American* 253 (1985): 51–59.

5. Terata (an investigation of birth defects). *Mother Jones*, January 1985, pp. 3–9.

6. National Research Council, *Toxicity Testing: Strategies to Determine Needs and Priorities* (Washington, D.C: National Academy Press, 1984).

7. Robert Sharpe, *The Cruel Deception: The Use of Animals in Medical Research* (Wellingborough, England: Thorsons Publishers Ltd., 1988).

8. René DuBos, *Mirage of Health: Utopias, Progress and Biological Change* (New York: Harper & Row, 1979).

9. See Sharpe.

CHAPTER 6

1. Carl Jung, *Memories, Dreams, Reflections* (New York: Pantheon, 1963).

CHAPTER 7

1. René Dubos, *The Wooing of Earth* (New York: Scribner, 1980).

2. Norman Myers, *The Sinking Ark* (New York: Pergamon, 1979).

3. Robert Allen, *How to Save the World: Strategy for World Conservation* (London: Kogan Page, 1980).

CHAPTER 8

1. John W. Grandy, "Ethical Issues and Future Directions in

Wildlife Management." *International Journal for the Study of Animal Problems* 3 (1982): 242–248.

2. Stephen R. Kellert, *Public Attitudes Toward Critical Wildlife and Natural Habitat Issues. Phase 1* (Washington, D.C.: U.S. Dept. of the Interior, Fish and Wildlife Service, 1980).

3. Message from His Holiness Tenzin Gyatso, Fourteenth Dalai Lama of Tibet, dated June 5, 1986, in recognition of World Environment Day and the year's theme, Peace and the Environment.

CHAPTER 9

1. Bill Devall and George Sessions, *Deep Ecology: Living as If Nature Mattered* (Salt Lake City: UT: Gibbs M. Smith/ Peregrine Smith Books, 1985).

2. Arne Naess, "The Shallow and the Deep, Long-Range Ecology Movement: A Summary," *Inquiry* 16 (1973): 95–100.

3. B. Neidjie, S. Davis, A. Fox, *Kakadu Man . . . Bill Neidjie* (New South Wales, Australia: Mybrood P/L, 1985).

4. See Matthew Fox, *The Coming of the Cosmic Christ* (New York: Harper & Row, 1989), and *Original Blessings* (Santa Fe, NM: Bear and Col, 1983). Also Thomas Berry, *The Dream of the Earth* (San Francisco, CA: Sierra Books, 1989) and Jay B. McDaniel, *Of God and Pelicans: A Theology of Reverence for Life* (Louisville, KY: Westminster/John Knox Press, 1989).

CHAPTER 10

1. *The Washington Post*, "Carbon Dioxide Curbs May Not Halt Warming," March 10th, 1990, p. 1.

2. *New Scientist*, "Fertilizers and Acid Rain Are Warming the World Too," October 7th, 1989, p. 29.

3. *The New York Times*, "Methane from Guts of Livestock Is New Focus in Global Warming" (the *Environment* section), November 21st, 1989.

4. *New Scientist*, "Are Cows Killing Britains' Trees?" October 23rd, 1986, p. 20.

5. Thomas Berry, *The Dream of the Earth* (San Francisco, CA: Sierra Books, 1989).

CHAPTER 11

1. Gilles Ailland, "Why Look at Animals," in *About Looking* by John Berger (New York: Pantheon Books, 1980).

CHAPTER 12

1. Yi-Fu Tuan, *Dominance and Affection: The Making of Pets* (New Haven, CT: Yale University Press, 1984). For further documentation on genetic disorders, see Ross D. Clark and Joan R. Stainer, *Medical and Genetic Aspects of Purebred Dogs* (Edwardsville, KS: Veterinary Medicine Publishing Company, 1983), and C. W. Foley, J. F. Lasley, and G. D. Osweiler, *Abnormalities of Companion Animals* (Ames, IA: Iowa State University Press, 1979).
2. Wayne H. Riser, "The Dog: His Varied Biological Makeup and Its Relationship to Orthopaedic Diseases," American Animal Hospital Association, 1985.
3. Survey from Pets Are Wonderful Council.
4. See Michael W. Fox, *Superdog.* (New York: Howell Books, 1990), and Michael W. Fox, *Understanding Your Dog and Understanding Your Cat* (New York: Bantam Books, 1977). See also *Cat Behavior and Psychology* and *Dog Behavior and Psychology* twenty-minute VHS videos prepared and distributed by The Humane Society of the United States, Washington, D.C.
5. American Veterinary Medical Association, "Policy Statement on Wildlife as Pets," *Journal of the American Veterinary Medical Association* 164 (1974): 272.

CHAPTER 13

1. *Science* magazine, April 10, 1987, p. 144.

CHAPTER 14

1. B. Devall, "The Deep Ecology Movement," *Natural Resources Journal* 20 (1980): 52–65.
2. A. H. Westing, "A World in Balance," *Environmental Conservation* 8 (1981): 177–83.
3. D. Williamson and J. Williamson, "Botswana's Fences and the Depletion of Kalahari Wildlife," *Oryx* 18 (1984): 218–22.

CHAPTER 15

1. Albert Schweitzer, *The Teachings of Reverence for Life* (New York: Holt, Rinehart and Winston, 1965).
2. Jeremy Rifkin, *Algeny* (New York: Viking Press, 1983). See also Jeremy Rifkin, *Entropy: Into the Greenhouse World* (New York: Bantam Books, 1989).
3. Peter Singer, *Animal Liberation* (New York: New York Review Press, 1990). See also Tom Regan, *The Case for Animal Rights* (Berkeley, CA: University of California Press, 1983).
4. R. G. Frey, *Interests and Rights: The Case Against Animals* (New York: Oxford University Press, 1980).
5. Christopher Stone, *Should Trees Have Standing? Toward Legal Rights for Natural Objects* (Los Altos, CA: William Kaufmann, 1974). See also Roderick Frazier Nash, *The Rights of Nature* (Madison, WS: University of Wisconsin Press, 1989).
6. Bernard Rollin, *Animal Rights and Human Morality* (New York: Prometheus, 1981), see also Bernard Rollin. *The Unheeded Cry: Animal Consciousness Animal Pain and Science* (New York: Oxford University Press, 1989) and Andrew Linzey, *Christianity and the Rights of Animals* (New York: Crossroads, 1987).

CHAPTER 16

1. Cited in Doug Boyd, *Rolling Thunder* (New York: Delta, 1974).

Index

About the Author

DR. MICHAEL W. FOX has long championed the cause of animal rights and protection. He is currently a Vice President of The Humane Society of the United States and director of their Center for Respect of Life and Environment. He has pioneered scientific techniques in the investigation of how society uses animals in the laboratory, on the farm, and in the home. Dr. Fox has disseminated his ideas about the ethical treatment of animals in over thirty books over the years, and is also the author of several children's books in which animals are treated with love and respect.

Dr. Fox is a Contributing Editor to *McCall's* magazine, where his column "Pet Life" appears monthly. In addition, he writes a nationally syndicated column called "Ask Your Animal Doctor." Dr. Fox is a consulting veterinarian who gives lectures, seminars, and presentations to groups concerned about animal welfare, ethology, and conservation both in the United States and abroad.

He holds a veterinary degree from London's Royal Veterinary College, obtained his Ph.D. in Medicine from the University of London in 1967 and his D.Sc. in Ethology/Animal Behavior from the same institution in 1976.

He lives in Washington, D.C., with his wife, Deanna. They have two mutts, twenty-year-old Loppy, from the frozen wastelands of Minnesota, and ten-year-old Friday, from the Lower East Side of New York City.